P9-DDF-204

HARD ON THE WIND

HARD ON THE WIND

THE TRUE STORY OF A BOY WHO WENT TO SEA AND CAME BACK A MAN

Otto Phipp, 11 September 1984
501 Eardley Ave
Pacific Grove, Ca 93952 93050.

RUSS HOFVENDAHL

WILLIAM MORROW AND COMPANY, INC.
NEW YORK   1983

Copyright © 1983 by Russ Hofvendahl

All rights reserved. No part of this book may be reproduced
or utilized in any form or by any means, electronic or mechanical,
including photocopying, recording or by any information storage
and retrieval system, without permission in writing from the
Publisher. Inquiries should be addressed to William Morrow and
Company, Inc., 105 Madison Avenue, New York, N.Y. 10016.

Library of Congress Catalog Card Number: 83-61565

ISBN: 0-688-02165-4

Printed in the United States of America

First Edition

1 2 3 4 5 6 7 8 9 10

BOOK DESIGN BY ELLEN LO GIUDICE

For Bev

1

The schooner drove toward the Golden Gate outward bound, hard on the wind on a starboard tack.

I stood at the lee rail watching the Mediterranean white of San Francisco's Marina District and Pacific Heights sliding by. Next to me stood a tall, muscular, dour-looking man. He wore a peaked cap, nondescript clothes, and smelled of cheap wine. It was difficult to estimate his age, but the way he balanced with the motion of the vessel it was obvious that he had spent a long time at sea.

Trying to sound saltier than I felt, I spoke to him.

"What's our first port?"

He looked at me at first unbelievingly, then with sardonic amusement.

"Ya be lookin' at it."

"No, you didn't understand me. I mean what's the first port we hit?"

"Gottdamn, boy, I tell ya. This be it. Frisco!"

I felt a lurch in my stomach that had nothing to do with the ship's motion. I knew by then that the schooner *William H. Smith* was bound for the Bering Sea on a codfishing voyage— but there had to be some port, somewhere!

Chris Olsen read the dismay on my face. But he had survived a tough school at sea—I later learned—and no one had ever spared his feelings.

His accent was heavily Scandinavian, like most of the fishermen on the schooner who had shipped out of Norway, Sweden, and Denmark years ago as young boys.

"Ve be back five monts. Maybe earlier—if de cod run, ve hit de right grounds."

"Five months!"

He nodded and then turned to stare again at San Francisco. It was April 27, 1937.

I was struck dumb by the information I had just received. At age fifteen, five months, in any circumstances, seemed like a lifetime. As the realization sunk in that this vessel was going to be my world for what seemed forever then, living in that fo'c'sle with a crowd of skid-row drunks, I almost wept.

How in the name of God had I gotten myself into this?

2

Five days earlier, Herb Ainsworth and I had cut our afternoon classes at Commerce High School and wandered along the Embarcadero. It was a sparkling April day and we stared longingly at the *Mitsubishi Maru* out of Yokohama, the *Deutschland* out of Hamburg, and all of the other merchant ships tied up, foreign and domestic.

By then, in 1937, it was almost impossible to ship out on an American-flag vessel except through unions. The shipping was tight, and there were too many American seamen on the beach for the unions to accept new members. But we had heard that once in a while it was possible to get a berth on a foreign vessel. Neither Herb nor I had any well-defined plan. We both had an intense desire to go to sea, and the specifics of how we got there were very definitely secondary to the fact of simply shipping out.

This particular day had been a real disappointment. We hadn't even been able to get aboard one of the foreign ships. Finally, about three in the afternoon, we turned off the Embarcadero and were walking rather disconsolately up Clay Street when Herb saw a group of men bunched on the sidewalk outside the Union Fish Company. He quickened his pace.

"Come on, Russ, let's see what's going on!"

Just as we got to the outside of the group, a man standing behind a table placed in the entrance spoke in a strong voice.

"OK, last berth. We need a messman for the *Smith*."

Herb was somewhat bigger than I, a quick thinker, and he moved decisively. Before anyone in the group responded, Herb had shouldered his way through the crowd and was standing directly in front of the table.

"I'll take that berth."

The company representative eyed him appraisingly for a moment. Herb was obviously a cut above the rest of the men bunched there.

"OK, kid, sign here. You check in with your papers by Friday morning."

Herb signed the ship's articles and emerged from the crowd with a big grin for me.

We continued up Clay Street. Herb was euphoric.

"I finally made it!"

"Where's this ship going, Herb?"

"Who cares? The main thing is getting that first trip. They didn't say a word about the union, but once I have this trip under my belt I know I'll be able to ship out again."

The Embarcadero smell of fresh roasting coffee was strong, to the west the top of the Clay Street hill defined the skyline, the sky was a bright blue, but for me the day had turned cold and dreary. Herb was shipping out, and I was not. I tried to look pleased for his good fortune but it was no use.

Herb stopped walking and laid a hand on my shoulder.

"Look, Russ, if one of us gets to ship out, that gives us a leg up. I'll be able to help you when I get back."

I wasn't convinced, but I appreciated the thought. We headed for our homes—Herb's in Hayes Valley, mine in the lower Mission District.

About two hours later, just as I was getting ready to leave for my night job at the St. Francis Hotel, the telephone rang. It was Herb.

"Russ, my father won't let me go."

"Why not?"

"I don't know." He sounded almost in tears. "Says I'm too young." Herb was a year older than I, sixteen, and while we both knew that you had to be eighteen to get a seaman's papers, that was another one of those bridges we would cross later.

Suddenly I was as decisive as Herb had been earlier that day.

"Look, Herb, are you sure your father isn't going to change his mind?"

"No way."

"Do me a favor. Don't say anything about it. I'm going to see if I can get that berth myself."

As disappointed as he was, Herb showed plenty of class. "Good luck, Russ. I hope you can pull it off!"

Remarkably, I did.

At eight o'clock the next morning I was at the Union Fish Company office. I told them my friend Herb Ainsworth had changed his mind, and I wanted the berth. Perhaps the casual decision to accept me in Herb's place should have told me something about this voyage, but it didn't.

I never learned the name of the man who had signed on the crew.

He drew a line through Herb's name.

"OK, sign here. Be back tomorrow with your papers. You got foul-weather gear?"

I tried to sound casual. "Not too much."

There was a glint of amusement in his eyes. "All right Son, I'll give you a note to Johnson's Outfitters. They're on Third Street between Mission and Howard. You can get what you need on the cuff, and the company will square it when you get paid off."

"Thanks a lot!"

"Don't mention it."

I headed for the United States Maritime Commission offices. There I learned that I needed a birth certificate to establish my United States citizenship and the fact that I was at least eighteen years of age. This seemed to be a body blow but, as it turned out, was the easiest hurdle of them all.

In those days, if you had been born in San Francisco, as I had, you simply went to the City Registrar of births, filled out a form in your own handwriting, and the clerk, after verifying the data against the original record, signed and sealed the record of your birth.

With this document safely in hand I found a quiet corner of the city library, very carefully eliminated the last two digits of my year of birth, 1921, with ink eradicator, and substituted "18" for the "21."

I held my breath when the official at the Maritime Commission studied the record of my birth, but it was only for the purpose of entering the information on his own records. By four in the afternoon I was officially Russell L. Hofvendahl, ordinary seaman. The only vessels I had ever been on were the ferries that plied San Francisco Bay.

3

That evening, before I left for work, I casually informed my uncle, Jerry Sleight, that I would be shipping out in a few days.

He was a widower, having been married to my mother's sister, and although we weren't related by blood, we were very close. He had railroaded from one end of the country to the other, and he had a real empathy for what I wanted to do, but he had a sense of his family responsibility also.

"Where's this ship going, Russ?"

"I don't know yet."

"What kind of ship is it?"

"I don't know that either." Suddenly I was beginning to feel a bit foolish.

"Jesus H. Christ, son, don't you think you ought to find out?"

"I will, Uncle Jerry. It's just that shipping is tough now. Any berth is hard to get. Once I get this trip under my belt it will be a lot easier next time."

"I know how you feel, Russ, but . . ." His voice trailed off. "I've got to let the rest of the family know."

My heart sank. My father had died when I was four years old, my mother had been hospitalized with tuberculosis since I was nine, and I had lived with various aunts and uncles in the intervening years. No one has ever been blessed with a greater group of surrogate parents, but I knew them for the practical, hardworking individuals they were. I was certain they would not understand this yearning for the sea the way my Uncle Jerry did—and they didn't.

But I convinced him, and he was able to convince the rest of them, that if they blocked me on this I would take to the road and would ship out somewhere, somehow.

It was a relatively short, intense family confrontation, but my family were pragmatists, and they perceived in me the same hardheaded characteristics that marked their own personalities.

By Sunday my seabag was packed stowed with, among other things, foul-weather gear, seaboots, and an old Navy pea coat— all acquired at Johnson's on credit. I had given notice to my boss at the St. Francis Hotel and had even managed to line up my cousin, Bill Sleight, as a replacement for my job.

Sunday night, with an unerring instinct for precisely the wrong thing to do, I set out for the San Francisco tenderloin to lose my virginity. With all of the exotic ports my ship was undoubtedly bound for, and with a youthful antipathy for appearing inexperienced before my shipmates, this was an obviously necessary step.

In 1937 the San Francisco Police Department maintained the safety of the city's citizens with maximum efficiency. Any out-of-town thug was known to the department within hours of his arrival and given a limited amount of time to vanish. At the same time, there were beat patrolmen reputed to be worth hundreds of thousands of dollars as the police controlled bookmaking and prostitution with an equal degree of efficiency.

As a consequence, I felt not the slightest fear for my personal safety as I strolled along Turk Street looking for a suitable bordello. In those days they were literally found on every block of the tenderloin. There were no red lights, and it is difficult to describe just why or how they were so identifiable, but they were. I decided on the Pearl Hotel. Like most of these establishments, the street marquee with the "hotel" name was well lit. The Pearl, again characteristically, had a rather long flight of stairs running from its single, curtained-door sidewalk entrance to the second floor.

As soon as I was inside the front doorway the rather heavy but quite pleasant scent informed me that I had made no mistake.

The madam greeted me at the second-floor landing. "Good evening. May I help you?"

I was equally courteous. "Yes, ma'am." For a moment, although I appeared older than my years, I had exactly the same feeling I had experienced at the Maritime Commission two days earlier. What if she knew I was only fifteen?

But after a brief, appraising look she invited me into the parlor.

It was fairly busy for a Sunday night, and a blond girl, Arlene, was sitting by herself there. She was dressed in black lingerie with a transparent negligee adding to an effect I was finding quite stimulating.

I am certain that the madam perceived my total lack of experience. She made no suggestion that perhaps I could make myself comfortable until some of the other girls were available for selection.

"This is Arlene. I'm sure you two will get along fine."

I almost started to say "Pleased to meet you" but decided that wasn't quite right. By then I was just about speechless anyway.

Arlene rose from her chair, took my hand, and led me to her room at the rear of the second floor. She must have been all of twenty-two, but to me she had the grace and poise of Madame Pompadour.

She locked the door behind me and with a sweet smile said, "That will be two dollars, please."

I gave her the money and, after the routine short-arm inspection and disinfectant wash, she was out of her very limited clothing gracefully but immediately.

Then she was lying on the bed totally naked. I believe my speechlessness gave her some intimation of just how inexperienced I was.

"Come on, dear. You'll like it!"

That I was sure of! But things were going so fast I didn't know quite what to do next. Arlene took care of that most skillfully and, awkward as I was, I thought it was the most wonderful thing I had ever felt!

When it was over she didn't hurry to disengage herself but lay there for a moment looking up at me. "I think I got me a cherry. That right?"

It didn't matter to me now. I simply nodded.

I left the Pearl Hotel feeling I was now ready for the sea and all of the exotic adventures it would bring.

4

The next morning my family was at the Ferry Building to say good-bye as I waited to board the ferry to Sausalito. There were no tears, and I was much too charged up to pay any heed if there had been.

The only directions I had were to find my way to the west side of Belvedere Island, located on the north side of San Francisco Bay and totally removed from the busy Embarcadero, serving merchant shipping. The *William H. Smith* would be waiting for me. I still didn't know what kind of ship *it* was or where it was bound for.

I caught a bus at the ferry terminal in Sausalito and got off in Tiburon, just a short distance from the bridge that connected Belvedere Island to the rest of Marin County. It was a steep walk to the top of the island with my seabag slung over my shoulder, and when I got there I paused for breath. Looking down to the edge of the island bordered by Richardson Bay, I saw a wooden shed with some sort of loading dock running into the bay. I decided that this must be my destination and headed down the hill for it. Today there are no homes on Belvedere Island that cost less than five hundred thousand dollars. At that time, this part of Belvedere was the codfishing terminal of the Union Fish Company. When I reached the shed I became aware of what was to me then the strongest smell of fish I had ever encountered. It was not unpleasant, just all-pervading. There was only one man on the premises, and I told him that I wanted to locate a ship called the *William H. Smith*.

He looked at me a bit derisively, I thought, and gestured south toward the entrance of Richardson Bay.

"There she be."

I looked in the direction he indicated, and for the first time that I could recall I saw a sailing ship swinging at anchor.

I had expected to see a modern merchant vessel, freshly painted, cargo booms fore and aft, like all those ships I had stared at so longingly on the San Francisco Embarcadero, the long street abutting the bay with pier after pier jutting out into the water. This was something else.

What I saw was a low-lying dark silhouette in the water with four masts reaching skyward. By then I was growing weary of displaying my inexperience—and I was not about to show my disappointment, although the words of my uncle Jerry came back to me: ". . . don't you think you ought to find out?"

I spoke to the man. "How do I get aboard?"

"I'll take you. Stow your gear in the dory there."

I tossed my seabag into the sharp-prowed, flat-bottomed boat. I didn't know it then, but this eighteen-foot dory was a duplicate of the fishing dories that the *Smith* carried.

Soon we were approaching the *Smith*. As we neared her, those sides which looked so low from a distance began to assume rather impressive dimensions. I couldn't see a gangway, but as my pilot maneuvered the dory to the starboard side of the schooner I could see a Jacob's ladder dangling with the bottom rung about two feet from the water.

Apparently I hadn't convinced this one of my experience either. "Make sure your feet are planted on that ladder before you start up. There's more of a surge than it looks like."

"What about my seabag?"

"Don't worry about that. Just get yourself aboard and we'll get your gear on."

I grabbed for the ladder, and just as I had my right foot planted, the dory dropped out from under me. Fortunately I was hanging onto the rope sides of the Jacob's ladder for dear life, but it was as if an elevator had suddenly descended, leaving me hanging there. I hung on, got my left foot braced, and started up. The bulwark was massive, at least fourteen inches across, and when I got to the top I scrambled over and looked around. There was not another soul on deck. The smell of tarred rigging, more than any other sensory impression the mark of the windjammer, scored itself into my subconscious. It was then about noon.

As I looked curiously about me I heard a shout from the dory: "You want your goddamn seabag—bear a hand!"

I looked over the rail, and my seabag came flying toward me. I managed to grab enough of it to hang on and roll it over the rail.

I looked aft. The quarterdeck looked exactly like movies I had seen of the stern of sailing vessels. There were two ladders leading from the main deck to the quarterdeck. There was a low, white taffrail surrounding the entire area, and a large wheel directly amidships, about halfway to the stern. I could see two companionway entrances leading aft to somewhere. Instinctively I knew that was not where I would be living.

Just forward of where I stood, and running almost to the foredeck, there was a squarish white deckhouse. I approached it from the starboard side. I saw there was no entrance on that side and looked through a porthole. There were two young men, fairly close to my age, sitting at a table in what looked like a small mess hall, and they were eating something.

I shouldered my seabag and went around to the port side of the deckhouse. There was a hatch with a sill, like all entrances from the main deck on the ship, about twelve inches high to keep out some of the seawater when the decks were awash. I dropped my seabag on deck and went in. To my right was a dim-looking hole. To my left was the ship's galley. Directly ahead was an entrance into the mess area.

The young men looked up. I learned later that they had been aboard since fairly early in the morning. This naturally gave them a great advantage in seagoing experience over me.

The smaller of the two, a blond, good-looking, rather stocky youngster, gave me a pleasant grin and stuck out his hand. "Hi, I'm Roy Brewer. How do you like the *Smith?*"

"Can't hardly say yet. I just got aboard." I tried to make it sound as if this was only the latest ship in my experience and I was reserving judgment. "My name's Russ Hofvendahl. Glad to know you, Roy."

The other boy shoved out his hand. He was sitting down but he had a broad frame and I guessed he must have been about six-feet-three. "My name's Gus Kalnin. They call me Trotsky."

"Glad to know you, Trotsky. Where do I bunk?"

They looked at each other with small grins. "We'll show you. Why don't you eat something first. The food's not too bad."

There was a large slab of salt pork on the table and a loaf of bread. That was all. The cuisine on the *Smith*, as I was to learn, did not run to niceties. I made myself a sandwich and it really did taste pretty good.

Roy spoke up as I finished eating. "The rest of the dress gang went ashore this morning. I think they'll be smashed by the time they get back. Come on. You better get a bunk. I'll show you." This was the first time I had heard the term "dress gang." It referred to that part of the crew whose primary duties in the codfish grounds would be cleaning or dressing fish.

He led the way through the dim hole I had first noticed. "Drag your seabag behind you. This ladder is steep!"

Indeed it was, and when I got to the bottom of the ladder I was in the forecastle, invariably referred to as and pronounced "fo'c'sle," of the *William H. Smith*. It was dimly lit by one bulb dangling overhead. At least they had electricity aboard.

There were bunks, three-high, running along the port and starboard bulkheads. There were no portholes. Most of the fo'c'sle was below the waterline. There was another series of bunks, also three-high, running athwartship at the after end of the fo'c'sle. I could see in the dim light that all of the fore and aft bunks on the port side had various items of gear strewn about and were obviously occupied.

It was equally apparent that most of the fore and aft bunks on the starboard side were empty. I started across the fo'c'sle to pick out a bunk on the starboard side when Trotsky stopped me.

"For Christ's sake, don't pick one of those bunks. That's the fishermen's side. They'll be coming aboard today sometime."

"Where in the hell am I supposed to bunk?"

"Well, the only ones left are these bunks running from port to starboard. That's what we had to take."

"What's the difference?"

"I don't know. They all look about the same."

Neither Roy nor Trotsky knew then what the difference was, nor did I, but we were to learn in the heavy weather ahead. The rolling motion of a ship is much more apparent than the pitching motion. There were many nights to come when I crawled into my bunk, wet and miserable after a night watch, only to be stood, alternately, on my head and my feet as the schooner rolled almost on her beam ends in a heavy sea. Lying on your back, spread out in a berth running fore and aft, you also felt the roll, but it didn't jam your head into the end of the bunk as it did where I tried to sleep.

One of the top thwartship bunks near the fo'c'sle ladder was still available, and I tossed my seabag into it. About one third of my life in the months ahead would be spent on that shelf.

At the time I had no particular reason for selecting a top bunk near the only source of outside air for the fo'c'sle, but during the next week I was very glad I had.

18

5

Trotsky, Roy, and I sat on deck talking, and I learned that they were San Francisco boys like myself, had never been to sea before, and really didn't know much more than I did about this voyage.

About three o'clock in the afternoon I heard the outboard motor on the dory which had brought me to the ship.

We walked over to the rail and watched the dory approach. The same man who had ferried me to the ship shouted as he got within hailing distance, "Grab the bow line and make it fast!"

Trotsky grabbed the line as it came flying over the rail, and as he was frantically looking for a place to tie it, a large, red-faced man snatched the line from his hands. "Yesus Chreest, lubbers! Vot ya tink de belayin' pin for, huh?" He expertly took a turn-and-a-half hitch around one of the belaying pins thrust through the resting holes on the inboard side of the rail. We learned later that this was Paul Myers, the first mate.

He looked over the rail at the human cargo in the dory and shook his head. He called down, "Toss de stern line! Ve belay it and giff ya slack, ya best be secured fore and aft to get dem aboard!"

I looked over the rail and couldn't believe my eyes. Five of the drunkest, sleaziest skid-row bums I had ever seen in my life were sitting or sprawled in the dory. Even from the deck I could smell them. One of them was perched on the bow and tilting a bottle of muscatel wine. It reached the vertical as I watched, and he swayed there in the dory for what seemed a long time getting down the last drop of the cheap wine.

Behind me I heard an authoritative voice: "Mr. Mate, when you get 'em aboard, shake 'em down for booze. I want none aboard."

19

"Aye, aye, sir!"

This was my first look at Captain Thomasen O. Thomas, master of steam and master of sail. He paid me no more attention then than he did the rest of the voyage, but his air of command was unmistakable. He was the master of this vessel.

He wore a peaked skipper's cap, and this was his only badge of authority. No one else aboard, including the mates, wore headgear like this. He looked briefly at the three of us.

"You men give Mr. Myers a hand in getting the crew aboard."

The mate's response to the skipper affected all three of us.

"Aye, aye, sir," we piped, practically in unison.

I thought I saw a brief flicker of amusement in the cold blue eyes. Then he turned on his heel and strode aft. Captain Thomas was six feet tall, about fifty five years of age, in good physical shape, and with a hard, deeply lined face weathered by many years at sea. I felt that a real seaman commanded this ship.

I was jerked back to our immediate duty by the peremptory voice of the first mate. "All right, vun of ya on each side de Yacob's ladder, pull dese sailors over!"

Trotsky and I scrambled up on the rail. The afternoon wind had risen, and there was much more of a surge than when I had come aboard earlier.

Somehow, like the blind leading the blind, one of those drunks in the dory would guide the hands of another onto the sides of the Jacob's ladder. It seemed as if they became part of the ship as they touched her. Despite their condition, and far more adroitly than I had done earlier, they timed their step off the dory and onto the Jacob's ladder. It was about ten feet from the waterline to the top of the rail. Slowly and arduously, one by one, they made it to the top, where Trotsky and I waited to haul them over the rail, and the mate and Roy pulled them on down to the deck.

Eventually we had all five aboard, and their seabags followed. They were all sprawled on deck as the mate patted them down.

He found two bottles of wine in inside coat pockets, two more in seabags. He methodically smashed the bottles on the outboard side of the rail and dropped the fragments into the bay. The fishermen by then seemed oblivious to what was happening.

"Grab a foot, boy, ve haul 'em to port side, dey can get below later." With one of us hauling on a leg it wasn't too much of a task to drag the five men to the other side of the schooner near the entrance to the deckhouse. This cleared the area where the dory tied up on the starboard side to unload more human cargo later.

I had seen plenty of skid-row drunks in San Francisco, but I had never been that close to so many at one time. I knew absolutely nothing about how this sailing ship operated, but looking at countless coiled lines, at that rigging, it seemed ungodly complicated to me, and I could not imagine how the *William H. Smith* would ever get under way with that kind of crew. In a sense it was fortunate that I was worrying about this, because it kept me from realizing fully, at least for that moment, that I would be living with this human flotsam in that unventilated fo'c'sle belowdecks.

Two more times that afternoon the scene was repeated until most of the fishermen were aboard. Then at about six o'clock the rest of the dress gang came rolling aboard. Almost all of them were drunk, but they were younger American types. Obviously they had had one last binge rather than God knows how many months ashore living on cheap wine and Salvation Army handouts.

At first Trotsky, Roy, and I were making cracks about the drunken fishermen, but as the afternoon wore on it seemed to me that their expressions were becoming as somber as I am sure mine was.

I could not avoid a feeling of strong apprehension. It was unbelievable that we were about to commence a deep-sea voyage with this crew.

There was no evening meal that night, but there was still

plenty of salt pork and bread in the mess. Finally, at about seven o'clock, we decided to get something to eat in the mess area.

Two tables were bolted to the deck there. Benches on each side were also bolted down. There was a space between the two tables and just barely room behind the benches to squeeze by. Above each table were long, narrow wooden containers gimbaled to swing with the motion of the ship and containing knives, forks, spoons, and condiments. The two tables accommodated twenty men at a time.

The three of us sat at the forward end of the more forward table chewing on the salt pork sandwiches. I had noticed that afternoon that Roy Brewer was particularly neat and clean about his person, and I had observed the look of disgust on his face as he had been required to handle one evil-smelling drunk after another. He was the first to speak.

"You know, I really want to go to sea, but my God, I didn't think it would be like this—with a bunch of bums!"

Trotsky and I nodded glumly.

Then I had an idea.

"Let's climb the rigging and get a look at the city." I got up and left the mess and they both followed me.

It was cool on deck and we clambered onto the rail and started to climb the foremast rigging. The wind had died somewhat, but there was a good breeze blowing, and it seemed to me as I climbed higher and higher, Trotsky and Roy following along below me, that it was cleansing the smells and unpleasantness of the afternoon out of me.

Without thinking, I did exactly as I should have done. I climbed up the rigging without ever looking down. Some instinct informed me that I should grip the side cables with my hands as I ascended, *not* the crosspieces lashed to the vertical cables. The lashing was seamanlike and secure, but salt water and weather deteriorate the lashings. It is not unheard of for a crosspiece to break away. If that happens, the seaman going aloft had better be locked onto those stays. Finally, almost to

22

the tops'l crosstrees, I paused for breath. The rigging close to the deck was wide, and it was a good arm spread to grab onto the stays on both sides. The crosspieces at the bottom were widely spaced, and the spaces narrowed only slightly approaching the crosstrees as the cables narrowed to their intersection at the very top, where they were secured to the mast just under the crosstrees. At this point the rigging was barely wide enough for both my feet on one of the cross braces. I stared across the bay at San Francisco as the lights in the city came on, and never did it look more beautiful.

Then I looked down and almost fell off the rigging. The main deck of the *Smith*, which had seemed so substantial when I walked on it earlier, now looked like a sliver of wood below me. I hung on for dear life as the vertigo momentarily made me dizzy. I called down to Trotsky and Roy.

"This is a lot higher than I thought it was!"

Only Trotsky responded, and briefly. "Yeah!"

Roy was the lowest on the rigging, and I think he was feeling about the same way I was. I heard his voice rather faintly: "I'm going down."

Neither Trotsky nor I said anything; we simply watched him descend the rigging. When Roy was about halfway down, Trotsky started down. Finally, and very carefully, step by cautious step, I went backing down myself.

When we were all standing on the deck again, we looked aloft to where we had been.

Trotsky spoke in a soft voice. "That's a lot higher than I thought it was when we started up!"

Roy and I nodded agreement. None of us voiced the thought that was very much on my mind and I suspect on theirs: What was it going to be like working aloft in that rigging when the ship was sailing?

We decided to go below and turn in.

There was a straw tick and pillow in my bunk, and I had brought my own blankets, as we all had. I had made up my bunk earlier in the day and stowed my gear around and under the tick. Included in my limited possessions were three inexpensive, lined writing tablets for my letters home from the foreign ports I would be seeing. When I learned there would be no foreign ports, I had decided to keep a diary. I didn't enter anything for the first few days, but after that, quite privately, I made fairly regular entries.

As I started down the fo'c'sle ladder that first night aboard the *Smith* my stomach lurched as I caught the smell, particularly of the fishermen. But surprisingly enough, despite the drunken snoring of most of the sleepers and the growing stench of that close environment, I dropped off to sleep almost immediately.

6

At 0900 *the next morning,* or two bells on the third watch, as time was to be reckoned on the *Smith*, we were mustered on the main deck just forward of the quarterdeck. Captain Thomas and the three mates stood there staring at us. The mates were going to select the men for their watches. Karl Miller, the second mate, was a stockily built, quiet German. Jim Bewla, the third mate, was a powerful six-footer, a Swede with a surprisingly impish look, and deep dimples on the few occasions he smiled.

Most of the fishermen were still sleeping it off in the fo'c'sle, but the entire dress gang was there as well as the only three fishermen who had come aboard sober.

While I had signed on the *Smith* as messman, I had already been euchered out of the job. With the exception of the fishermen, who were paid strictly on the basis of the number of fish they caught, the compensation for the rest of the crew, from the captain down, was on shares. The messman got sixty cents per ton of codfish; the ordinary members of the dress gang got forty cents per ton. I had been told earlier that morning by Frank

Simmons, the head splitter, that John Gunderson put in for and obtained the messman's job and that I would be one of the dress gang. It really didn't matter all that much to me, and eventually I learned it was one of the luckiest things that happened to me on the voyage.

In addition to the shares per total tonnage of codfish, each member of the dress gang received about ten cents per fish caught, the same rate as the fishermen. Since the dress gang could fish off the side of the vessel while the fishing dories were out, and since the messman received a higher tonnage rate because he was not likely to have much time for fishing, I figured I could make up the difference in shares by catching codfish. Also, by then, I was beginning to accept with resignation whatever came my way on this ship.

Thus I stood on deck as a member of the dress gang.

The captain spoke. "All right, Mr. Myers, you have first pick." He selected Walter Jensen, a quiet Dane and one of the three sober fishermen, for his watch. Then it was the second mate's turn and finally the third mate's.

We were all young and healthy, and while some of the dress gang had prior seagoing experience, I learned later that none of them had ever shipped on a sailing vessel before.

There wasn't much reason or basis for the watch selection, but this was the way it was done.

The first mate's watch commenced at midnight and ran until four in the morning. The second mate's watch commenced at four in the morning and ended at eight. The third mate's watch commenced at eight in the morning and ended at noon. Then the first, second, and third watches repeated themselves until midnight.

Time was told by the bells struck on the ship's bell on the small house just aft of the wheel. Struck by the helmsman usually, or the mate on watch if the weather was heavy and the helmsman couldn't turn from the wheel, those bells thereafter tolled the passing hours.

After the watches were selected, Captain Thomas addressed

us briefly. He was a Norwegian but had hardly a trace of Norwegian accent.

"I know that most of you don't know how to work a sailing vessel. We won't expect you to look too smart at the beginning. Rather do it right than fast. Mind what your mates tell you to do and you'll get along. We'll be hoisting sail about noon when the wind comes up. Stand by for orders."

I felt a thrill of excitement as I listened to him. This wasn't what my idea of seagoing had been, but some of the feel of this old sailing ship was beginning to sink in.

Later that morning the sails went slowly up as we lay to anchor. The sheets were free and we swung headed into the wind—first the foresail, then the mainsail, then the mizzen, and finally the spanker. The fore, main, and mizzen were all gaff-rigged, the spanker was triangular or leg o'mutton. As the spanker was going up, the captain gave the order to start hauling anchor. There was no auxiliary engine on this ship; it was wind power or nothing. But we did have a deck engine to provide power for the generator, which supplied our rather limited electrical system, to haul anchor and to work our bilge pump. As the anchor thumped into place against the bow, the first mate took the wheel, spun it to port, and the sails slowly filled. We didn't set any of the foresails or topsails then. What we had set was enough to get us out to sea, and with the limited number of experienced hands then available, there was no point tempting Fate trying to handle the additional sails with green men.

Following the mates' orders, we hauled on the sheets until all four of the sails were sheeted in and I could feel the *Smith* moving to a freshening nor'westerly.

We made a bit of leeway at first, sliding toward San Francisco, and then I could feel the ship start to drive. It was blowing about thirty knots, not unusual for San Francisco Bay at that time of year, but not that frequent either. It was a bit too heavy for pleasure craft but good sailing weather for this 170-foot, gaff-rigged schooner. It was 170 feet at the waterline but considerably longer overall if the long jib boom and the projection of the spanker boom over the stern were taken into account.

As we began to move, with the four major sails set and drawing, I went over to the port rail to look at the city. That is where I first met Chris Olsen.

7

That night, about a half hour after I heard six bells strike on the second watch, there was a bellow outside the deckhouse.

"Third watch on deck!"

Instinctively I moved with alacrity. When I got topside Jim Bewla was standing forward of the house which contained the deck engine. This was located between the main- and mizzenmasts. He was standing on the weather starboard side where the deck was clear. On the port side, even close-hauled, you had to duck under or walk around the sheets.

"OK, ve set up vheel vatches now." He shone his flashlight on a list he held in his hand.

"Hofvendahl!" His tone was peremptory.

"Yes, sir!"

"Dat sound lik' good Svenska name." He seemed to soften a bit in his tone.

"My grandfather shipped out of Goteborg, Sweden, sir."

It seemed to me that I was off to a fairly good start.

"Ve see. Ya take de first turn."

All of a sudden the size of this ship hit me. I hadn't even steered a rowboat. Now I was going to handle the wheel of this schooner.

Just about then I noticed the mate staring at someone behind me. It was Chris Olsen, and he was swaying slightly where he stood.

Bewla started to say something, then changed his mind. He assigned the next three wheel watches, told me to report to the wheel promptly at eight bells, turned on his heel, and disappeared through the companionway into the stern quarters.

I went below, got my pea coat and watch cap on, and waited just forward of the quarterdeck. As eight bells started to strike I was on my way up the ladder heading for the wheel.

By then, and again characteristically for this part of the California coast, the wind had died with sunset and we were just barely making steerageway.

I didn't realize then how much easier it was to hold a heading for this vessel with a good wind, and I was secretly relieved that it had lightened up.

Just as I reached the wheel I heard the second mate give the course to the third mate.

"Course 310. Full and by. Pretty light now, but she's movin' some."

Bewla repeated the course: "310."

As I reached the wheel, which stood about four feet in height from where the wheel post joined the deck to the topmost spokes, the second-watch helmsman turned to me and gave me the course: "310." The ship's compass was divided into sections starting at 1 degree, just east of due north, and continuing around the compass to 360 degrees due north. A course of 310, then, was northwesterly, 50 degrees west of north.

Mechanically I repeated the course "310" and took my position behind the wheel, my eyes glued to the lighted compass in the binnacle just forward of the wheel. The vertical line all the way forward in the compass assembly had to center on the numerals in the compass reading 310 if I was to keep her on course.

Bewla stayed fairly close to me for the first half hour, and I think the main reason he was so patient was that we weren't really going anywhere. The current had set us down slightly south of the Golden Gate, and in those rare moments I took to steal a look at the city, I saw the Richmond District and Sunset District separated by the dark mass of Golden Gate Park. The

28

streets were sharply defined by the illuminated streetlights as they marched eastward in ordered ranks toward the first rise of hills. I had never seen this view of the city before, and it fascinated me.

I had little time to enjoy it, however. As I watched the compass swing to 305 degrees I began to spin the wheel to starboard, watch with satisfaction as she came back to 310 degrees and then with dismay as she began inexorably to move to 315 degrees, then to 320 degrees. Frantically I spun the wheel to port. There was no hydraulic system on this wheel, and it turned hard. Very soon I broke a sweat.

After about ten minutes of my battle the mate stepped up to the wheel next to me.

"Yesus, boy, don't fight her so. Look!"

Expertly he gentled her back on course. "She go off a point, let her go, she come back. Don't move her so much."

"Aye, aye, sir!"

It looked so easy when Jim Bewla did it. For me it was a constant struggle. But I was learning. After forty-five minutes I wasn't handling the wheel like the mate, but I was holding her within five degrees of our course.

About ten minutes before my hour at the wheel was up the mate spoke to me. "Ya tink ya keep her on course long enough for me to get coffee?"

"Yes sir."

He nodded and started down the starboard ladder to the main deck.

Just as he disappeared, I saw a large man coming up the port ladder to the quarterdeck.

Thinking this was my relief coming a bit early, I gave him the course: "310."

Instead of a brisk acknowledgment I heard the slurred voice of Chris Olsen. "I know de course. Ve take dis scow back to Frisco!"

Pushing me aside, he grasped the wheel. I could smell the stench of cheap wine strong in the cold night air.

Expertly he spun the wheel hard to starboard, and slowly the

Smith began to come about. The headsails, when we set them later, required careful handling, letting go at just the right moment when tacking and sheeting home when she was through the eye of the wind. Now with only the fore, main, mizzen, and spanker set, all sheeted home amidship, they were self-tending. The volunteer helmsman's change of course threatened no harm to the vessel, but God alone knew what would happen to me!

At just the instant she came through the eye of the wind, the precise directional point from which the wind blew, I realized I'd better do something and tried to grab the wheel again and turn her to port. Chris Olsen was drunk, but he was a large and powerful man. As I tried to wrestle the wheel from him he placed one large right hand against my chest, gave one push, and I was sent sprawling.

Fortunately for my standing on the third watch, Jim Bewla was pounding up the ladder to the quarterdeck at just this moment, took in the scene at a glance, and raced to the wheel.

Olsen, intent on going back to harbor, never knew what hit him. Lying on my back on deck, I saw the mate stop just to Olsen's right, draw his fist back, and smash it into Olsen's temple. He went down like a poled ox. None too gently the mate got his foot under him and rolled the inert body out of the way.

As he spun the wheel to port I could hear the captain's roar from the skylight above his cabin at the very stern of the vessel.

"Mr. Bewla! What the hell is going on?"

The mate raised his voice so the captain could hear him in his cabin.

"Vun of de vatch—drunk, Cap'n. Tried to take us back to Frisco. She be on course again."

Captain Thomas' voice dropped in volume, but he could still be heard quite clearly on deck.

"Don't let it happen again, Mr. Bewla!"

"Aye, aye, sir!"

The mate glanced at me. "You OK, kid?"

"I guess so."

30

"Don' vorry 'bout it. Bastard got some booze on board some-how." He glanced down at the unconscious form. "Olsen a good man ven he be sober. Ve let him sleep it off here for now. Tak' dis vheel." There was a small grin. "Course 310."

"Aye, aye, sir!" Thank God he didn't know I had voluntarily surrendered the wheel to Olsen, thinking he was my relief. Halfway to the galley for his coffee, Bewla had felt the ship coming about. As he reached the quarterdeck he saw my brief struggle for the wheel, took in the situation at a glance and probably felt a slight feeling of relief that I hadn't fouled up so badly by actually taking her about after all his instruction.

In another couple of minutes my relief was approaching the wheel.

"Course 310."

"Course 310." Then seeing Olsen's inert form stretched out, "Who the hell is that?"

I was physically and emotionally drained. My answer was terse. "Ask Mr. Bewla. He'll tell you."

So ended my first wheel watch on the *William H. Smith.*

8

When we came on deck after breakfast for our watch the next morning, a steady northerly was blowing and we were heeled over on a port tack. For now, with the wind pouring over our port side, we were sailing toward the coast. Eventually we would be tacking out again and, even though I didn't realize it then, we would be tacking close-hauled all the way to the Bering Sea.

We usually didn't see much of Captain Thomas, but he was on deck studying the wind this morning. I could see him talking to the third mate, who was soon giving us an order.

"OK, men, ve goin' to put on de heads'ls. Olsen!"

"Aye." Chris Olsen stepped forward. He didn't look healthy. He had about three days' heavy black stubble, I could see the bruise on his right temple, and his eyes were bloodshot. But he did look sober.

"Take Hofvendahl and set de flyin' yib."

The flying jib was the headsail farthest forward on the jib boom. At the forward tip of it, the footline angled up to the end of the jib boom, unlike the footline nearer the bow, where you could stand on the footline and brace your middle against the jib boom. At the forward end, there was no way a seaman could stand on the jib boom footline and do what he had to do with the sail. Depending on the job to be done, one way out there was to straddle the end of the jib boom and hook your feet in the footline for whatever degree of safety that provided.

We were rolling along that morning and, while the sea was not breaking over the jib boom, the pitch of the vessel brought the end of the jib boom almost into the swells one moment, then lifted it high toward the sky the next.

There may have been life belts on the *Smith*, but in the five months I sailed on that vessel I never saw one. Certainly there were no boat or fire drills, and we didn't have life belts on that morning or at any other time. I didn't realize it then, but working the heads'ls from the jib boom was one of the most dangerous sail-handling jobs on the ship. A misstep, or a heavy sea raking the jib boom, and any seaman who went overboard in those seas, with his heavy clothing and seaboots, would be irretrievably lost before the *Smith* could ever be brought about to retrace her course and find him. Yet it never bothered me the way working aloft on the tops'ls did.

Olsen knew the hazards from long, hard experience, and I am sure that my cheerful attitude that morning added to his already black mood. Still, just before we started out on the jib boom he gave me the classic sailing man's advice.

"Ven ve out dere, kid, don' forget: Vun hand for de ship, vun hand for yourself."

"I'll remember!"

Chris Olsen started out on the footline first, pulling the tack of the flying jib with him. I followed along behind, pulling the rest of the stiff canvas.

It was a long, tough job getting the tack of the flying jib secured to the shackle, then getting the shackles on the luff secured to the outer forestay. Finally it was done, and then the halyard was locked on. Out watchmates on the foredeck ran her up and sheeted her home. It was amazing to me, as little as I knew about sailing then, how this outer heads'l, so small in comparison with the four major sails, pulled us into the wind. Captain Thomas knew from long experience that it was going to be a beat all the way to Unimak Pass and that we would need those jibs. The sails would be hauled in hard to the line of the vessel, and the jibs, with the aerodynamic effect of headsails on a fore- and aft-rigged windjammer, would be of monumental importance in propelling us close to the direction the wind was coming from. The "beat" is aptly named, a hard point of sailing, unlike the run, with a vessel running free with the wind behind it.

After the flying jib was set and drawing, the mate gave orders to set the outer and inner jibs. We moved aft on the jib boom, one of our watchmates handed out the tack of the outer jib to us, and we repeated the process.

The work was progressively easier as the foot line descended to a level from the jib boom that made it easier to work. Finally the flying jib, outer jib, and inner jib were all set and drawing. Chris Olsen and I had finished our job, and I couldn't remember anything I had ever done that gave me more satisfaction. I could feel the *Smith* under me heeling more, pulling up to windward, and moving.

I knew better than to expect any compliments for what was no more than part of the day's work for a real sailor. But it didn't hurt when we were finally back on the foredeck and Chris looked at me, gave a slight nod, and almost smiled.

Then the watch set our staysail from the foredeck, all heads'ls were set and drawing, and the *William H. Smith* was really sailing hard on the wind.

9

It was still fairly early in the year, and we were not yet far
enough north for the long days that provided full daylight
until ten or eleven at night when we were in the Bering Sea
later that summer.

It was usually quite dark when our night watch commenced,
and when we went on deck that night I couldn't believe my
eyes. The lee deck was alive with phosphorescence as the seawater rushed through the scuppers and swirled aft along the
deck. Like thousands of sparkling diamonds carried in a dark
stream, it was a breathtaking sight. Even more beautiful and
spectacular was our bow wave thrown up by our heeled-over,
driving hull. The white water was illuminated from within the
wave as if some lighting system of the sea gods were switched on
for the benefit of the crew of this lonely schooner. Farther away
from the ship, the effect of the phosphorescence dwindled. It
was near and on the vessel that the effect was so dramatic.

Roy Brewer had been selected for the third watch also. We
spent many of the idle watch hours together when we were not
standing a wheel turn, working sails, or doing ship's work. Like
me, he could hardly believe what he was seeing this night.

"That's one of the most beautiful things I've ever seen," he
said.

"Me too. How come it's not always like this?"

"Damned if I know. Let's see if we can grab some!"

Like two small children trying to put salt on a bird's tail, we
stooped over the deck trying to capture some of the phosphorescence in our hands. It was no use.

I learned later from Captain Thomas, on one of the few occasions that I dared to ask him a question while he was on the
quarterdeck during one of my wheel turns, that the scientific

explanation is fairly prosaic. Although an infrequent occurrence, the phenomenon is caused by the luminescence of small marine organisms and is more common in tropical waters than in northern latitudes. The fishermen had probably seen it countless times during their years at sea. I suppose they had grown used to the sight, because I never heard them remark on it.

For me the effect was startlingly beautiful and magical.

For Doggy Anderson it was a precipitating cause.

At about ten o'clock, just after four bells on our watch had sounded, Roy and I were sitting in the mess having coffee. Above the sound of the wind and the creaking of the hull we heard Jim Bewla's shout.

"Get de bastard out of de riggin'!"

We ran out on deck. Jim was just aft of the mains'l standing rigging, and he was shining his flashlight about halfway up.

We looked up and saw a figure clinging to the rigging. As we watched we saw his right hand raised high above his head, and we could see the belaying pin clutched in it. With a violent downward swing he clubbed at something and almost fell off the rigging.

We had been brought on deck by the third mate's shouted order to the rest of the watch clustered by the rigging. Now he changed his mind.

"Didn't know he had dat belayin' pin. De hell wit' it. He kill himself, not goin' to send vun of my men up for him!"

Paddy Whelan, the only Newfoundlander aboard and one of the three sober fishermen I had noticed the first day, materialized at Bewla's elbow. He was not on our watch.

"I'll get him," he said quietly.

Bewla looked at him briefly. "If ya vant. I'm not orderin' anyvun."

Paddy nodded and started up. He was probably about fifty-five years old, but he went up that rigging like a boy. As he got near the upper figure he slowed down and then stopped. There was one halfhearted swing at him with the belaying pin, and then we could tell that Paddy Whelan was talking to our be-nighted shipmate. Paddy's words were lost in the sound of the wind, but he kept talking for what seemed a long time. Finally Paddy started down, and the man above started down after him.

As Paddy reached the rail he stepped off the rigging onto the rail and nimbly down to the deck.

Paddy was Irish with a trace of the brogue in his speech, and there was a glint of amusement in his eyes now as he spoke quietly to us.

"Don't spook him, lads, when he gets close. Just stay quiet."

As Doggy Anderson reached the rail I recognized him as one of the first fishermen we had hauled aboard two days earlier. It seemed like a lifetime ago now.

Paddy spoke to him reassuringly. "Let me have the belayin' pin, Doggy, till ye get down."

Docilely, like a child, Anderson handed the heavy pin to Whelan, then climbed down on deck, where he swayed and looked as if he would fall.

Roy and I supported him, one on each side, as Jim Bewla took command again. "Get him into de mess and get some coffee down him."

If anything, Anderson smelled worse than he had when he first came aboard, but we ignored the smell. He obviously was in bad shape.

When we got him into the mess and seated at one of the tables, Paddy got coffee. He filled one of the mugs half full, added a lot of sugar and canned milk, and then carefully cupped his hands around Doggy's. Anderson's hands were shak-ing so violently there is no way he could have drunk that coffee unassisted.

I learned later that Doggy Anderson was at least sixty-five years of age, the oldest man on the ship, and this codfishing voyage to the Bering Sea was the only berth he had been able to secure for the past five years. Paddy Whelan was a close friend of his and bunked just above him on the fishermen's side of the fo'c'sle. Paddy had awakened to find Anderson's bunk empty, had gone on deck to find him, and had immediately perceived the situation when he saw our watch clustered around the mainmast rigging with Bewla's light playing on it.

Now, sitting in the mess, Anderson's eyes were darting about, and he spoke in gasps. "Don't let 'em get me, Paddy!"

My reaction was involuntary. "Who?"

For the first time Doggy's eyes focused on me. "All kinds of strange little bastards. Ya see 'em on deck wit de lights on der heads."

I started to explain about the phosphorescence, and then I became aware of Paddy gently shaking his head, the same amused look in his eyes.

Doggy Anderson was in the throes of a full-scale attack of delirium tremens, the sort of attack that would have had a doctor and nurses in attendance at a sanitarium, hypodermics at the ready.

Out here, on the *William H. Smith*, Anderson would have to survive this on his own. Paddy Whelan knew this, he had seen plenty of other shipmates go through the same thing and survive—particularly on the codfishing schooners. There was amusement to be had in Doggy's hallucinations, and Paddy accepted it matter-of-factly, without cruelty.

Suddenly Doggy screamed.

"Dey comin' over de table, get dem cocksuckers!"

Paddy grabbed him around the shoulders and spoke reassuringly.

"I won't let them get ye, Doggy. Rest now, lad."

Gradually Doggy subsided, and about a half hour later we helped Paddy get him down the fo'c'sle ladder and into his bunk.

I couldn't forget the terror in Anderson's eyes as he perceived with horror those small demons, invisible to the rest of us, coming after him.

The gamut of emotions, from the striking beauty of the phosphorescent sea to Doggy Anderson's attack of delirium tremens, had tired me out more than I had realized. I was asleep as soon as I hit my bunk.

10

It has been said that conditions in the fo'c'sle of a codfisher in those days were such as to make hardened seamen turn pale. Our quarters in the *Smith* bore out this observation in spades.

A shift in the wind and the withdrawal symptoms of acute alcoholism finally made the conditions in the fo'c'sle of the *Smith* insupportable for me.

During my two nights in the fo'c'sle, I had become sufficiently used to the throat-grabbing smells of vomit and incontinence that somehow I could crawl into my berth and go to sleep.

About two hours after I had climbed into my bunk and gone to sleep during this third night, I awoke with a splitting headache. For the short time that it took me to become oriented, I felt as if I were entombed with the stench of the dead engulfing me. I couldn't figure out what had changed.

Then I became aware of a dripping sound on the fo'c'sle ladder and the fact that there was no fresh air coming from the port-side entrance to the fo'c'sle. Early on the first watch, following our night watch, the wind shifted to the west and increased markedly. This left us on a port tack but heading much more directly for Unimak Pass, the entrance to the Bering Sea. While I was sleeping, a giant comber had broken over the port rail and had cascaded down into the fo'c'sle. With the wind making up there was no choice for the watch on deck but to batten down. What had awakened me was the absence of fresh air and the stench of the alcoholic fishermen.

Somehow I had thought that the worst was over. It was probably due, among other things, to the fact that Chris Olsen had been sufficiently operational to set the jibs the day after having been drunk enough to attempt to sail us back to San Francisco single-handedly.

However, he had an iron constitution and, while he probably had not drunk any less than his shipmates during the winter on the beach, he had obviously recovered faster.

Probably because my bunk was closest to the fresh air we normally got in the fo'c'sle, I found it impossible to go back to sleep now. Also, while I was beginning to realize that I was not subject to seasickness, my stomach was turning over uncomfortably as I lay in my bunk trying to breathe as little of that air as possible.

Finally I pulled my clothes on, stepped from the rail on the bunk below to the fo'c'sle ladder, and went topside. I peered through a port-side porthole of the deckhouse and could see the seas breaking over the weather rail. I went to the starboard side in the mess area and stared out of a porthole. The lee rail wasn't under, but we were really heeled over, and the deck was awash.

The hatch leading to the deck was secured, as were all of the ports. The air in the mess was close, but it wasn't like that horror below in the fo'c'sle. There was no way I could get comfortable, but I sat down on one of the benches, put my head down on my folded arms on the table, and dozed intermittently for the rest of the night. Every once in a while I would awake with a start when we dropped off a swell and slammed into the trough, as if the ship were hitting a brick wall. I couldn't quite bring myself to admit that maybe my relatives were right—after all they hadn't known any more about this voyage than I had—but there were times that night, and more than once, when my uncle Jerry's admonition that I ought to find out something about this ship came back to me.

The captain; the three mates; the cook; the radio operator, "Sparks" (I never knew him by any other name); and Frank Simmons, head splitter and dress gang boss, lived in the stern quarters. The rest of us, thirty-six at the start of the voyage, thirty-three when we dropped anchor in San Francisco the following September, lived in the fo'c'sle. From time to time various members of the dress gang were assigned cleaning duties in those stern quarters. Nothing ever looked more palatial to me than those cramped two-man cabins that the mates and the other high-ranking ship's company shared. Captain Thomas' cabin, occupying the full beam of the ship, all the way aft, with stern windows and his own bathtub in solitary splendor, seemed downright luxurious to me. In the first days the one factor that impressed me above all others was that these quarters were all above the waterline, they all had ports, and you could breathe the fresh sea air!

I didn't go below again that day. After our morning watch I was sitting on the forward hatch staring at the wild sea and the gray sky when I suddenly became aware of a commotion near the deckhouse on the weather side.

Oscar Quarten, the second salter, was the center of a small group of men who were moving in my direction. He was gesticulating wildly, and it seemed as if they were trying to get their hands on him. Oscar was fairly short but very sturdily built, and he was effectively keeping the others at bay. I realized as the group neared me that these were all fishermen; none of the dress gang was involved. In the instant it took me to perceive the scene, I got the impression that Oscar was not physically intimidating the others so much as there was something going on that had them backing off.

Then Oscar's eyes caught mine, and he came striding up, shouting at me in Swedish. I didn't understand the words, but his meaning was unmistakable. As he got close to me I could see that his eyes were wild, there was foam at the corners of his mouth, and he looked like a maniac. This was my second encounter in as many days with an active case of delirium tremens. I wasn't about to argue with him, particularly when I saw him draw back his beefy right fist. This pitching wet deck was no place for a fight, even if there was a reason for one. In the split second I hesitated, trying to decide whether to back off or hit him first, his eyes suddenly rolled up in his head and he collapsed on his back on the wet deck. As he lay there his legs and arms twitched violently, he continued to drool, and he moaned and groaned. There was nothing anyone could do, but Chris Olsen suddenly snatched out his sheath knife and forced the handle into Quarten's mouth.

"Dere. He not bite off his tongue, anyvay!"

It seemed like hours, but I am sure the incident didn't last more than a minute.

Oscar Quarten finally gave one last convulsive shudder, his arms and legs gradually subsided into stillness, and he lay on deck.

For a while we weren't sure whether he was alive or dead. Then, as we took a swell over the weather rail, the icy salt water dashed into his face and he was sitting up with a bewildered expression.

At first he spoke only in Swedish, then with a sheepish grin he looked at me. "Vot ya do to me, boy?"

I simply shook my head.

Oscar slowly got on his feet. He looked as if nothing had happened to him. He hadn't shaved since coming aboard, he smelled as bad as most of the fishermen, but other than his disreputable appearance he looked fit and healthy.

By unspoken agreement—it was as if Oscar's attack were a signal they were waiting for—the fishermen turned to in the fo'c'sle that afternoon. Fortunately the wind had lightened so that they were able to keep the deckhouse hatch open. Soiled blankets were doused in seawater, then rove through the sheets and standing rigging to blow dry in the wind. They formed a bucket brigade and took turns passing fresh buckets of salt water below, taking out dirty buckets of salt water into which the swabs had been wrung out. They worked steadily for three hours with the undirected but coordinated effort that long years at sea had taught them. By the end of the first watch the fo'c'sle had been thoroughly scrubbed down and aired out.

Then the fishermen shed their clothes and scrubbed off in salt water. Their soiled clothes were tied to light lines, secured to the standing rigging at one end, and tossed over the side for the sea to beat them clean. It would take a while for them to dry, but they all had at least two changes of clothing with them.

There was a limited supply of fresh water aboard, and it was strictly for drinking. For washing and shaving it was either rain-water or salt water.

We had one rain barrel standing under the drain spout coming off the forepeak deck and another standing at the aft starboard corner of the deckhouse. They were each about a third full of brackish water, probably half rainwater and half seawater. Standing naked in the wind just aft of the forepeak, the men shaved with straight razors, staring into the metal mirrors wedged into the after edge of the forepeak deck, their feet spread, braced to the roll of the ship. It was a remarkable sight to me, since I had concluded, with the dogmatism of youth, that these men had never been clean in their lives and had no desire to be. They were all of North European extraction and their bodies, surprisingly well muscled considering the months of dissipation on the beach, were lily white, contrasting sharply with their deeply weathered faces, necks, and forearms.

Just before night chow I went below and could hardly believe the evidence of my own senses. The fo'c'sle actually smelled clean—not fresh, because seawater doesn't do the job that fresh water does—but really clean. I heaved a sigh of relief and realized as I did so that it was the first deep breath I had inhaled in the fo'c'sle since I came aboard.

There were to be times to come when the weather required us to batten down and the air below became heavy. When the salted cod began to mount in the main hold just aft of the fo'c'sle bulkhead that smell, added to the smell of thirty-six infrequently washed male bodies, made our living environment a bit pungent. But somehow that was an honest, hardworking smell. With but two exceptions, I never again had the slightest difficulty going to sleep in my bunk below.

11

The second wheel turn, at two bells on the night watch, was mine. By now I thought I was getting the feel of it. Still, from time to time Jim Bewla would mutter an oath and step to the wheel.

"Gottdamn, boy, ve vant to go like dis," he thrust his arm straight ahead, "not lik' dis"—he made a waving motion with his hand. "Look at dat vake!"

I looked aft briefly and I could see a curving line of white foam disappearing into the black sea.

"Yes, sir. I'll try to do better."

Jim nodded and stomped off.

Grimly I concentrated on our course. It was now 355 degrees, almost due north. The wind had lightened but it was still blowing steadily at about twenty knots, more than enough to keep her driving full and by.

I was learning not to overcorrect the helm now when she went a point or two off course, and toward the end of that wheel turn I really began to enjoy this experience. One sensation that never ceased to exhilarate me was when the stern lifted and we ran down one of those long North Pacific swells. Then I was standing at the wheel with the whole length of the ship running downhill from where I stood. The red port running light and the green starboard running light defined the foremast rigging where the running lights were mounted. It seemed a long way to those lights from the wheel on the quarterdeck. It only lasted a few seconds, and then our bow was either crashing into the sea ahead or climbing the next swell, but there was something about having the length of that schooner laid out at my feet that lifted my spirits higher than the stern lifting on the sea.

While I really concentrated on keeping a course during my

wheel turn, it was a time by myself. The ship was alive, the sea was immense, and I was part of it all.

When my relief appeared I gave him the course and went down to the main deck. It was a moonless night, but the stars were bright in a dark velvet sky.

We did not go below on our watch, except momentarily to don foul-weather gear or for some other good reason. I was tired out from my almost sleepless night the night before. I wasn't in the mood for talking to Roy, and privacy was hard to come by on the *Smith*. Then I thought of the forepeak deck. With the lightening wind the seas were no longer breaking over the bow, and the forepeak deck would be a good place to stretch out and relax.

I lay on my back with my hands clasped under my head, staring up at the night sky. After a while I became aware that the entire diamond-studded sky was gently rocking as I watched the stars above the silhouette of the foremast reaching to the sky. It is one of those sea-begotten illusions that requires special circumstances. The roll of the ship cannot be too violent, as in a storm, and there must be some vertical part of the ship's structure thrusting into the sky to provide the fixed point of reference. Then it seems as if the ship and I are one, sailing on a delicately balanced course, with the night heavens gently rocking to and fro above.

It was a pleasant, dreamlike sensation, enhanced no doubt by my drowsiness, despite the hardness of the deck. Then, as was to happen to me many times at sea, I began to think about and speculate on the immensity of this universe.

I thought about my one year's attendance at a Lutheran church while I had lived with my Aunt Erna. I had no strong antipathy to the church; in fact, I rather enjoyed the hymn singing. It was just that I could never understand how the pastor could be so certain he had all the precise answers to profound questions, the answers to which are so patently unprovable.

As I lay there on the deck of the *Smith*, whatever religion I was ever to have began to develop within me. It seemed to me

44

that all of the ordered immensity of the heavens could not have happened simply by chance. That North Star was placed in the night sky by design, not by accident. My realization was not a profound awakening. It was a gradual awareness, only beginning then.

Despite the environment of the ship, whatever was to come on this voyage, and God knows it had been a beginning I had not expected, I felt at peace with the world as I looked up at the stars rocking gently in the heavens that night.

12

For three more days the *Smith* sailed on; not a fair wind because we were still close hauled, but on a heading of 355 degrees, very close to our course for Unimak Pass—the entrance to the Bering Sea.

With all of the fishermen operational, the watches settled into a steady routine. The topsails were set late on the second watch early one morning. When I came on deck later that morning I could feel the added drive of the ship, and for a moment I was puzzled—the wind did not seem any stronger. Then I looked aloft. All of the tops'ls were set and drawing. The *Smith* was an old vessel—her sails were worn, stained, and patched. Still, with every stitch of canvas set, hard on the wind she was a thing of beauty.

My feelings, when I looked up and saw the tops'ls set, were a mixture of relief and disappointment. I was relieved that the earlier watch had bent on the tops'ls; I had a vivid recollection of how high those crosstrees seemed when I had climbed up there when we were still at anchor, but still I had a feeling of disappointment that I had not had the chance to test myself working aloft. I need not have worried; my time would come.

Roy and I spent a lot of time together on watch when we

were not otherwise occupied, and one of the habits of the old-timers that had interested and amused us was their continual measured pacing of the deck, from one end to the other. Fore and aft they went—hour after hour.

One morning I noticed Chris Olsen walking by himself, adjusting his gait to the motion of the ship. As he completed his walk to the forward end of the deck, and turned aft I fell into step beside him. Although he was not the type of man to invite or encourage casual conversation, I felt a certain affinity for him. He had given me the first word on what this voyage would be. Although it was never mentioned, he had commandeered the wheel during my first wheel turn, and we had set the heads'ls together. I am sure that to Chris I was just another one of the green hands aboard, but he gave me a friendly enough nod when I fell into step beside him.

"Chris, how come you walk like this all the time?"

"Vat else to do, boy?"

"I don't mean just you, all of the fishermen."

Chris seemed to be thinking as we continued to walk, reached a point just forward of the port ladder leading up to the quarterdeck, and he turned to walk forward again. About half-way forward he finally replied.

"Don' know. But ya go to sea long enough, ya be doin' it too."

He was right. It wasn't too long after my conversation with Chris that Roy and I found ourselves, without quite realizing what we were doing, walking from one end of the deck to the other as we talked about girls, the world, the voyage, and all the other topics of conversation we found to explore. We were doing it before we realized that we were walking exactly the same way the fishermen did. I decided that we probably did it out of a subconscious need to exercise the body. Also, it did help to pass the sometimes monotonous hours.

Late in the morning watch a few days later I fell into step with Chris Olsen again. I don't recall that he ever started a conversation, but he was friendly enough once we were talking.

"How long will it take us to get to Unimak Pass now?"

He just looked at me. By then he was using my first name occasionally, but it came out sounding like "Roos."

"Not too long if de vind hold. But dese bloody vindyammers, de vind never holds!" He was so right!

The next morning I awakened to find my chin driven into my upper chest, the top of my head solidly planted to the headboard. A moment later I was sliding to the starboard end of the bunk, where my feet jammed into the headboard of the next bunk. A moment after that and my head was jammed against the port headboard again.

As I struggled awake I could hear muttered oaths and, more than anything else, the sound of the *Smith* creaking and groaning like a soul in torment. For days now we had been heeled over to starboard, rolling and pitching to some extent, but basically with a feeling of continued equilibrium.

This was a totally different sensation. We were wallowing. I didn't realize it until I went up on deck and saw the huge glassy swells and the sails slatting. The *Smith* was becalmed.

Becalmed she stayed for what seemed like forever. She never stopped rolling, and our rotund German cook accumulated one burn after another on his arms as the motion of the ship threw him against one hot part of his large coal-burning stove after another. He was not a good-tempered man at best, and I avoided looking in his direction as I hurriedly passed the galley on my way to and from the fo'c'sle.

For the fishermen this was simply an expected part of a voyage on a windjammer. For the rest of us it was as trying a time as we ever had on the *Smith*. With the continual rolling in those swells it was difficult to walk on deck, and a wheel turn didn't mean anything except standing there and battling the wheel as the spokes, quiescent one moment, would suddenly spin as a surge caught the rudder the next.

The calm was responsible for my learning about one of the oldest sailing superstitions.

Roy Brewer had a good singing voice and an encyclopedic

memory for all of the current songs of the day. Very often on a night watch we would sit on one of the hatches and simply sing along. He also knew at least fifteen verses of "Abdullah Bulbul Amir," not to mention "Frankie and Johnnie" and other old ballads. On occasion, rather than sing, I would provide a questionable musical accompaniment by whistling as Roy sang. On our second night watch during the calm we were sitting on the aft hatch, Roy singing, me whistling, when Chris Olsen and Skys'l Sam, another fisherman on our watch, appeared without warning.

We had about half a moon that night, and our faces were quite visible.

Skys'l Sam grabbed me roughly by the shoulder. His face was hard. "Knock off de vhistlin'—hear!"

"What for? We're not bothering anyone." I was indignant, but I didn't feel like challenging him.

"Ya vhistle up de vind, dat's vhy!"

It was ridiculous. "Why not? We could sure use some wind."

Skys'l Sam's face was set, and his voice was menacing. "Ve get enough vind vhen it come. Ya keep up dat damn vhistlin', ya vhistle up a blow. No more vhistlin'!"

I could see Chris Olsen's face and, it seemed to me, he looked somewhat embarrassed, but his face was equally grave.

Neither Roy nor I could believe it. Roy asked, "Are you serious?"

They both nodded emphatically.

The whistling wasn't that important, and the quarters were too close on this ship. It was easy enough for a fight to start under any circumstances, and the whistling simply didn't mean that much. They turned away and continued pacing the deck.

Roy and I just looked at one another and shook our heads. I never again whistled aboard the *Smith*. More than that, I have never been able to whistle on any other ship. Their superstition, although I thought I didn't accept it, had become part of my life at sea.

During the third morning that we were becalmed, Frank Simmons approached me on deck. As head splitter and dress gang boss, he controlled the work assignments for everything but sailing the vessel.

"Russ, this is up to you, but you can have that messman's job back if you want it. We've got to get Johnny Gunderson out of the galley."

"I don't want it, Frank. I like it on deck. Not right now with this damned calm, but I don't want to work in the galley."

Frank nodded. I had a feeling that after the summary method of dispossessing me from the messman's job in the first place, he wouldn't insist.

"It's OK. I've got Eric Johnson lined up, but I thought I'd give you first crack at it—higher shares if you want it."

I shook my head and, as Frank turned away, asked him, "How come you're taking Johnny out of the galley?"

"He's got a dose."

"He's what?"

Frank said, grinning, "Got himself a dose of clap in Frisco just before we shoved off."

My blood ran cold. Suddenly I thought of the men I had worked with at the hotel who had gotten themselves infected with gonorrhea. No one ever had a better sex hygiene education than I had received working at the St. Francis. I recalled with horror their stories of that first drip of the penis, the pain on urination, the ones who had developed strictures and had their urethras reamed out with a surgeon's instrument.

I remembered Arlene, probably the same Sunday night that Johnny got himself infected.

Frank looked at me curiously. I don't know whether I had turned pale, but I was sure feeling that way.

"I didn't know Johnny was that good a friend of yours, Russ. Don't worry. When we get into the Bering Sea one of the Coast Guard cutters will take him off."

I must confess I wasn't thinking of Johnny Gunderson right at the moment. "How long will that be?"

Frank looked at the sails' slatting. "God knows if we don't get some wind."

There was no one to blame but myself. Bitterly I thought that was really a stroke of genius, getting myself laid the first time in my life and then shoving off on a voyage for five months with no access to a woman for the entire time. Now this possibility! I knew that Arlene's perfunctory examination of my penis, and the wash in the disinfectant solution, were no guarantees whatsoever that some prior customer had not left her infected. Still, I just had not thought of it until now.

Frank tried to be reassuring. "I don't think there's a chance he could pass it to the rest of us. It's just that there isn't anything the cap'n's got that will do him any good. The cap'n figures the best thing to do is keep him off his feet and hope it doesn't get too bad before a cutter takes him off."

I nodded, and Frank continued to reassure me. "Far as I know there's only one way to get clapped up, and that's by dippin' your wick in the wrong hole."

Probably I didn't groan at this point, but when Frank turned to go aft to his quarters, I didn't stop him. I had had enough of this conversation.

Johnny Gunderson was at least seven or eight years older. I hadn't had much to do with him before, and he probably was mildly surprised by my evident concern for his condition. This wasn't his first dose, he had never suffered the really traumatic effects that some men I knew had, and basically he was fairly relaxed. However accurate or inaccurate his medical information was, I learned that he had indeed, in all probability, contracted gonorrhea sometime during that last Sunday night in San Francisco. Naturally, he was sure it had happened in a tenderloin whorehouse. The only thing that puzzled him was that it had taken quite a bit longer for the symptoms to manifest themselves this time. While he didn't put it in those words, the effect was that he must have been at the very end of the incubation period when he noticed the discharge from his penis. He had figured, if he ever thought about it, that he was home free.

No one on the *Smith* ever knew what I went through during the next few days. Every time I urinated I imagined a burning sensation. Carefully, privately, and continuously, I examined my equipment—nothing untoward.

Eventually I decided that I was probably still healthy. The constant worry finally left me. With it went my preoccupation with the virtues of a celibate monastic life.

Then, four days after we were first becalmed, the wind came out of the northeast, and we were moving again. We were still close hauled, this time on the starboard tack, but we were making northerly day after day.

13

The wind held steadily. We sailed on a long slant west by northwest. The prevailing wind, after the days we were becalmed, was like a tonic.

The evening meal was the one time that the entire ship's company filled the mess in two sittings. My third watch was the only watch that permitted a daily routine, as to time at least, roughly like a life ashore. We could never sleep a full eight hours, but at least we slept during the night, when most people ashore did.

Many of the first watch, coming off duty at 0400, didn't want to break their sleep to get breakfast.

In the same way, many of the second watch would eat breakfast as they came off watch at 0800 and then sleep through the noon meal.

For the first ten days we had eaten fresh meat—that is, fresh frozen from some cold-storage house in San Francisco, but still fresh meat. After that, with no refrigeration aboard, we didn't taste fresh meat again until the middle of August, when we traded a load of fresh cod for some frozen meat with a company steamship in the Bering Sea.

Still, with a sense of duty I didn't appreciate at the time, our German cook varied the meals with the limited resources he had to command.

There were always platters of salt pork or corned beef on the mess tables between meals along with the bread the cook baked to provide a mug-up for the watches.

The potatoes lasted a surprisingly long time. Those and onions were about the only fresh vegetables we had. The *Smith's* hold was packed with rock salt, which would be used to salt the cod, and the fresh stores were stowed below directly on the salt. The icy waters of the North Pacific created a cold-storage effect that kept the hold of the *Smith*, if not refrigerated, at least cool enough to preserve the type of stores we carried.

One of the minor disadvantages of the third watch was that practically all of the store-handling and moving chores were assigned to the morning section of the third watch, from 0800 to 1200. I thought that was fair enough and the captain's way of compensating for the more irregular sleeping hours of those on the other watches.

All of the work details on our watch were handled by the dress gang. The fishermen were real seamen, they performed when it counted in a blow, and this was simply another basically unspoken compensatory device to equalize duties and responsibilities.

Both Roy and I were willing workers, and it seemed as if we drew more than our share of this duty. Fourteen days out of San Francisco I began to welcome these assignments. After the frustrating, nerve-racking days when we were becalmed, I would never again complain about monotony, but with the *Smith* sailing on a steady course, the watches repeated themselves with little variation, and any break in the routine was welcome.

The breakfast meal was consistently the best, with generous platters of bacon and eggs on a fairly regular basis. The sides of salt bacon kept well in the hold, and one of our regular chores was to go down into the hold to turn the large wooden crates of eggs upside down from their prior position about once a week. I was told that this kept the eggs fresh. I don't know whether this is a fact or another superstition of the sea. I do know that almost five months after we shoved off from San Francisco, and just before we dropped the hook for the last time in that beautiful bay, we were still eating eggs that tasted good to me.

There was little dinner conversation in the mess. The cook and the messman were intent on getting us in and out. The sooner the first group was out, the sooner the second could be fed. The sooner the second was fed, the sooner their workday was over.

The eating was serious and to the point. There was something about that sea air, and probably my age at the time, that kept my appetite ravenous. I was never embarrassed by my appetite. My shipmates turned to with equal determination.

One night, a little more than two weeks out of San Francisco, I finished my evening meal, carried my plate and utensils to the slop bucket that stood near the galley sink where the messman labored, scraped my plate clean, and dumped the plate and utensils into the bucket of salt water standing near the sink.

If the weather was reasonably fair the crew tended to gather for a while after the night meal near the forward hatch, talking and smoking.

By then, on this particular evening, I was no longer tortured by the fear that I had contracted gonorrhea at the Pearl Hotel. The *Smith* was heeled over and driving. My stomach was full and, somewhat to my surprise, I realized that I was content. Looking at my shipmates, particularly the fishermen, I was even more surprised to realize that these were a remarkable group of seamen. They were rough-hewn and uneducated, but they were men, and they knew their job.

Gone were the skid-row bums who had been unceremoniously hauled aboard the vessel just two weeks before. They were clear-eyed, healthy, and hard-muscled now; the metamorphosis was little short of unbelievable.

By then I had learned something about how the ship's crew would function once we were in the codfish grounds in the Bering Sea. I didn't really know then that the fishermen quite literally risked their lives every early-morning departure when they pushed off in their dories. I had learned enough, however, to realize that they, and all of us, had better be in shape for the daily routine to come.

I had developed enough respect for the skill it took to work this windjammer to realize how well founded my concern had been about commencing this voyage with the fishermen in the condition they were in when they came aboard.

I had also learned that this was standard routine for a West Coast codfisher. I began to appreciate that Captain Thomas was too good a seaman really to risk his ship. He had relied on the weather reports, the probabilities that we wouldn't hit a blow in the first week or so, and his past experience.

He knew that sooner or later (and really much sooner than I would have believed possible) the alcohol would metabolize out of their systems, the sea air would restore them, and the *William H. Smith* would be sailed by a crew of old windjammer hands who knew exactly what they were doing.

By the time the ship had shaken down, us lubbers were beginning to learn too and, in most instances, did more good than harm working this vessel. It didn't just happen; it was a product of many years' collective sailing experience that the captain, the mates, and the fishermen had accumulated. None too gently, but effectively, they passed the knowledge on to us.

The *Smith* was now an efficient commercial sailing vessel.

14

The next day the weather began to make up on our morning watch, and the wind steadily increased.

To the extent possible, the captain tried to schedule the sail handling for the daylight hours. We were making long tacks across the broad reaches of the North Pacific, and it really didn't matter whether we came about on a new tack at midnight, or six or seven hours later, when there was daylight for sail handling. There were no navigational hazards for him to be concerned about where we were sailing.

This time, as so often at sea, the elements surprised him. We had all assumed that this was a strengthening of the wind that would hold at thirty to thirty-five knots and get us to our destination that much sooner. Instead, very gradually, the wind velocity increased. By the time we reported on deck for our night watch we were still carrying all sails, and the decision had just been made to take in the tops'ls. This led directly to the most dangerous mistake I ever made on the *Smith*—almost my last.

By the original selection of the mates each watch had an equal number of fishermen. The dress gang members on each watch just about equaled the number of fishermen. By tacit understanding, each fisherman basically paired off with one of the green hands. It was an efficient means of instruction, and it provided a margin of safety to have an experienced man working with a green hand. Roy Brewer usually worked with Skys'l Sam on the two-man assignments. Ever since we had set the heads'ls together I had been paired with Chris Olsen.

One of the men on the third watch had already taken over the wheel. Jim Bewla assembled the rest of the watch on the weather deck. He had to shout to make himself heard over the howl of the wind.

"Skys'l, take Brewer and get in de fore tops'l. Olsen, take Hofvendahl and get in de main tops'l." In another moment he had given the orders for the mizzen and spanker tops'ls.

We moved off to our respective jobs. I should have known by then that there was no real urgency about getting the tops'ls in. We obviously had to reduce sail—it was blowing about forty knots by then—but a few minutes made no difference.

I also had learned by then, I thought, that it is always better at sea, absent the most calamitous crisis, to take a moment to study a situation.

Despite this knowledge, without saying a word to Chris Olsen, or waiting for his instruction, I made my way to the port-side leeward rigging of the mainmast and started up. I was wearing my heavy seaboots and foul-weather gear.

It was a combination of factors. Those soaring topmasts of the schooner had intimidated me ever since I had climbed the rigging while we were still at anchor in San Francisco Bay. Subconsciously I knew I'd better start up without thinking about it too long. Then too, Chris had led the way out on the jib boom, and I wanted to show him I was an able hand, that I didn't have to wait for him to lead me.

It was awkward going with my gear on, but surprisingly as I climbed the rigging in the lee of the mainsail it was as if the wind had stopped there and the sound had died.

When I got about halfway up I thought I heard a shout on deck. It was a black night, and when I looked down I could just barely see someone standing by the rail where the rigging was anchored.

Then I decided it had been my imagination and kept climbing. I wanted to be in those crosstrees before Chris got there. I was also pleasantly surprised to learn that even though I had looked down at the deck I wasn't hit by the vertigo that had bothered me the first time.

I kept climbing. I could see the gaff of the mainsail, inboard and just above me. The gaff was smaller than the boom but performed the same function at the head of the sail as the boom did at the foot. The rigging narrowed, and it became more difficult to find a foothold. The crosstrees were about six feet above me. Holding on with my left hand, my left foot planted on the cross bracing, I was reaching for another handhold with my right hand, my right foot stepping up for the next rung. In this position I cleared the mainsail gaff with the upper part of my body.

The wind hit me with a blast that almost, but not quite, tore me from the rigging. Aloft there, close hauled as we were in a heavy sea, the roll was probably three times as great as it was on deck. I was luckier than I deserved to be: The *Smith* rolled to starboard just as that blast of icy air caught me. If the roll had been to leeward, as the force of the wind struck my upper body, that would have been it. As it was, it tore the right side of my body from the rigging. All that saved me was the fact that my left foot slipped off and inboard through the rigging, and my left hand clutched the tarred cable with a deathlike grip.

I hung there, straddling the cross bracing, both hands now gripping the vertical cables of the rigging. I was just below the gaff, out of the force of the wind again. My heart was pounding, and I was sweating under my oilskins.

For one crazy moment I was trying to figure out how I could traverse that space between the gaff and the crosstrees—through the force of that wind. Then it hit me what that shout had been about. I forced myself to think, finally. Of course. If you ever went aloft in a blow you *had* to climb the weather rigging. The force of the wind then would be constant all the way up. It would press you against the rigging. If the topping lift on the gaff let go, or the sheet for that mainsail, the gaff would slam into the leeward rigging and take anyone on it flying into space. On the weather rigging you would be safe. I shuddered as I thought of my stupidity.

Very carefully I planted my right foot on the rung below where I was straddled, extricated my left leg, and started back down.

I didn't know what to expect when I got back on deck. At the least a tongue-lashing, at worst permanent ostracism as a dangerous fool—unfit to work with.

To my surprise Chris Olsen was waiting for me on deck. I could just barely make out his features. The expression on his face was an odd combination of relief and anger.

"Yesus, Roos, don' never climb dat lee riggin! Ya don' know—"

I interrupted him. "I know now, Chris." For a brief moment I thought I was going to be sick.

Then we heard Bewla's roar. "Olsen, I tol' ya get dat main top in!"

Chris looked at me, and I could see genuine concern on his face now. "I get anudder hand to vork de tops'l. Ya stay on deck."

I shook my head. It was one of the toughest decisions I ever made, but I knew if I didn't go back up now those topmasts would forever defeat me.

"No, Chris. I'll go back up." I tried to smile. "You go first this time and tell me what to do."

Chris grinned at me and nodded.

Just then Bewla appeared. "Vat de hell ya men doin'? I giff' orders to get dat tops'l in."

Chris just looked at him. "Ve goin', mate."

This time Chris started up first on the weather rigging. I followed—carefully. The wind tore my breath away, but it did press me to the rigging, and I marveled that I had survived that earlier climb on the leeward rigging.

Under Chris's expert guidance I finally clambered into the crosstrees. Working slowly, one hand for the ship, one hand for ourselves, we fought that canvas. When the tops'l halyard dropped the sail, it was like a live thing thrashing in the screaming wind, but finally, little by little, we had it secured.

Holding onto the cross members, I lowered myself out of the crosstrees, feeling carefully for the rigging with my feet. Finally I was climbing down and, after forever, I was back on deck.

Chris Olsen was down a moment later and looked at me. "Ya be a good hand, boy." He nodded to emphasize the accolade.

Nothing anyone ever said to me on the *Smith* meant more than these few words from Chris Olsen.

15

The wind continued, ever stronger. By the time we took over the watch the next morning all of the heads'ls except the stays'l had been taken in.

We sailed close hauled on a port tack our entire watch with the wind blowing a steady forty-five knots. I drew the wheel turn at six bells on our watch, and it was the toughest wheel turn I had yet. It was hard work to keep the *Smith* from running up into the wind with the heads'ls down—a constant struggle forcing the wheel to starboard against the direction in which she wanted to go. The effort kept my body warm, but my feet felt like two blocks of ice.

The worst effect was the wind—almost constantly on our nose. It made it difficult for me to get my breath, and about halfway through my wheel turn I became nauseated from the effort of breathing. I stayed that way until finally relieved by the first-watch helmsman.

The nausea passed, but I was exhausted. After the midday meal I hit my bunk and passed out as if someone had slugged me with a belaying pin.

I was awakened a couple of hours later by a commotion in the fo'c'sle. Men were swarming up the ladder, others were pulling on seaboots and oilskins. Some like myself were sleepily sitting up on their bunks. From the top of the fo'c'sle ladder I heard the bellow, "All hands on deck!"

It was quite apparent that this wasn't the first call. I recognized the first mate's voice. "Gottdamn, men, move it!"

The ship was heeled sharply to starboard, and it was almost as if it were pinned there. I was one of the last out of the fo'c'sle. The ladder, which had a normal angle to port, steep but nonetheless an angle, was almost vertical. It was difficult getting up and out on deck, but I finally made it.

When I reached the deck I saw that the sea was a boiling fury. The *Smith* had suffered what in a small racing yacht would be termed a knockdown. But she wasn't righting herself, and it was apparent, even to me, that some of her sails had to come down fast.

Looking over the leeward rail, the visual effect was as if the sea were running uphill from the rail, which was almost under. The thirty-seven-foot beam of the *Smith* gave an illusion of space and solidity, and as I hung onto a port weather shroud I was essentially in a vertical position with the gray, wild sea running uphill from the starboard rail to the horizon.

There was no time to ruminate on this unique experience. Paul Myers was barking orders, and I went slipping and sliding down the canted deck, then groping my way aft to join the third watch in getting the mizzen down.

About halfway through the afternoon first watch the wind velocity had increased, this time suddenly and without warning, screaming out of the northwest. I don't know what the velocity was, but it was close to or at gale force. We were pulling in everything but the stays'l and spanker. We had to get her off her beam ends and get her standing on her feet.

Getting the three gaff-rigged sails down was always ticklish. It was not possible simply to release the halyard, as with the heads'ls and the spanker, and let her drop. That heavy gaff was almost as large as the boom, and it had to be controlled carefully as the sail was lowered. If it got loose in a blow like this, the effect could be lethal.

We were grabbing canvas as she dropped and then, almost down, a fierce gust caught the sail and blew it over a dory hung on the starboard davits just abeam of the mizzensail. It was impossible to pull it off from the deck against the wind.

Our mate was incisive. "Hofvendahl, ya and Brewer, get into dat dory. Get dat sail free!"

Bitterly I thought, why in the hell is it always me? But this was a job that required no knowledge, just muscle. The seamen were needed to handle the mass of lines that were still a puzzle to the green hands.

The *Smith* was beginning to stand up again, but there was still a sharp heel to starboard. I looked at the dory slung on those davits and prayed that the davit lines would hold.

Roy and I fought the mass of sail little by little up off the dory and inboard as the rest of the men pulled on it from deck. Probably due to my experience aloft the preceding night I was proceeding cautiously with my legs solidly braced against the leeward side of the after end of the dory. Roy was working in the midship section of the dory and became so focused on our job that it was as if he had forgotten where we were. But I was ever conscious of that angry mass of swirling sea rushing by. I had heard the stories of men who fell overboard in much lighter winds than this and who never had been recovered. I knew, without the stories, that a drop into that sea meant the end.

With the last heave on that heavy canvas, Roy was facing directly inboard and, as we finally freed the sail from the dory, the *Smith* took another roll to starboard.

The effort he was expending in pushing the sail suddenly left him with no handhold on anything just as the sail was pulled off the dory and aboard and the ship rolled to starboard. He staggered back against the side of the dory hanging out over the Pacific. The top of the dory rail hit him just above the back of his knees. His scream was torn away by the wind, and there was an agonized look on his face as he started to go backward off the dory. I had been moving gradually forward in the dory as I had worked the sail off of its stern. I was just within reaching distance of him as he fell backward. Fortunately for both of us, I had to lunge for him and in doing so fell below the dory rail as my left hand caught in one of the spaces down the front of his oilskin jacket. The jacket was secured by clips rather than snap buttons, and I was holding against the clip. For an agonizing instant we hung there; then the *Smith* started to come back to port and he was fighting for his balance, finally coming upright and then collapsing on top of me in the bottom of the dory.

We lay there panting for a moment, wrung out. Then we heard Bewla's voice on deck.

"I didn't send ya up dere to sleep! Ve need everyvun on deck! Get yer asses down here!"

I just shook my head and wondered how many of us would survive this voyage. Roy was incapable of saying anything.

By the time we were back on deck the fore-, main-, and mizzensails were down and in the process of being secured.

With only her stays'l and spanker up the *Smith* wasn't making much way, but at least she was back on her feet.

It wasn't until we were on watch that night that Roy tried to talk about it.

"Russ, I . . ." his voice broke and there were tears in his eyes.

"Forget it, Roy. You would have done the same for me."

He just nodded.

I walked the deck a long time that night, thinking. What I had done that afternoon had been purely instinctive, a simple reaction without time for thought. Yet Roy believed, with some justification, that he owed his life to me. Maybe he did, but there was no courage involved.

Yet, when I had made the decision to go back aloft the previous night, that had required all of the courage I could summon, and no one would ever know.

This voyage was teaching me a lot of lessons—almost on a daily basis, it seemed at times. One of them was that life is hardly perfect—and rarely as fair and just as I would have had it.

16

The wind blew steadily, occasionally with roaring blasts that rolled the *Smith* hard over to leeward, more often with a steady but unremitting force that made me wonder how long it could continue. All that day, through that night, through the next day and night, it came out of the northwest. Finally, on our watch two days later, it started to lighten. We ran up the fore, main, and mizzen. That afternoon the first watch hoisted the jibs. Early on the second watch, in the late afternoon, the tops'ls were set, and by the time we came on watch that night the *Smith* was sailing again with everything set and drawing.

On the rather infrequent occasions when Captain Thomas

could get a noon sun sight I had seen him balanced on the quarterdeck sighting through his sextant. By now I had philosophically placed myself in the hands of Fate and Captain Thomas.

All I could see in the vast distances visible from the deck of the schooner was an unbroken expanse of sea. How Captain Thomas was going to get this windjammer to a place which its very name suggested must be a narrow opening—Unimak Pass—I didn't know. Somehow I had confidence that he would do so.

That night, after my wheel turn, I was walking on deck with Chris Olsen again.

"Good thing the crew turned to the way they did the other day, huh, Chris? We would really have been up against it if we hadn't gotten those sails down when we did."

Chris spat, somewhat contemptuously, I thought. "Hah! Dis number of hands ve ought to be able to get 'em down. Used to do it wit' six A.B.'s and two mates many a schooner I shipped on."

By then I was growing used to the male point of view, perhaps the human point of view—male and female—that no matter how tough things were, the narrator had known it tougher. Still it didn't seem physically possible that only eight men could handle a vessel this size.

"Come on, Chris, you mean to tell me that eight of you handled the sails on a four-master like this?"

"Dat's right." Chris chuckled briefly. "Course, it vas all hands on deck damn near every vatch, but ve get de yob done."

"How would you get those sails down with just eight men, Chris?"

"Vun at a time, dat's how. Cap'n took de vheel. He tak' a vatch too. Mates hauled on lines lik' everyvun else. Ve do it, Roos."

He convinced me, and I really began to appreciate the old reference to wooden ships and iron men. My God, I thought, we worked hard enough hauling on those halyards and sheets.

63

What it must have been like on those West Coast schooners, handling sails in a blow with less than a fourth of the hands we had, was almost beyond my grasp.

By then I could steer a steady enough course that I felt free to talk to the mate, if he encouraged me at all, when I stood my wheel turns.

By casual questions, directed to Jim Bewla and later to Skys'l Sam, I learned that what Chris Olsen had told me was indeed the fact. The fore- and aft-rigged schooners usually sailed with just the number of hands that Chris had said they did. In fact, disabling injuries were so common that these ships were often sailed, and effectively, with even fewer men than that. Of course, the crews rarely slept through two off-duty watches as we did on this floating luxury palace, and the wheel turns were two hours long for each able-bodied seaman each watch, watch after watch. No wonder these fishermen had developed the muscles they had.

My respect for these old sailors was growing. They rarely volunteered anything about their early days at sea, but they seemed willing to talk and to respond to all the questions I had.

One night in the mess I was having coffee with Skys'l Sam. He was a Dane and obviously one of the most knowledgeable seaman aboard.

"Skys'l, how did you get your name?"

He chuckled briefly. "First time I ship out she be a skvare rigger out of Copenhagen."

I interrupted him. "How old were you?"

"Tvelve year." He went on. "Ve hit heavy veather first veek or so. Den ve catch fair vind. De mate ordered me aloft vit anudder han'—set de fore skys'l."

I wasn't familiar with the square-rigger nomenclature, but somehow that sounded high to me. There was little question that the fore- and aft-rigged schooners were far more efficient than the square-riggers at beating to windward. But the paintings I had seen of the old square-rigged clipper ships, with their sails fixed to the yards swung on the masts across the line of the hull to take full advantage of a following wind running free, were beautiful to behold. Their masts towered into the skies.

"Which sail was that, Sam?"

"De highest. You tink dese crosstrees high, nuttin'." He shook his head vigorously.

"Anyvay, I climb up, do vhat dey tell me, ve get de sail set, den I look down." Again he chuckled reminiscently. "I can't move. Mate on deck hollerin' at me. Didn't matter. I yust hung dere."

"Jesus," I said. I thought how the relatively modest height of our crosstrees, only a hundred feet or so above the deck, affected me.

"How did you get down?"

"Same vay I vent up, vit my hands and feet."

"How long were you up there?"

Sam thought for a moment. "Maybe t'ree, four hour. Long time. Anyvay, I finally back on deck. My mate he started callin' me 'Skys'l Sam.'" He chuckled again. "Been 'Skys'l Sam' ever since."

Skys'l Sam was as rugged as the rest of them, but he wasn't nearly as large a man as Chris Olsen or Jim Bewla. I could picture an undersized Danish boy, twelve years of age, clinging in terror to that rigging high above the ship, hanging there hour after hour, those topmasts rolling through great arcs in the sky. It was sobering to me even to think about it.

After a while, when it became obvious that I was truly interested, they would spin their yarns by the hour. Probably half of them had the same experience that Skys'l Sam had of freezing in the highest rigging of a square-rigger their first time aloft. None of them came down any other way than under his own power and without assistance. I learned that not all novice sailors did get down safely, either. It was infrequent, but not unheard of, to lose a new hand like this, whose terror froze him to the rigging until finally the elements and exhaustion cast him off into the sea. It was simply a part of life on those ships in those days. There was only one way to break in a new hand for the tops'l work, and that was to send him up.

The great majority of those who went aloft came down eventually, and for the few who didn't—better to lose a green hand than risk another hand trying to help him down.

As far as I know, and at least on the *Smith*, Skys'l Sam was the only old sailor who carried his mate's sarcastic christening with him for the rest of his life.

I had never kept a diary, and I don't really know what impelled me to do so on this ship. I suppose it had something to do with not wanting to waste something I had paid good money for in that depression year. For whatever reason, within a day or so of coming aboard, I started to log in one of my writing tablets in pencil—which was all I had—what transpired on this voyage.

It is a sketchy outline at best, and there were many days when we were dressing fish in the codfish grounds in the Bering Sea that there are no entries at all. Yet, like the evocative strains of a favorite song, a glance at the diary I kept on the *Smith* awakens a rush of memories.

The sounds and smells, the faces of my shipmates return as if I were walking the deck of the *Smith* with them only yesterday.

Many of them, despite the fact that I lived with them for almost five months in the close quarters of that fo'c'sle, were known to me only by their first names, often as with Skys'l Sam, by nicknames that identified them forevermore in my diary and in my mind.

I didn't own a camera, and one thing that didn't get into the diary was who did. Nonetheless, sometime after our return to San Francisco I came into possession of an unusually clear and informative group of snapshots of life aboard the *Smith*. These too keep the memories green.

Another thing that didn't get into my diary was the sea stories these old sailors told, but I have never forgotten them. I was an avid reader and, long before I shipped out on the *Smith*, I had read the *Bounty* trilogy by Nordhoff and Hall, Jack London's *Sea Wolf*, and Dana's *Two Years Before the Mast*, among others.

As fascinated as I was by these books, they inspired no desire to ship out on a sailing vessel. I wanted to go to sea, almost desperately, but it had never crossed my mind that I would ever ship out on a windjammer.

Now, during some of the off-watch hours, I sat on the bench in front of the potbellied coal-burning stove in the fo'c'sle and listened to the fishermen's yarns. I heard firsthand what it was like to beat around Cape Horn on a square-rigged sailing ship through the roaring forties, those awesome latitudes approaching the cape where the wind roared and the seas built up to mountainous waves. Without exception, each one of my Scandinavian shipmates had done it—in the hard direction from east to west, almost invariably beating into the wind. Many of them had done it more than once. Now they laughed about some of it, and if two or more got yarning together they would sometimes lapse into Swedish, Norwegian, or Danish. The languages were slightly different, but they were understandable among them. Then I would interrupt and remind them I couldn't understand their bloody language with the long "ooo" sounds. Good-naturedly they would go back to their Scandinavian-flavored English.

The usual stories were personalized—tough skippers and mates, character shipmates they had shipped with. It was their shop talk. I am sure that coal miners and steel mill workers talk in a similar way in their own frames of reference.

These men saw no romance in their lives. Without exception they decried their lives at sea. Yet, when I heard them swap stories about Hong Kong and Hamburg, Sidney and Shanghai, the references as casual and commonplace to them as street names in San Francisco were to me, I was fascinated.

All of them held able-bodied seamen's papers in the United States merchant marine, and their stories of life aboard a modern American merchant vessel sounded too good to be true—fresh meat every day, ice cream for dessert almost every day (the farther north we got the more the talk seemed to turn to food), hot showers, and fo'c'sles with portholes or at least funnels to get the fresh sea air in.

I didn't want to be laughed at, and it would only have emphasized my lack of experience, so I never volunteered to say that by now I didn't think the *Smith* was all that bad.

They did think it was bad, or at least said they did, and I deferred to their experience accumulated during long years at sea. It would have surprised them to hear anyone speak well of this old windjammer.

They would have been even more surprised if I had told them that day by day I was seeing them ever more sharply defined as the unique individuals they were. These men were good shipmates. I have never forgotten them.

17

Jack Anderson had the aftermost top bunk on the dress gang port side of the fo'c'sle. The aft section of his bunk extended behind the headboard of my bunk. Thus we were in a convenient juxtaposition for conversation when he was stretched out in his fore-and-aft bunk and I was stretched out in my thwartship bunk. The bunks formed basically a right angle, and when I was in my bunk, head to port, we could converse quietly across a distance of only a few feet.

In the course of a number of off-watch talks like this I learned that Jack was twenty-three years of age, had been born in New Orleans, and like many young men of that time, he was resourceful. He had done many things, including retail sales, some merchant shipping out of the Gulf Coast ports, and a stint in the generator room of a public utilities company. Although he didn't look the part, he had an affinity for equipment—particularly gasoline engines.

Like almost everything on the *Smith*, at least as it seemed at the time, our deck engine was cranky and uncertain. It was utilized mainly to pump out the bilges every other day but was also used to pump seawater aboard, to hose her down, and to hoist the anchor. God only knows when the *Smith* had last been hauled and had her bottom caulked and painted. I know that when the bilge pump was operating the water from the bilges seemed to pour out in a never-ending stream.

Frank Simmons had assumed command of this ship's function and had managed, finally, to get that engine running almost every other day, but there were days when no matter how he cursed and labored it simply would not sputter into life.

On one of these occasions Jack was watching him and made a quiet suggestion. At that point Frank had just about had it.

"All right, goddamnit, get in here and see what you can do!"

Jack shrugged, went into the deckhouse, and inside of half an hour had the engine purring. I didn't know anything about the functioning of an internal-combustion engine, but it was obvious even to me—I had been standing nearby on the deck watching Frank work—that it sounded better than it ever had.

Frank Simmons was an effective administrator, and he knew when to make a decision.

"Anderson, you want to take charge of this sonofabitch?"

Jack barely nodded. "Suits me."

"OK, you keep her running, I'll talk to the cap'n, we'll take you off watch. This'll be your main duty from now on."

That decision, so casually made, was to have a monumentally important consequence for the *Smith* in the not too distant future.

It was interesting to me that Jack enjoyed working on the engine because he was easily the most fastidious man on the ship. He had a very pale complexion, almost white-blond hair, and rather piercing brown eyes.

No matter how begrimed he got working on that engine, he always cleaned the grease off thoroughly in gasoline. While he could not afterward have washed in anything other than the salt water the rest of us used, when he was through cleaning up he managed to look as if he had just stepped out of a hot shower.

Nicknames were bestowed casually on the *Smith*, and rarely could I remember when or where any of them started. Probably

69

because of his personal habits, pale complexion, and very blond hair, Jack became "Powderpuff." The first time I heard someone address him so, I was sitting next to him in the mess. I could see his jaw muscles tighten for an instant, then relax.

The name was not intended cruelly, although it may have had that effect to some extent. It was merely descriptive and clearly did not carry any implication of homosexuality.

If it had, that would have started a fight for sure. I appreciated the fact that he always dealt with me as an equal, and I never called him anything but "Jack."

"Powderpuff" he became and eventually, with a maturity and judgment far beyond whoever had hung that name on him, he responded to it as if it had been given him at birth.

Despite his skill, at times the engine refused to start even for him. On one particular day, as if intent on proving its dominance, the sole source of mechanical power on the *Smith* had absolutely refused to give out one starting cough. Jack had neither the tools nor the space for a major overhaul, but he had patiently gone through the fuel system and was now working on the ignition.

It was not quite six bells on our morning watch, about a week after Jack had become deck engineer. I had finished a wheel turn at four bells and was standing at the hatch of the deckhouse watching him work. We were heeled over to port, sailing close hauled on a starboard tack.

"What're you doing now, Jack?"

"Cleaning the plugs. Think that's what she needs. It better be. I've tried everything else."

He had by then cleaned all four of the plugs on this four-cylinder engine, had replaced two of them, and was about to replace the third when we both heard the shout—almost a scream.

"Fire! Fire in the lazaret!"

For an instant my heart seemed to stop beating. I had heard the stories of fires at sea. On the old, wooden windjammers there was no hazard more terrifying.

I ran to the starboard rail and looked aft. I could see smoke pouring out of the port lazaret hatch about three quarters of the way aft on the quarterdeck. That was where our gasoline drums were stored. I had helped Jack pump out five-gallon jerry cans there to fuel the engine. If that fire hit those drums we wouldn't even have time to get the dories launched before the *Smith* went off like a bomb.

I could hear feet pounding on the deck and some shouting. Probably there were a relatively small number of men aboard who knew about the gasoline in the lazaret, but they all reacted to the cry of fire.

The helmsman was already turning her into the wind to lessen the air draft.

Automatically the crew had roughly assembled into watches, joining their watchmates for this crisis effort.

I saw a bucket flying over the port rail at the end of a line.

Most of my watch were already assembled at the starboard rail just aft of the deckhouse where the engine was located.

Chris Olsen was swinging a bucket into the sea at the end of a line. Skys'l Sam shoved an empty bucket into my hands before I fully realized what was happening, and I found myself part of a bucket brigade.

I never heard a command uttered. There had never been a fire drill aboard either, but as always these men, fighting for their lives now, did exactly what had to be done.

Even as I saw the first bucket of seawater hit the lazaret, I knew it was no use. The smoke was heavier now, and I could see the first orange flicker of flame. It would take far more than these puny buckets of seawater to get this blaze under control.

As I passed the bucket, grabbed an empty one, and waited for Chris to dump the next seawater in, I looked through the hatch into the deckhouse housing the engine. Jack had just finished seating the last spark plug. I could see that he was working rapidly, but he was in total control. Every movement was intense but focused on the job at hand. His concentration was palpable.

The captain's bellow sounded from the quarter deck. "Get the engine running! We need water!"

It was as if Jack Anderson never heard him. His expression didn't change, his movements didn't alter. He knew as well as every other man on the ship that our lives depended on him and the engine. He continued his tightly controlled, intense efforts.

Watching him, I knew that he would perform. I didn't know whether it would happen in time, but I knew if anyone could do it, he could. I dropped my empty bucket and ran for the hose coiled on deck.

"Come on, Chris, let's get that hose."

Chris started to swear when he saw me drop the bucket. However, one glance at a bucket of water at the end of our line dashed onto that flame flickering out of the lazaret and he knew it was no use.

Before we reached the hose, Skys'l Sam already had one end connected to the seawater intake valve. Chris and I grabbed the nozzle end and raced for the quarterdeck, dragging the hose behind.

Just as we topped the ladder and reached the quarterdeck I heard the engine roar into life. Suddenly the hose was like a twisting snake in our hands. Jack had really revved up that recalcitrant monster.

We held the stream of water on the lazaret hatch as two of our watch pulled the hatch open. The flames shot out and I thought again of those gasoline drums stored below. I think I prayed. I really was too young to die.

As the hatch opened we could feel the heat spring out at us like a live thing, the flames licking at the deck. It was a fair day and none of us had foul-weather gear or gloves on. I was at the very end of the hose, the seawater was really shooting out, but I couldn't force myself closer to that intense heat. Then I thought of those gasoline drums once again. We could train the hose on the hatch opening, but somehow we had to force that stream of water down into the lazaret at the source of the fire.

I was wearing my old Navy pea coat with the large collar. Pushing up the collar with one hand, I held onto the hose with the other. Chris and I were choking from the smoke, and I could barely talk.

"Hang on to me, Chris!" I said, gasping. Then I backed to the hatch opening, my head hunched down behind my collar. I felt the edge of the hatch with the heel of one foot and would have fallen into the inferno below but for Chris Olsen's iron grasp on my coat.

Then we forced the nozzle into the hatch, paid out about three more feet of hose until the seawater was pouring directly into the lazaret, and sprawled on top of the hose on the quarter-deck to hold the hose in place. The smoke was now intense, and I didn't know how long we could hang on. Then, little by little, the flames subsided. I could hear the crackle and hiss of whatever was burning below as the water hit it.

We thought we would win now, but that hose was going to stay in place no matter how long it took.

Finally it was over, and we knew we had won.

That night at our evening mess I didn't hear one man refer to him as "Powderpuff." They knew that we were still afloat thanks only to Jack Anderson and his knowledge of that temperamental engine.

As for Jack, he responded to "Anderson" with precisely the same demeanor that he had responded to "Powderpuff." He was a man in control.

18

Johnny Tango and Sam Culleson had nothing in common except premature baldness and skilled boxing ability.

Johnny was a White Russian who had fought his way ever east with a Russian cossack troop as the Bolshevik Revolution consumed the motherland. Like many of his compatriots I knew at the St. Francis Hotel (there were Russian counts and countesses among our elevator operators and room maids if their stories were credited), he finally made his way to Shanghai. He was then eighteen years of age. During those chaotic years following the end of World War I he had managed to survive by one means or another. Finally he had decided to leave China and had signed on a Norwegian tramp steamer as an ordinary seaman.

He told me once about his first sight of San Francisco. It was 1922 and he had just turned twenty-one.

"Ven I see dot ceetee bootiful, vhite—I know dot's for me."

He jumped his ship in the city, hid out with some Russian emigrés he had known in Shanghai, and stayed with them until his ship left port.

In the stable society of California, Johnny found it more difficult to live by his wits than it had been in Shanghai. He had a strong, compact, muscular build, and he drifted into professional boxing. Fighting as a heavyweight, it was easier for him to get a fight than the lighter-weight boxers.

He had an unpronounceable Russian name. "Johnny Tango" had been his professional fighting name, and he continued to use it. He spoke with a strong Russian accent; in some respects it was like the Scandinavian language, replacing the "w" sound with a "v." However, he also left "h" off many of his words that demanded it in English, and he had a way of reversing nouns and adjectives that made him a bit difficult to follow.

Although Gus Kalnin—Trotsky—was native born in the United States, his parents had emigrated from Russia, and he could speak some Russian. Much of Johnny Tango's background came to me secondhand through Trotsky.

Unlike most of the Russians I had known, Johnny was invariably cheerful.

It was as if all that he had been through in his early years, including the brutal grind of fighting semiwindups in small-town fight arenas year after year, had left him with a basic conviction that life had to be better now.

74

I was a dedicated fight fan. Although I was attending high school with Ray Lunny, an accomplished professional lightweight of that era, I really hadn't known any other pro fighters, and Johnny Tango fascinated me. Also, he had an ingenuous way about him that made it impossible for me not to like him.

Sam Culleson was an amateur fighter, but the AAU tournaments of those days were almost as tough as professional boxing. He had had over a hundred amateur fights as a lightweight and was seriously thinking of turning pro when he ran afoul of the law in Napa County. He was fairly closemouthed about just what he had done, but I gathered that he had participated in an attempted armed robbery of a liquor store. I believe that Sam was basically more ashamed of his ineptitude than the fact that he had been caught and had done a solid year in the Napa County jail.

His cellmate during that sojourn was a professional gambler and card shark. During the six months or so that they had shared living accommodations, Sam's cellmate had taught him just about everything he knew. Sam was a willing pupil because I have never, before or since, seen anyone more adept with a deck of cards.

Johnny Tango was a bit over six feet tall, and both his ears were slightly cauliflowered. Despite his pro boxing experience, these were about the only marks of his trade he carried. His deep-sunk eyes and rather broad nose did not show the marks of the ring so characteristic of many professional fighters.

Sam Culleson was about five-eight, had sharp, rather aquiline features, and his nose was slightly flattened at the bridge. The septum had been spread about on the inside also, because Sam was forever exhaling through his nose with the brisk sound so often heard at ringside. It was so automatic with him that I don't believe he was aware he was doing it.

It was Sam's theory that, since a man's beard obviously grew heavier with repeated shaving, then exactly the same thing should happen with the hair on top of a man's head. He had gotten his head shaved twice while doing time and was convinced it had done some good.

Johnny Tango was easily persuaded of practically anything. He was also growing rather bald for his thirty-six years, and Sam prevailed upon him to exhange head shavings. One of the important factors was that Johnny shaved with a safety razor—Sam didn't relish the thought of a straight razor applied to his skull even while the motion of the ship was relatively steady and predictable.

They were both on the first watch, and one afternoon after the midday meal they took turns shaving each other's heads.

Johnny Tango was exhilarated as he rubbed his hand over his shiny pate. "Ze 'air she coom bak' 'eavy—lik' beard." He nodded emphatically.

Sam grinned and looked at me. There were five of us interested spectators. "Come on, Russ, you don't need it like me and Johnny, but it'll guarantee you a good head of hair the rest of your life."

That made sense to me. I had a safety razor packed in my gear and, with a couple of packets of single-edge blades that would more than last the voyage at the rate I was shaving then, I had the implements at hand.

Among his other talents, Sam was an accomplished jailhouse barber, and he had brought with him a good set of scissors and also clippers.

I hesitated for a moment, then said, "What the hell. Go ahead, Sam."

Since I had a good youthful head of hair at that time it took considerably longer than it had for Johnny and Sam. Sam had my hair off with reasonable dispatch. However, it was the shaving that took the time and about half my supply of blades. About midway through the operation Sam gave way to Roy. At one point Roy was taking one long sweep across the top of my head when we heeled rather sharply, the bench on which I was sitting slid to port on the now wet fo'c'sle deck, and I could feel the corner of the blade sink into my scalp.

Roy looked genuinely concerned, and I knew why when I felt a stream of warm liquid running down my cheek in front of my left ear.

76

Johnny Tango was in charge, however. "Iss h'OK. Ve got powder for dot." I felt the bite of alum rubbed vigorously into my scalp. Roy was a bit shook by the mishap and gave way to Sam again.

Finally, about forty-five minutes after they started, it was done. I rubbed my hand over my head and it did feel smooth and clean but for the traces of dried blood here and there.

Roy Brewer was sufficiently vain about his appearance that it rather surprised me when he decided to have his head shaved also. By then, most probably based in large measure on Roy's decision, about half the dress gang decided they too would go the route. We spent the rest of that afternoon turning a good portion of the *Smith*'s crew into reasonable facsimiles of the inmates of a prison ship.

I was a bit startled when I looked into my metal mirror the first time, and my watch cap had a tendency to slide up on my head, but in general I found it a most interesting effect, and eventually the scalp wounds healed. For no good reason other than the way life is lived in an all-male society, there was a small but perceptible bond among those of us who had taken this step to ensure a healthy head of hair forevermore.

It was late that afternoon, when all the barbering was done, that I first observed Sam's skill with a deck of cards. The shaving of the heads had put him in a somewhat nostalgic mood, and he began to tell us about his cellmate.

"Blackie could do the most unbelievable things with cards of anyone I ever saw. You guys get this place dry and I'll show you one of the things he taught me."

We soon had the deck dry and clean and were squatting in a small circle around Sam. After shuffling the cards he proceeded to deal four kings to me, four aces to Roy, four queens to Trotsky, and four jacks to himself. It was amazing because we were practically on top of him and none of us could detect anything unusual.

Then he showed us what he called three-card monte. It is a variation of the shell and pea game, only using cards. Sam displays a king, a queen, and a jack face up in a row before him.

He then turns them face down and rather slowly, or so it seems, moves them around until the three cards are again in a row with one of us guessing the identity of the selected card. No one of us guessed right, and Sam was obviously delighted with the attention.

Johnny Tango was a fascinated observer and finally requested a turn. Sam hesitated for a moment and then let him try his luck. Johnny missed the first two times and then, to our surprise, he picked the right card.

"Aha! I know dot's de vun," he chortled.

I wasn't quite so surprised when I noticed the appraising look in Sam's eyes. Johnny was like a child with a new toy. He wanted to go on, but Sam refused.

"No, Johnny, you've already figured it out. Besides, I'm tired. All this hair cutting has me wore out."

I didn't realize it at the time, but I was seeing the hook. It came much later in the voyage, but in due course I would observe the sting.

19

Sparks was an affable, quiet man who had little to do with the rest of the crew. He was of medium height and build with regular features and rather bloodshot eyes. He was our one link with the outside world. I had seen his table with the wireless equipment at one end of his cabin, but I never recalled seeing him sitting there operating. I had learned that, when we got to the grounds, he would be the ship's tallyman. He would keep the running individual counts of codfish caught. On the voyage up to the Bering Sea, besides whatever he may have provided Captain Thomas on weather information, he had little or no impact on our lives. Twice that I recall during that thirty-day voyage he hand-printed a news bulletin and tacked it to the mess bulkhead. Sparks may have considered that the summer of 1937 was a quiescent time in the world and not really worth our attention. It was the year after the Berlin Olympics, the year before the Austrian *Anschluss*. There were, of course, momentous events occurring in Asia that year and throughout the world. For those of us on the *Smith*, particularly the younger members of the crew who would be profoundly affected by the ultimate force of those events in just a few short years, we may as well have been living on another planet.

It wasn't merely a matter of personal inertia or disinterest. There were a number of times when I observed Sparks swaying slightly standing on the deck just forward of the hatch leading to his stern quarters, a rather beatific smile on his face. This suggested to me that, although there was no liquor in the fo'c'sle, at least one member of the crew had a private cache in those stern quarters.

It may have been the memory of the fire, perhaps an unspoken realization of just how vulnerable this old vessel was to the vicissitudes of the sea, but no one ever voiced resentment of the ship's radio operator. He was obviously indispensable if we required emergency help. Regardless of how little effort it would have required for Sparks to provide a daily news bulletin, the fact that he did not evoked no verbalized animosity from the crew. He was pleasant and courteous enough, despite the little contact he had with us. But, more than that, it was almost a superstition, like not whistling up a blow: No one complained about Sparks. On May 19, 1937, he put out the word, via hand-printed notice tacked on the mess bulkhead, that the schooner *Louise* had reported her position about 260 miles due north of us. The *Louise* was a three-masted schooner also owned by the Union Fish Company. She had left San Francisco two weeks ahead of us, and it began to look as if we might catch her and beat her into the Bering Sea.

The word spread through the *Smith* that we were probably about five days sailing from Unimak Pass, and we began to make ready for the grounds. The wind came consistently out of the north and we were taking shorter tacks now, closing in on the entrance to the Bering Sea.

During our morning watch on this day I started to go into the mess for a cup of coffee when Ole Johansen blocked my way.

"No vun in de galley. Ve pourin' lead."

Then I realized why the breakfast was over so quickly that morning, with the cook and the messman leaving the galley almost immediately. The fishermen were pouring lead weights for those of us in the dress gang, and a new fisherman like Johnny Tango, who did not have his own gear.

What the company provided for each man was two spreaders, four large barbed hooks, the line for our reels, and a pair of nippers needed to haul that wet line and preserve the palms of our hands. Everything else was assembled or manufactured on board. The fishermen who had made this voyage before had their own gear, and they had the know-how to equip us new hands.

I watched through the deckhouse port as Walter Jensen expertly melted lead in a long-handled steel container thrust over an open section of the cook's large coal-burning stove. The weights we used were large—about ten inches long, an inch and a half in diameter where the eye hook was set in the molten lead, and weighed about six pounds. Aside from the fact that it was a lot cheaper for the company to have its own unpaid crew doing the fabricating, it is doubtful if there were any weights like these to be had anywhere. They had to be specially made.

We would be fishing for the cod about a fathom or so off the bottom, and it took a heavy weight to drop the hooks down where they belonged and hold them there against the tides in the Bering Sea.

As Walter waited for the scrap lead to melt, I could see Ole fashioning a cone of old newspaper roughly the size and shape of a weight. Very carefully he placed this in the center of an empty bucket, and Sven Johnson, another fisherman, just as carefully packed rock salt around the cone, maintaining its shape. There was just room in the galley area for the three of them to work, and I thought momentarily, with a shudder, of the consequences if Walter slipped or the ship gave an unexpected roll as he was handling that molten lead. Nothing untoward happened. They worked with careful efficiency. As soon as a paper cone was ready in the bucket of rock salt, Walter poured the lead into it rapidly. Sven had backed off by then, and Ole was ready with an eye hook to which the spreader assembly would be attached later. As the melted lead reached the horizontal top level of the cone Ole, wearing a heavy glove, thrust the shank of the eye hook into the lead, held it steady for a moment until the lead began to harden, and then carefully withdrew his hand. After the lead had set and cooled, each weight was distributed to one of us with directions to file off the paper remnants and rough edges. Very carefully, with a rattail file we worked a hole into the smaller end where the fishing line would attach.

It took them three mornings to pour about eighty weights, enough for the dress gang and with some to spare. Weights would be lost occasionally, and it was too much of a project to take over the galley to set up this molten-lead procedure any more often than necessary.

The method of compensation for the dress gang had some interesting socioeconomic implications. With this part of the crew on shares, based on total tonnage caught, it was in everyone's interest to assure that anyone who could fish was equipped and did so. Even though the fishermen were paid solely on the number of cod each one caught, they worked hard and willingly to outfit us and teach us. As far as the fishermen were concerned, the sooner we caught our cargo the sooner we headed home. Every fish a member of the dress gang caught added to the total catch, and this was incentive enough for them.

With payment for the dress gang based also on the number of fish an individual caught, he was motivated to work at the fishing and thus increase his personal economic reward in addition to what he was paid on shares. There are probably few fields of economic endeavor that lend themselves so effectively to such a socialistic-capitalistic amalgam. I don't know how or when the system was developed for the dress gang members of the codfishing schooners in the Bering Sea, but it worked effectively.

My uncle Jerry was a dedicated member of the Brotherhood of Railroad Trainmen and had lost no opportunity to indoctrinate me with the virtues of the workingman and the culpability of the bosses, usually referred to by him in a pejorative sense as "the company." Whether this method of compensation might be a carefully crafted design by the company to extract such willing labor from a part of the crew never bothered me in the slightest.

The one thing that did disturb me was the salt cod served at least one meal a day and sometimes twice a day ever since the fresh meat had gone. To my Scandinavian shipmates, the salt cod was akin to mother's milk. It had formed a staple part of their diets as children, and they genuinely enjoyed it. They did prefer the fresh cod and they assured me, with enthusiasm, that when we got into the grounds we would have some real eating—all that fresh fish.

For starters, I didn't much care for fish in any form, although I enjoyed seafood such as crab and shrimp. By the fourth week aboard the *Smith* the smell of that cod almost turned my stomach. I could only nod glumly as Chris Olsen would chomp away contentedly, and benignly encourage me between mouthfuls. "Dis goot chow, Roos." I am sure my less than enthusiastic appetite for the cod was apparent to him. Once in a while he would grin slightly and say, "Eat, plenty more vhere dis com' from!"

It was one of the few times in my young life when I ate to maintain my strength and that was about all. Bitterly I thought of my uncle Jerry's emphatic statements that the company would screw its men at every turn. The Union Fish Company was really doing it to me with their goddamn salt codfish unsold from last year's catch, and now providing the most inexpensive possible larder for this year's crew.

On the other hand, in 1937 the Union Fish Company (despite its name it was anything but unionized) probably could have funded this voyage only by doing exactly as it did—cutting every possible corner.

With the distribution of the weights the environment on the ship quickened. We would soon be where the cod were. This was the reason for the voyage. The men who had been there before knew the dangers, the cold, and the long, backbreaking hours of labor. Yet taking cod out of the Bering Sea was our reason for being here. Like a military combat unit just before battle, the veterans knew what they would be confronting, and they did not minimize anything in passing on their knowledge to the green troops.

For the dress gang the ultimate tests were the ten-thousand-fish days. These were the days when the cod poured aboard in a never-ending stream. Then the dress gang toiled and labored until every last cod was dressed and salted in the hold below. It might take ten, twelve, or fourteen hours, but the work went on until it was done. Frank Simmons could not have enjoyed the prospect of these exhausting days. Yet he took a perverse delight in telling us, "Wait'll we get ten thousand fish coming aboard in one day. You guys think you've worked before. Just wait!"

With a perversity that matched his, we were waiting expectantly for the chance to prove we could do the job. However inexplicable the reasons, the entire crew was eager—indeed, anxious—to get into the Bering Sea to start catching codfish.

Two fishing lines were passed out to each one of us. With Skys'l Sam's help I constructed two wooden reels. These were simply wooden rectangles about thirteen inches long by about seven inches wide, with the four ends projecting a couple of inches to hold the line.

The spreader was an opened horseshoe-shaped bronze alloy piece of metal. It was about five inches from one end around the horseshoe to the other end. It was about three-quarters inch across the metal and about one-quarter inch thick. It had an open eye hook at the top of the horseshoe attached to the round eye hook fixed in the end of the weight, and then it was clamped shut. From each end of the spreader, tied to a swiveled eye hook, we attached about seven inches of braided line with the hook at each end. Basically the function of the spreader, as the name implies, was to keep the hooks separated or spread so that when the cod were running, we could catch them two at a time. The single fishing line leading from a reel was attached to the weight by tying a bowline through the hole we had carefully worked and smoothed in the narrow end of the lead.

When we were all through, each of us was equipped with two reels of line, each line with a weight, a spreader, and two hooks at the very end.

As we worked on our personal gear I could hear the occasional roar of the outboard motors as the fishermen tuned them and worked on them where they were hung in the wells in the dories.

One morning, about midway through our watch, I called up to Chris Olsen in his dory.

"Chris, can I come up and watch you?"

"Yah. Vhy not?"

I climbed up the standing rigging to where I could, carefully, step off onto the stern of Chris's dory. He had his powerful outboard motor disassembled in the midship section of the dory and was painstakingly examining each component.

"Thought I heard your outboard running yesterday. What're you doin' now?"

"Yust makin' sure! Dey ain't all dat much, but dey be all ve got vhen ve get out in de grounds. I make sure dis vun get Chris Olsen back!"

"How long you been comin' up here, Chris?"

"First time fifteen year ago. Shippin' off dat year, and dis de only berth I can get. Den I didn't ship on vun of dese scows for anudder ten year." Chris shook his head bleakly. "Last five year dis de only berth I can find. Vun t'ing, vhen I come back at least ve have dese outboards, no more dose bloody sails."

"What was wrong with the sails?"

Chris sometimes looked at me as if he wondered if there was

84

a brain in my head, then occasionally he would remember how new all of this was to me. This was one of those times.

Wiping his hands on a greasy rag, he leaned back against the side of the dory and started talking. I think it was just about the longest stretch he ever talked to me. His tone was somber.

"Roos, de Berin' Sea, she be bad vater. Strong tides, qvick blows. De dories been usin' outboards up here only 'bout ten year. Vhen I shipped in 1922, all sailing dories. Dese dories got no keels. Ve can only go as far upvind as ve can get from de schooner. Hope ve get fish dere. Den if she blow ya can run down on de ship." He paused and stared hard at me. "And hope ya make it de first time, oars not much goot vith dose tides, udderwise . . ." He shook his head without finishing his thought.

"If a fisherman missed, couldn't they go get him?"

"Vith vhat?" His categorical question exploded. "Ve lose four men dat first trip. Dat's vhen I decide no more fer me."

Then he seemed to relax a bit. "In 1933, needed a berth, vhen I find out no more sailin' dories I decide to take a chance vhen I couldn't get anudder berth. Man's got to eat."

I changed the subject slightly. "How long they been fishing cod in the Bering Sea, Chris?"

"Don't rightly know. Dat first trip of mine—dere vas vun old hand, been comin' up here more dan t'irty year den."

The conversation with Chris had sobered me. I thought of these old sailing dories trying to reach the mother ship against an adverse tide, frequently with a squall coming. My God, what terrible odds! Then I thought of some of the weather I had already seen on this voyage. I knew we would never launch the dories in those seas. But what if our fishermen got caught out in a sudden blow like that?

I knew now why the fishermen treated those outboards as if their lives literally depended on their reliability. The way they tended those small engines was eloquent testimony to that dependence.

Although it was never a topic of general conversation, I had heard enough stories about the sudden blows in the Bering Sea to realize that each year some fishermen never returned. To the extent possible, the fishermen on the *Smith* were doing all that could be done to ensure that none of them would be lost this year.

20

Although Chris Olsen could not have been described as antisocial, there was only one man on the ship I had ever seen him seek out for companionship. This was Karl Miller, our second mate. It had been only a few times, but occasionally after the evening meal (which was about the only time most of the crew were on deck at the same time), I had seen them leaning on the rail, staring out to sea, and talking.

Everything I learned from and about Chris came by dint of persistent questioning. In a way I am sure Chris regarded me as a nuisance but, on the other hand, it is rather flattering to have an individual take such an interest in one's personal life.

I was nothing if not brash, and one morning on watch I walked the deck with Chris and asked him point blank, "You don't seem to have much to do with anyone aboard except the second mate. How come?"

Chris looked at me with surprise. "Nay, Roos, I . . ." He hesitated briefly, then grinned. "I all de time talkin to ya. Dat right?"

I had to smile. "That may be, but that's only because I'm always asking questions. Have you shipped with Karl Miller before?"

He nodded. "Aye. Ve vere on a freighter two year. Bot' on deck, shippin' from de East Coast to Rio mainly. He sav' my life in a bar down dere vunce." He shook his head at the memory. "Karl a good man. Drinks some, but not like some udders aboard." His eyes clouded, and I could tell he was not excluding himself. He went on talking.

"Karl vork hard, get his mate's ticket, but no yobs for mates dese days. Dat's vhy he be on de *Smith* fishin' cod. He be my friend." He looked directly at me, and I decided to drop this line of personal interrogation.

"When do you think we'll be in the grounds, Chris?"

"Gottam, boy, I be tellin' ya and tellin' ya, ve be dere vhen ve get dere. Don' vorry about it!"

"I know, Chris. But when do you think?"

It was our morning watch, the day after the lead pouring was completed. We continued to pace the deck. Chris studied the sails, looked at the sea.

"If ya didn't ask me, ve probably be dere tree day now, but . . ." He broke off with an accusing look that very clearly implied I had jinxed our progress with my continual questioning.

Sure enough, about six bells on our watch that night a sudden squall hit, we were momentarily laid over on our beam ends, and it was "all hands on deck" again.

This time we were on watch anyway, and I didn't have to roll out of a warm bunk. But it was also a dark night, and I found myself far out on the end of the jib boom with Chris battling the flying jib into a secured bundle. Skys'l Sam and Roy were just aft of us, fighting the outer jib, while the rest of our watch were getting the inner jib and stays'l down. It was tough for all of us out on that jib boom, plunging into the sea one moment, then soaring up toward the sky the next.

It was a measure of how well the new hands had been taught that within about ten minutes, the rest of the crew working on the main and the spanker, we had the *Smith* sailing under fore and mizzen alone.

With all of that sail down the vessel was under control but making much less way than we had before the weather hit.

When the first watch took over I stood by the top of the fo'c'sle ladder for a moment before going below, and my eyes caught Chris's as he came into the deckhouse peeling off his oilskins. He nodded once brusquely, as if to say, "I told you not to tempt Fate by asking so many damn fool questions about when we were going to get there."

This time I hadn't done it. When I came on deck for our watch the next morning we were heeled over on a port tack, all the sails were set and drawing, and the sun was out. We had very little sunny weather on our voyage thus far, and this seemed like a good omen. The *Smith* surged through the sea like a live thing, the spray flung by our bow wave sparkled in the sunlight, and the sea was a deep indigo blue instead of the perpetual gray water streaked by white to which we had grown so used.

Early that afternoon Frank Simmons mustered all of the dress gang to start setting up the deck to dress codfish. The first watch was already on deck, the second watch was done out of their normal afternoon sleep, and those of us on the third watch normally didn't sleep then anyway.

The hatch cover came off the forward cargo hatch, and six of us were ordered below to handle the lumber. These were basically two-by-twelve sections which would form the checkers into which the fish would be tossed while awaiting dressing down. While the checkers and other wooden fixtures in place on the deck did not prevent sailing the ship, as we moved from anchorage to anchorage in the Bering Sea, they did impede free movement on deck. For this reason they were not set up until we were almost to the codfish grounds, and they were knocked down as soon as the decision was made at the end of the season to sail for home.

As undirected as many of the endeavors on the *Smith* seemed at times, everything worked with precision now. Frank Simmons, as head splitter, was in charge of the dress gang, and he directed this effort.

Axel Swenson was the head salter, and Oscar Quarten was the second salter. Besides Frank, they were the only two men in the dress gang who had ever even seen a codfish dressed for salting before.

It was up to Frank to organize these inexperienced men into two dressing crews—one port side, one starboard side—assign the men to specific tasks, and get the entire operation ready to dress fish.

The first step was to set up the checkers and construct two sets of heading boxes, splitting tanks, and drying racks, one for the port side, one for the starboard side.

The lumber looked to me like it had been used the previous season—I could see the nail holes—and it was heavy. It took us a couple of hours to move the lumber from where it had been stored on top of the rock salt on deck.

Then Axel Swenson put Roy and me to work at the forward end of the hold shoveling rock salt aft in the hold to clear the way for the first cinch (pronounced with a hard "c") of salt cod. This was a cleared area in the very bottom of the hold, up against the forward bulkhead, where the salter would place the first fileted cod and little by little build up the stack with carefully placed triangles of freshly dressed cod. His function was absolutely critical to the success of the voyage. Too little salt and the cod would rot, too much salt and we would lose weight—and money for the crew.

At the far aft end of the hold Oscar Quarten had Trotsky and Sam Culleson shoveling salt to clear the area for his first cinch of fish.

All afternoon we toiled, and when I looked at the area we cleared, I prayed for steady weather. I didn't much relish the thought of the *Smith* pounding into heavy seas and shifting that salt on us again.

By the time we climbed out on deck, just before the night meal, there was an aft checker in place on the port side nailed to the deck, and one in place on the starboard side.

The stars were bright that night, and the wind held. Midway through our watch we came about on to the starboard tack. Then the next morning I was awakened by the feeling of sliding gently down to the starboard end of my bunk as I felt the *Smith* lose way briefly, heard the shouted commands from on deck, the slat of the sails as the ship came through the eye of the wind, and felt her fill away on a port tack. I stretched out with a feeling of satisfaction. These short tacks had to mean we were getting close.

The sun continued to shine, the wind held, and we continued to work on the deck, setting up for dressing fish.

Late on our watch we heard a shout from the foredeck, "Sail ho!" It was the *Louise,* dead ahead, and about five miles distant. As we closed on her I looked past the *Louise* and in the far distance could see the vague white outline of a snow-covered mountain. It was the first land we had seen in almost a month.

The *Louise* tacked away from us, and eventually we lost sight of her. By the end of that day the checkers were nailed in place on deck, and the heading boxes, splitting tanks, and drying racks were almost completed for each side. There wasn't too much to be done now, and we would be ready.

On May 25, 1937, at four bells on our morning watch, I was standing on the forepeak with Chris Olsen, staring ahead.

I saw what looked like two smudges on the horizon with a stretch of clear water between directly forward of the jib boom.

On the twenty-eighth day out of San Francisco, Captain Thomas had navigated this windjammer through blows and calms, tacking across thousands of miles through the trackless waters of the North Pacific, precisely to Unimak Pass, the entrance to the Bering Sea.

I was excited. "Chris, is that it? When—" Then a glance at the stern, admonishing look on his face, and I shut my mouth.

Whatever the reason (for once I had stopped asking questions), the wind shifted to the southwest, the sheets were slacked off and, almost for the first time since we had left San Francisco, we were sailing on a broad reach. It was a fair wind and we sailed through Unimak Pass like an express train.

Unimak Pass is about eight nautical miles across its Pacific entrance and runs for about twenty nautical miles northwesterly to its egress at the Bering Sea.

To starboard we could faintly discern the settlement of Unimak on the southwestern corner of the island of the same name.

To port we were close enough to Ugamak Island to see the waves crashing on that barren rock. Even on a bright, sunny day like this the low-lying silhouette had an ominous look about it. I was too exhilarated by our swift passage through the pass to pay much attention to that particular island then. One day less than three months later, the sight of it would be etched on my memory forever.

Seeing the land slide by on both sides of the ship gave us a sense of distance traversed, of really getting there, that we hadn't known before.

Sailing through, with that blessed, steady beam wind, we cleared the pass in about two hours. At six bells on the first watch there was open water abeam to port and to starboard. We were in the Bering Sea.

21

The wind continued to hold from the southwest and we slacked off the sheets until we were running, heading in a generally northerly direction to wherever the captain decided to drop the hook and start fishing.

With all of the checkers and other gear secured to the deck, there wasn't much room for walking. Most of the time on deck at this time we leaned on the rail and stared out to sea if we weren't working the ship or standing a wheel turn.

Just after our night meal, salt cod again, I was out on deck staring aft when I saw a smudge on the horizon. It grew larger until I could make out the shape of a ship which seemed to be bearing on us. I hadn't really thought too much about John Gunderson once I realized I didn't have the clap myself, and he seemed to be making it all right. Now I remembered. He might be doing it the hard way, but he was going home. I went below.

Johnny was just finishing packing his seabag.

"How you doing, Johnny? Can I give you a hand?"

He looked at me, then smiled pleasantly. "I'd appreciate it, Russ. I have felt better to tell the truth." He paused briefly and looked at me. "You know you're damn near the only one on this ship who wanted to know how I felt and acted like he meant it!"

As usual, the light was dim in the fo'c'sle, and I was glad Johnny couldn't see me too distinctly. I could feel the blood rush to my face as I thought of the real reason I had been so concerned about his health.

"That's OK. Let me get that seabag topside for you."

I balanced his seabag on my right shoulder, held onto the draw lines at the end with my left hand, and carefully ascended the ladder, hanging onto the rail with my right hand.

Johnny followed slowly. Other than coming up to the mess for meals, or going on deck to relieve himself, he had spent most of the preceding three weeks in his bunk. Whether it was the enforced idleness or the gonorrhea, he really did not look well.

By the time we got up on deck I could see the trim lines of a Coast Guard cutter slowly easing up off our weather quarter. Gently our helmsman turned the *Smith* into the wind, and we hung there with the sails luffing. Then, with the superb, disciplined seamanship that the Coast Guard always seemed to display, that sleek white cutter maneuvered into position. Bow to wind, paralleling our position about one hundred yards off our port beam, I could see their motor launch descending from the davit lines with smooth efficiency. At this distance I could hear the quiet thunk of her engines, and it seemed to me—although it may only have been an olfactory illusion born of my enforced diet of salt cod—I could smell fresh bread.

The white paint and the metal fittings positively sparkled. Compared to the *Smith*, she was like an antiseptic dream. Coming to our succor like this, summoned by the invisible magic of Sparks' wireless, I was reminded of seeing a well-dressed man on the downtown streets of San Francisco giving a handout to a seedy, down-at-the-heels panhandler.

As the launch approached, the Jacob's ladder was put over the port side between the fore and main standing rigging.

There wasn't anyone aboard who would have traded places with Johnny Gunderson, given his physical condition, but still he was going home. I thought longingly of the ice cream I was sure that cutter had stowed aboard.

There wasn't too much of a sea running, but there was enough to test the skill of the Coast Guardsmen. Expertly the coxswain brought the launch alongside. He looked up at us and grinned.

"You got a sick man aboard?"

It was apparent that Johnny's affliction had not been treated with top-secret security.

There were answering shouts from the *Smith*. "That's right!" "Sonofabitch would do anything to get off this scow!" "Johnny, you keep that cock of yours secured when you get back to Frisco!"

Johnny smiled weakly, laboriously climbed up on the rail, and started down the Jacob's ladder. There were four men aboard the launch. Two of them—the coxswain in the stern, the other in the bow—used long boathooks to hold the launch to the *Smith*, expertly pulling her in and holding her off as the sea moved their small boat. The other two stationed themselves amidship in the launch waiting for our shipmate. As the launch rose on a surge, with Johnny just about at the foot of the ladder then, one on each side of him, they plucked him off and set him on a midship thwart.

His seabag followed, again passed easily from the rail of the *Smith* to the two men amidship in the launch at just the right instant when a swell carried the launch up to where it was only a few feet from the top of our rail.

The coxswain pushed off with his boathook at the same time the Coast Guardsman in the bow pushed off with his, and the launch was chugging powerfully across the stretch of water separating the two vessels.

I could feel the *Smith* bearing off to starboard as the sails filled. Johnny turned once and waved. He shouted something, but it was lost in the wind. It was the last time I ever saw him. Now there were thirty-five men in the fo'c'sle.

With the wind coming from our stern quarter there was much less of a driving sensation through the sea, but we were still making knots. All that night we sailed and then about 0600 I was awakened by the rapid, loud clanking of the anchor chain going through the hawsepipe. There was no electrical or electronic gear on the *Smith* to tell Captain Thomas where the cod were. It was strictly trial and error, and obviously we were about to make our first try.

Paul Myers, the first mate, was one of the most consistently successful fishermen aboard, season after season, and I suspect the captain listened to him when it came time to make the decision to drop the hook and try our luck.

The Bering Sea, compared to other bodies of water, is relatively shallow, although it has some very deep areas within it. Codfish are basically a bottom fish, and usually we anchored five to ten miles off the Alaskan coast, sent the dories out, and hoped for the best.

As I came on deck that morning about half the dories were already launched and fanning out from the ship. Two fishermen handled the fore and aft davit lines for the other fishermen until the last dories were ready to go, and then the dress gang took over lowering them into the water.

Once the routine was set, the fishermen were shoving off at about 0500 each morning and returning with their first catch about four or five hours later.

Until the first cod were pughed aboard, the dress gang had no duties, but most of us fished off the side for at least a couple of hours each morning.

This morning, however, Frank assembled us for final instructions.

"When that first dory gets in, I don't care whether it's starboard or port, I want you idlers looking lively! Get that dory's lines secured to the thimbles and hold him in until he's unloaded."

94

The main dressing operations were concentrated about amidships on both the port and starboard sides. Each one of the idlers (God only knows where that term was generated) was equipped with a pugh stick (pronounced with the "ew" sound as in church pew). This was like a pitchfork but with only a single tine, which was constantly filed and refiled to a sharp point. I was a portside idler.

Just forward of the main deck checkers and just aft of them were four fish ports, two to a side. The bottoms of the ports were just a couple of inches above the ship's deck and measured about ten feet long by about three feet high. These slid open so that when a dory was secured to the thimbles in the mooring line, run through blocks located about six feet fore and aft of the ports, an idler could hold a dory roughly opposite the open ports while the fisherman in the dory pughed his fish aboard as the idler took the count. When not in use the mooring line lay slack on the running board. When counting in a dory it was held about waist high by the idler.

We had constructed running boards about three feet above and paralleling the deck and about eighteen inches wide. These were secured to the inboard side of the ship's bulwarks so that when an idler was standing on a running board he had a much more elevated view of the dory, the mooring line he was controlling from his position on the running board, and the fish he was counting in. Also, however, the top of the ship's rail hit him just below the knees. When the sea was running, that stance on the running board felt none too secure as the mooring line jerked the idler fore and aft on the slippery surface as he tried to hold a dory in place opposite the port.

The basic dress gang crew for each side consisted of a splitter, header, gutter, and four idlers.

The operation commenced with an idler counting in a dory, and the other idlers pughing the fish from the open deck area into the checkers, where they couldn't slide out the port and over the side. From the main checker the cod were pughed into the heading box where the header, working with a brace of knives constantly resharpened with a stone kept at his station, split the fish up the middle and cut off the head. This operation required a certain amount of muscle, and Trotsky, probably because of his size and strength, was our portside header. The gutter, working between the header and the splitter, took the carcass from the header and simply pulled all the guts out of the fish. From him the fish was passed to the splitter who, like the salters belowdecks, had a key job. Rapidly making an incision on both sides of the backbone where it had joined the head, he freed enough of the bone with his razor-sharp knife to enable him to grasp the end of the bony column with his gloved left hand. Some fish required further incisions along the backbone. He finished the cut the header had started by splitting the fish all the way to its tail with his knife, then ripped out the spinal column with one pull of his left hand. This too required strength. The skill came in making the incisions so that very little, if any, of the meat came out with the backbone. When the splitter was through there was a large, boneless, roughly triangular filet of cod lying on the splitting table. The splitter pushed it off the splitting table into the saltwater splitting tank just adjacent to his station. From there an idler would pugh the split and boned cod, now washed free of blood, into a drying rack. The rack was about three feet wide and nine feet long. Despite its name, the purpose was not to dry the cod but simply to permit the excess water to drain off before the dressed cod were pughed through the hatches to the cargo hold below. Down there the salt passers would pugh the dressed cod from where they had landed on the tarpaulins stretched out on the bottom of the hold to the cinches where the salters were working. I never had any reason to time this entire operation. However, for a nonmechanized procedure, we turned a codfish, often still exhibiting some signs of life, into a large fish filet salted down in the hold of the *Smith* in a remarkably short period of time.

The first dory in that morning was a portside dory—Sven Johnson's. Frank Simmons didn't shout, but his tone was authoritative.

"OK, Russ, count him in. Watch that pugh stick when you hand it down."

I climbed up on the running board, caught Sven's bowline, and secured it to the forward thimble with a bowline knot. This wasn't too intricate a knot, and I had practiced it beforehand. It was calm enough this morning that the knot didn't matter too much then, but there would be days when it was imperative that the dory bow and stern lines be secured with knots that would absolutely hold and, at the same time, could be untied rapidly no matter how much strain they had been subjected to.

When I had Sven's lines secured to the thimbles I passed him the pugh stick, handle first, and he began to pitch the fish aboard. I counted each fish aloud in increasing numerical order. Sparks had come out of his cabin and was standing on the quarterdeck with his tally board.

As Sven pitched the last cod aboard I turned aft and shouted, "Number eight dory, fifty-seven!"

It was not much of a catch, but it was the first time out this season, and at last we finally had codfish coming aboard.

When I was about through counting Sven in, Roy was catching the bowline of another portside dory forward and was starting to count him in.

When his dory was empty, Sven stepped agilely from his dory to the Jacob's ladder and aboard. He went immediately to his bow line as I untied his stern line and then let the dory drift all the way astern of the schooner, securing it to a long line that permitted it to drift astern of the ship while he got some food.

This was the normal routine each day after the morning catch. In the afternoon, when the dories came in for the night, they were hoisted on the davits because the weather was too unpredictable to risk leaving them in the sea all night.

Normally the portside dories counted in on the port side, the starboard dories on the starboard side. However, if they began to jam up on one side or the other, the captain would often hail a circling dory and direct the fisherman to the other side of the ship to keep the fish coming aboard as uniformly as possible.

After a brief meal in the mess, one by one the fishermen

hauled their dories forward, dropped into them, and shoved off for another half day of fishing.

We only counted in about a thousand fish that morning so we were through dressing down by the time the last fisherman had shoved off for the afternoon's catch.

It was just as well that we started with a light catch. I could hear Frank Simmons patiently instructing Trotsky, keeping an eye on how we idlers were doing, and in general maintaining control. From time to time Frank left his post at the splitting table and went over to the starboard side to observe the operation there.

One of the dress gang was a lanky, sinewy mountaineer from Tennessee. He was a quiet individual and obviously strong. Early on he was christened "High Pockets." That is all I ever knew him as and the only name that identifies him in my diary. Frank had designated him as the starboard splitter and, because of the degree of skill and strength required for this job, spent a good deal of time with him that first day, making sure he was handling it right.

The splitter was the key man on each side's section of the dress gang, and it was imperative that the right man be selected as the starboard splitter. By the end of the first day Frank was satisfied that High Pockets would perform.

By 1900 hours we had finished pitching the last dressed cod into the hold and were hosing down.

Frank seemed to me to be in a good humor. "Damn, I wanted to find out if you guys could work—two thousand fish, this is a bloody vacation!" But he grinned as he said it, and I am sure he was just as glad the first day's catch had been light enough for us to settle in.

I could feel it in my arms and shoulders a bit. Pitching those twenty-pound cod into the checkers and into the heading box was exercising muscles I hadn't had prior occasion to use, but I liked the variety involved in being an idler. As yet I had no idea of the dangers involved, but it sure beat standing there all day tearing the guts out of codfish. I was well satisfied with our first day in the grounds.

22

The next morning I decided to try my hand at fishing off the side. There was obviously no perceptible advantage to one fishing location over the next from the side of the ship. Still, some locations seemed to enjoy more success than others. Once selected, by unwritten law this was your fishing station for the duration of the time in the Bering Sea. I watched Oscar Quarten appropriate a spot farthest forward on the starboard running board just aft of the foremast rigging. Since Oscar was an experienced hand, I immediately moved into the space next to his. It was directly over the forward starboard fish port.

"Is it OK if I fish here, Oscar?"

He simply shrugged. "Vun place yust as good as anudder."

Still I felt I could learn from watching Oscar and that he must have an insight into the preferred locations. He did, but only in one limited sense. Since his lines off the side were forward of and clear of the port, and since his work as a salter below represented the last step in the dressing process, he could fish off the side until the very last moment. On the other hand, as soon as the first dories started coming in, the ports had to be cleared. Since the idlers were the first ones to work as the dories arrived, it didn't matter to me if I was fishing over a port.

The first day's fishing had commenced with white, fatty pieces of bacon used as bait. However, halibut was the favored bait, and at least half the fishermen that first day had returned with halibut for this purpose. They were cut up and distributed to the entire crew. Apparently the white surface of the bottom chunks of halibut attracted the cod. That skin of the halibut seemed as tough as shoe leather, and once a square white piece of halibut was firmly anchored on a hook, it would last for hours. There was no obvious effort to fish for halibut for bait, but there always seemed to be plenty available.

The cod is not a fighting fish, but when it takes the hook, the fisherman knows it. It was not sport fishing in any sense, but there was the fisherman's satisfaction in pulling in a fish. Also, it meant money in that depression year.

As Johnny Tango was fond of saying, "Joost lik' pooling up deems from vater." The pay for the fishermen for a single cod would be precisely determined when we weighed out at the end of the voyage, but it would be close to ten cents per fish, and it *was* like pulling dimes out of the sea. My hourly rate of pay at the St. Francis ran about forty cents, including tips. It actually was a very satisfactory rate for that time and my age. With that measure in my mind, every time I hauled a cod from the bottom of the Bering Sea, when I finally did start catching them, I was thinking with satisfaction that this represented a quarter of an hour of work back in San Francisco.

That first morning, after about an hour, Oscar had ten fish on deck behind his station and I had not had anything I could identify as a bite.

The fishing technique was simplicity itself. The line went over the side until the heavy weight carried it to the bottom. Then it was pulled up a fathom or so and the fisherman gently moved the line up and down until a cod, attracted by the white gleam of the chunk of halibut in those cold depths, took the hook.

Finally Oscar looked over at me. He was a born comedian and totally unaware of the comic effect he produced.

"Yesus, Roos, da vay ya yerkin' dat line no vunder ya don' catch fish. He can't grab de hook!" Unconsciously he pantomined a cod, mouth open, head bobbing up and down trying to grab my hook rapidly ascending and descending in front of his mouth.

With his walrus moustache and his eyes fixed on the imaginary bait, the sight of him almost broke me up, but Oscar was easily offended, and I needed his help. I kept a straight face.

"Maybe I don't have a big enough piece of bait on the hooks, Oscar. It's hard for me to know if I got a bite with that weight. Would you try my lines for a minute?"

100

Oscar nodded, let his lines hang, and moved to my station. In less than a minute he gave an upward pull on one of my lines and handed it to me. "Now—pull him in!"

We all had a pair of nippers. They were medium-hard rubber, grooved circlets that we wore around our wrists like bracelets. As soon as we hooked a fish we dropped them off our wrists down to where they crossed the hands at right angles and the line was pulled up hand over hand caught in the groove of the rubber. There was a definite technique involved in using the nippers. For the experienced fishermen they were like part of their hands. For the inexperienced like me, it was a long time before I was used to the nippers and hauling in that line with long, hand-over-hand pulls, letting the line drop at my feet in a smooth, unsnarled oval. Without the nippers that wet, heavy line would have sawed through a man's hands.

The nippers were really awkward for me that first time, but finally I caught the gleam of a swirling fish just below the surface. Oscar was watching me carefully. "Don' yerk too hard now, steady pull."

I almost lost my right nipper as I reached for the spreader end of my weight, but it caught on the spreader as it dropped off my hand, and I carefully hoisted my first codfish aboard. It was good-sized, probably close to twenty-five pounds, and it gave me a real sense of accomplishment. On a projected basis my first two hours of codfishing were not going to make me rich. I had four fish lying on deck when I heard the cry, "Dory comin'!" and hauled in my lines. At least I knew I could do it.

Sparks was walking up and down the deck tallying the dress gang's catch before the first dory came in. Again it was a port-side dory, and again I was counting it in at the aft port.

The swells were large, rolling with a long motion, glassy-surfaced. I was more used to the sudden pull of the mooring line now and held the dory more easily abeam of the port as it counted in. "Number six dory, forty-seven!" I yelled aft to Sparks, and this day's dress down began.

Our total catch for the day was just a few hundred more than on the first day. It was not enough. We knew that we would be moving the anchorage. A codfishing schooner could figure on about two and a half to three months of suitable weather in the grounds before the storms became too frequent to permit continued fishing. Even during these few months there would be blows that absolutely precluded fishing from those flat-bottomed dories. Sixty days of fishing was a reasonable average to expect up there, and 350,000 codfish for a schooner like the *Smith* was considered a good catch. At just over two thousand fish each for the first two days we were a long way from that kind of voyage.

When the last dory was slung to its davits and secured, and while the dress gang was still hosing down and squaring away, the anchor was hauled, the sails were set, and we were under way again.

The wind was light and we ghosted along, close hauled on a port tack, bearing generally northeasterly, working in closer to the Alaskan coast.

It was during this first change of anchorage in the Bering Sea that I fully appreciated my good fortune at being a member of the third watch.

We didn't sail too long or too far, but we did stand watch around the clock. The second watch stood their afternoon and early-morning watches from four to eight, although it was a foreshortened morning watch, since we dropped the hook at 0500, and the fishermen were shoving off in their dories in less than an hour. That meant that some of the fishermen on the first watch had about an hour's sleep when they came off watch at 0400 and were soon out again fishing for cod. Those of us on the third watch got close to a normal night's sleep. The weather was calm, and the time had to be utilized.

23

At about 0800 that morning I decided to try some fishing again. I put fresh halibut chunks on my hooks, dropped the first line in, and baited the second. As the weight carried my second line down I idly hefted the first line and was amazed at what I felt. It was as if I had hooked onto the anchor.

Oscar Quarten mounted the running board next to me as I started to haul in my first line.

"Man, oh, man, Oscar, I don't know what I got, but it sure weighs!"

Oscar eyed me hauling on my line for a moment, then rapidly baited his lines and had them over the side.

Just as his second weight hit the water and started down I could see two cod flashing on my spread set of hooks as I got them near the surface.

By then Oscar was steadily hauling in on his first line. He glanced once at me. "Ve in a skool, de cod really runnin'. Haul dem!"

And haul them we did. In about half an hour I had forty codfish thumping on the deck behind my station.

By then my arms and shoulders were aching. It was a long haul from the bottom of the Bering Sea. It was plenty of weight to lift from the depths, even with the buoyancy that the salt seawater provided. When two cod averaging twenty pounds each plus the lead weight broke the surface, I then had nearly a fifty pound load to haul from the sea up to and over the side of the ship. Depending on the roll of the ship at that moment, it was a distance of from six to ten feet or so. Until I could reach the spreader with one hand, all of that weight was being lifted on that wet fish line. As exhilarating as it was, it suddenly dawned on me that I had never worked so hard in my life.

This was direct money earned, specifically tallied for my personal fish count. It was not the impersonal pecentage of shares of total tonnage caught, and I really wanted to stay with it, but the call of "Dory comin'!" ended the dress gang's fishing that morning. As it turned out, it was just as well. Although we didn't know it at the time, we were starting our first ten-thousand-fish day.

Frank Simmons shouted at me just as I finished pughing my fish into the forward starboard checker and Sparks had tallied my count.

"Russ, count in this dory for'ard!"

I ran to the portside forward running board, climbed up, and stood by to catch the mooring line. It was Paul Myers, the first mate, coming in, and I could hardly believe my eyes. His dory was so loaded with fish that there couldn't have been two inches of freeboard between the top of his gunwales and the surface of the water. As he chugged in he expertly tossed the bowline to me, and I made it fast to the mooring ring with alacrity. Then I raced aft, caught his stern line, and had it fast. I hardly had the stern line fast when he was shouting, "De pugh stick, idler, giff' me de pugh!"

Not only was Paul Myers the best fisherman aboard, he also was a powerful, authoritative figure. He was impatient and demanding. None of the idlers wanted to count him in because he kept up a constant stream of abuse, directions, and invective. It was not an easy job at best to keep that dory centered on the fishport, and his demands didn't make it any easier.

This morning, however, all of the fishermen had hit the school, and Paul Myers saved his breath for the work at hand. The surface of the sea was smooth, but there were large, glassy swells rolling across the Bering Sea. Fish after fish I counted, holding onto the mooring line as the dory dropped six or seven feet below me one instant, then rose the next until the first mate, toiling with the pugh stick, was forking the fish directly over the rail, not even trying to miss me. I managed to duck most of these cod flying through the air, although the tail of one of them caught me a sharp slap across the mouth. Finally the dory was empty. "Number one dory, three hundred and six!" I yelled aft to Sparks.

By then dories were counting in at all four ports, and others were slowly circling, waiting their turn. As I climbed off the running board Frank Simmons was shouting, "We need fish in the heading box. Move it!"

I grabbed my pugh stick and started forking fish into the heading box.

About then I could hear Axel Swenson's bellow from below decks, "Gottdam, giff' us some fish below!"

There were split and cleaned cod in the drying rack, and I started to move toward it to pugh them into the hold when Frank called out, "One thing at a time, Russ! We need 'em in the box first!"

I stole a quick look at the deck inboard from the fishport. It was loaded with fish. If we didn't get them into the checkers soon we'd start losing them out of the port. The way it was going, fish were starting to back up to the port so that the next dory wouldn't be able to count in.

The entire vessel was alive with movement. Fish were flying aboard. The idlers were rushing constantly from one job to another. I didn't even have time to remember my aching muscles from my own fishing that morning. Hour after hour it went on. Finally, at about one in the afternoon, the decks were clear, the checkers were loaded with fish, the heading boxes were full, and there were mounds of split and dressed cod on the tarps under the fore and aft hatches. There were no dories coming in, so we had that much of a respite.

Frank Simmons expertly pulled the backbone out of one last cod, pushed it into the splitting tank, laid down his knife, and looked around him with a grin.

"How do you like it boys?"

I looked at him. "Is this how the ten-thousand-fish days start, Frank?"

He nodded, then raising his voice so he could be heard on

the starboard side, said, "OK, men, let's secure for chow."

Wearily we stacked the pugh sticks against the deckhouse, washed some of the fish blood off our hands and face in salt water, and trooped into the mess for food. For a change it was salt pork instead of cod, and the cook had prepared a tremendous dishpanful of some kind of cooked pudding.

As I sat down on the mess bench I began to realize just how tired I was. I could feel my legs trembling slightly, and I could feel the darts of pain running from my shoulders into my upper arms as I reached for the food.

We had a half hour for eating, and then it was back to work dressing cod. There was no way I could keep track of the number of fish we dressed, but the total seemed beyond counting.

At about two in the afternoon it looked as if we were finally catching up when I heard Sparks shouting from the quarterdeck, "Dory comin'!" It started all over with Paul Myers again counting in with over three hundred fish. He was an indefatigable worker and one of the four fishermen who went out three times that day. But even he began to recognize his own physical limits, and came in with only one hundred fish the last time.

I was too committed to my own responsibilities to give much thought to how hard those fishermen worked, but once or twice I saw those dories coming in with two hundred to three hundred cod aboard and I thought briefly of the forty fish I had caught that morning. The fishermen didn't have that last, long, heavy pull over the side of the ship that we had—it was a lot closer from the surface to the gunwales of their dories—but they were still hauling them all the way from the bottom hour after hour.

On and on we toiled. By about six in the afternoon I was beginning to feel numb. Still we worked. At one point in the midafternoon as I moved hurriedly from one section of the deck to another trying to respond to urgent, profane demands for fish in the heading box, fish below, fish off the deck, and fish into the checker, I thought of one of my uncle Jerry's labor stories. At the time I was working as hard as I was capable of working, almost beyond the point of feeling, side by side with Roy Brewer as we speared the fish with our pugh sticks, sailing them off the deck into the checker.

Roy saw me grinning as we toiled and obviously couldn't accept what he was seeing. "You cracking up, Russ? What's so goddamn funny?"

Like myself he was smeared with blood and fish gut from the soles of his rubber boots to the top of his head. "I can't tell you now, Roy, later."

But the story stayed with me. Working almost in a daze, I could visualize my uncle Jerry holding forth. He was a handsome man, tall, with an erect, vigorous build and flashing brown eyes. He could tell a story with zest and, particularly if it made a point for organized labor, his declamatory abilities were unequaled.

Henry Ford, whose company was one of the last of the automobile manufacturers to be unionized, was a favorite target of his.

As Mr. Ford was setting up his first production line, this initial mass-production endeavor proceeded by trial and error. Toward the end of his first line he had a worker using a lug wrench tightening two nuts on the left front wheel of the car as it moved slowly past him.

This didn't take too long and, little by little as Henry Ford monitored his production line, he increased the worker's job requirements until he was tightening all of the lug nuts on the front wheel, then rapidly devoting himself to the rear-wheel lug nuts as the car moved past his place on the line.

This represented just about maximum effort for this particular worker, but there was still a brief interlude of unoccupied time before the next vehicle arrived. Finally added to his work was screwing on the radiator cap. This kept him working to capacity every instant on the line, and Henry Ford was at last satisfied. He was getting the maximum work effort out of this man.

At this point in the story my uncle Jerry, an intent, serious expression on his face, was wildly spinning the imaginary wrench at the front wheel, spinning it at the rear wheel, then racing to the front of the vehicle before it got past his place on the line and screwing on the radiator cap.

Thus occupied, leaning over the hood of the car, working desperately, my uncle Jerry's apocryphal worker caught sight of Henry Ford himself, a satisfied look on his face, making a periodic tour of his production lines.

"Hey, Henry," the man yelled, "shove a broom up my ass and I'll sweep the floor in my spare time!"

This, I thought, perfectly described the circumstances of the idlers on a day like this.

There were long hours of daylight now in these northern latitudes, and on and on we worked.

Finally, at about nine that night, I pughed the last dressed cod into the forward hold and looked around. It didn't seem possible, but we were through.

Then the deck engine was turned on and we hosed down the deck, the running boards, and all exterior surfaces. It wasn't a matter of cleanliness particularly, it was basically to keep the buildup of fish gut and blood within controllable limits. It was the last task of the day for those of us dubbed "idlers," at some dim point in the history of codfishing in the Bering Sea, by someone with a perverted sense of humor.

Numbly we hosed ourselves off in the cold salt water, then made our way into the mess. The cook and the messman worked a long, hard day in the codfish grounds also. There was food on the mess tables for the fishermen, in from their dories, throughout the entire day. When the dress gang was finally through for the day, no matter what the hour, we ate as a group. Finally the galley was secured until the next day began at about 0400 for the cook and the messman.

I was sitting between Roy and Trotsky, too tired even to care much that I was eating boiled cod again.

Roy turned slowly toward me. "You know, I really didn't think anything was funny today, but something sure as hell struck you that way. What was it?"

I was too worn out to do justice to the story about Henry

Ford's production line, but I got the point across. It probably had something to do with their exhausted condition also, but it struck Roy and Trotsky as just about the funniest thing they had ever heard. Then again, as with me, the total relevance to the way we worked when we were dressing fish at maximum capacity probably had something to do with it.

It started with just Roy and me, then the other portside idlers picked it up and finally the entire dress gang.

From then on, when it really got heavy, when the pressure was coming from every direction, someone would call out, "Hey, shove a broom up my ass!" That and no more, but it released the tension like magic. My uncle Jerry would have been proud of me.

24

For six more days we labored. The weather held calm, the fishermen were shoving off by 0500 each dawn, and we were working from about 0830 each morning until about 2100, or nine o'clock, each night. The first day's catch at the new anchorage had tallied 10,153 codfish. For seven straight days, including that first one, we never dressed less than 9,500 fish each day. Most days the catch ran somewhat over 10,000. With only a half-hour break at midday we toiled for twelve hours every day doing the hardest type of physical labor.

I had awakened at about 0630 the second morning thinking I should get to my fishing station and start hauling in cod. As I started to roll out of my bunk I was suddenly aware of each separate muscle in my body—and each one of them was aching. I fell back on my bunk, deciding immediately the hell with it.

After about half an hour I raised my head slightly and looked over at Jack Anderson in his bunk.

"Jack, you goin' to do some fishing before the dories come in?"

He was lying on his back, one arm propped under his head, smoking a cigarette. He looked at me quizzically. "Don't think so, Russ. I did a day's work yesterday, and I have a feeling there's more of the same coming." Jack was also a portside idler, and I had observed that he worked hard and efficiently. He had a knack for being just where he was needed most.

Although he was not a particularly outgoing type, I counted him as a friend and someone I could rely upon. It was not just his ability with the deck engine that impressed me. There was a feeling of dependability about him that made me trust his judgment.

If Jack was going to conserve his energy, then maybe I wasn't being lazy by deciding to forgo fishing off the side this morning. I settled back with a sigh and drifted off to sleep again. I was awakened by Frank Simmons' raucous bellow. He was an ex-Marine and, while he usually ran the dress gang with an easygoing efficiency, he could be as peremptory and commanding as he had undoubtedly been as a buck sergeant in the Marine Corps. He was standing in the middle of the fo'c'sle.

"Come on, men, hit the deck! Them dories'll be comin' in soon, and we may have a few fish to dress!"

There were muffled groans from various parts of the dress gang side of the fo'c'sle, but soon we were all out of our bunks.

About half an hour later, finishing a breakfast of mush, scrambled eggs, and salt pork, we heard the shout on deck, "Dory comin'!"

Like souls condemned to a purgatory of hard labor, we stumbled out on deck, and the second day began.

I learned then that the best tonic for work-sore muscles was continued use. By noon of the second day my body was beginning to feel almost normal.

Chris Olsen usually counted in on the port side. He was one of the top fishermen, but he never went out three times in one day, as Paul Myers sometimes did.

Fishermen and dress gang were bone weary most of the time, and there was little inclination or time for idle conversation. Once in a while I did have a chance to talk briefly with Chris. One such occasion presented itself during the late afternoon of the third day. I had just counted in his dory. It was a good load, his second of the day, two hundred and ninety-five cod, and for once I was working steadily but not like a man possessed. The fish were going efficiently through our human mill, but there were no dories in sight. The heading box was full, there were plenty of dressed cod on the tarps in the hold for the salters, and I was pughing fish steadily from the deck into the nearest checker.

Chris was trudging wearily forward when he saw me. I plunged my pugh stick into a fish and leaned on it.

"You goin' out again, Chris?"

He shook his head. "Nay, I got over five hundred today. Dat's enough." It was almost as if he read my mind. "Paul Myers, he has vife back in Frisco. He got to make it up here." He looked briefly at the long, rolling, gray swells. "Ya never know ven she start to blow. I don' vant to be no more tired dan I am now if she blow up, and I out in dat dory."

I nodded, and Chris went forward to peel off his gear.

By then I was beginning to develop an appreciation of just how dangerous it was for those fishermen in the dories, alone in the Bering Sea. In clear or overcast weather they usually could keep the schooner in sight, but not always. The topmasts were visible to them from the dories when the fishermen had long since disappeared from our line of vision from the deck of the *Smith*. I had heard these flat-bottomed boats referred to as floating coffins by some of the fishermen, and that was just part of it. Sudden fogs could leave the men almost helpless, hoping that their last compass fix on the schooner had been accurate, that they wouldn't miss the schooner on the way in and take themselves far out in the lonely sea beyond any hope of rescue.

The next day we had an ominous indication of just how unstable the dories were. Chris had come in with a good load of cod at about 0900, had tailed his dory off the stern, and had gone into the mess for food.

We were working hard on the first of that day's catch when we heard Captain Thomas' shout from the quarterdeck, "Dory capsized! Get the fishermen on deck!"

I was working the forward end of the deck at the time and raced to the deckhouse hatch. Leaning in reluctantly, because I knew what a problem it was, I called out, "Someone's dory's capsized! Captain wants you on deck!"

No urging was needed. There was loose gear in some of those dories, and it would be a job righting one in the sea, which was starting to run.

There were eight fishermen in the mess at the time. Quickly but with no outward sign of concern, they were on deck, moving rapidly aft. The dories were all identical, painted a light yellow and with a green painted canvas cover forward stretched over a rib running about two feet fore and aft from the bow to a curved thwartship crosspiece of wood. The taut canvas kept some of the sea out when the weather got heavy. The number of each dory was painted in heavy white paint on this canvas forepeak. Chris's was number five. We had all stopped working to watch the fishermen on the quarterdeck. I saw Chris shake his head once, and I could hear one explosive "Yesus!"

It was his dory that had capsized. How it happened no one knew. It had nothing to do with poor seamanship. The only practical way to secure the dories for the brief interlude while the fishermen were aboard getting something to eat was to trail them off the stern of the schooner. Once in a while, when the weather suddenly took a brief heavy turn, the bow line of one dory would be stretched taut just as another dory swung into it. The sudden jolt could capsize one or the other, and something like that had happened to number five. Seeing that dory bobbing upside down sent a cold chill down my spine. It was a graphic reminder of just how vulnerable they were.

Working with their usual efficiency, the fishermen started to do what was necessary to get it floating right side up. Since it was Chris's dory, he had to accept the responsibility for the cold, wet task of working from another dory when they hauled that one and number five abeam of the quarterdeck to get lines fast to his capsized dory for the job of righting it.

Whenever I could, I took a look at Chris working alongside the ship. His expression never changed. He was used to a hard life, and this was simply another bad turn to overcome in the course of a day's work. Fortunately he had all of his gear well secured, and all he lost was one nipper in the capsize.

Eventually he had the dory bailed dry and was ready to go out again as soon as he had another nipper to complete the set he needed to haul his fishing lines.

He was the last of the fishermen to shove off for his second load, just as we were temporarily halting for our midday meal.

I cast off his bow line and called out, "Good luck, Chris!"

He gave me a sardonic grin, a wave of the hand, and then faced forward as he steered his dory away from the *Smith* for more hours of backbreaking labor.

On it went, a never-ending stream of codfish coming aboard, through our dressing process, and finally into the hold to be salted down.

With absolutely no contact with the outside world, no radio, no magazines, no newspapers, there wasn't much else to do except hit the bunk sometime after the night meal. This was usually about 2200 hours for the dress gang, and it did make for an ample night's sleep. With the ship at anchor there were, of course, no watches to stand each eight hours around the clock. By the fourth morning of this run I awoke at about 0600 and found when I moved that my muscles were not protesting. Sooner than I would have thought possible, my body had been worked into shape.

The relatively long hours of sleep each night, compared with the trip up to the Bering Sea when we didn't average any more than seven hours a night, if that, had another effect on me.

As I began to settle into the hard physical routine I found, toward the end of my relatively long nights of sleep, that I was beginning to have wildly erotic dreams.

Once it had been brought home to me, the day we sailed out

of San Francisco Bay, that this ship was going to be my world for the next five or six months, I had bitterly regretted my decision to patronize the Pearl Hotel that last night in the city. I had supposed that having learned just how desirable a woman's body could be I would be tormented by the memory. Somewhat to my surprise, the total absence of anything aboard the vessel even to suggest the female sex, along with the constant learning experiences and the somewhat foreshortened hours of sleep had combined to reduce my anticipated problem to a minimum.

Now, however, as I became conditioned to the hard work, I found that my reservoir of energy was replenished with a normal eight hours' sleep, and often toward the end of a night in my bunk my subconscious was taking over with understandably explicit dreams. I suppose it would have been the same whether or not I had known Arlene that last night, but there was no doubt that the memory of her lovely body provided a substance to my dreams that hadn't been there before.

The last three mornings at this anchorage I fished for an hour or so after breakfast. Although the cod never ran again as heavy as they had the first morning, I was averaging twenty fish a day, and when I secured my fishing gear the seventh morning with the shout of "Dory comin'!" I had caught a total of 102 fish.

The sky had seemed a bit darker to me when I went on deck that morning. There were occasional whitecaps in the distance, and when the fishermen were getting ready for their second trips I noticed that without exception they took a few moments to study the sea and the sky before shoving off. But the fish were still running in this part of the Bering Sea, and out they went.

By that afternoon the wind was blowing harder and harder and the *Smith* was beginning to pitch, bow into the wind, coming up short on the anchor line with an occasional jolt that made footing difficult on the blood-slick deck.

Headed into the wind there wasn't too much of a roll. Basically the vessel rose and fell on her anchor line, but there were times when an errant wave caught us broadside and rolled her over sharply.

114

About midafternoon, as I was pughing fish out of the checker into the heading box, I was facing aft and I saw Jack Anderson spear a heavy load of dressed cod out of the drying rack. He carried the fish on his pugh stick the ten feet or so it took to toss them down the aft hatch to the salters below. Just as he reached the open hatch the ship gave a roll to starboard and for a split second it looked as if he was going to catapult headfirst into the hold. With an instantaneous reaction to his danger he released his grasp on the pugh stick, with the load of dressed cod on the end, and dropped to his knees just at the edge of the hatch. As it was, the upper part of his body went over the edge of the hatch with its topside structure projecting about eight inches above the deck, and I thought he was going anyway. There was no time to help him. The pugh stick with the cod on it went sailing into the hold like a javelin.

Sam Culleson was Oscar Quarten's salt passer, and they were working the after end of the cargo hold. I could hear his outraged shout. "What the hell are you doin' up there, tryin' to harpoon me?"

Jack teetered on the port side of the hatch for a second or so, then regained his balance. He called down into the hold. "Sorry, Sam, lost my balance for a second."

In fact, he had saved himself a broken neck by doing exactly the right thing at the right time. He looked forward and saw me standing there transfixed, still with a whole cod on the end of my pugh stick. I could feel my heart racing at his narrow escape.

He shook his head slightly. "Let that be a lesson, Russ. Don't get too near the hatch when she's blowin' like this."

I nodded. There were indeed some things to remember.

The running boards had heavy sacking nailed to the surface to give the idlers a slight degree of purchase for the soles of their rubber boots. However, after three or four thousand fish had been counted aboard, inevitably enough fish blood and entrails had splattered on the surface to make it very slippery.

As we counted in the portside dories that afternoon it really got bad. The storm was coming, and the fishermen were almost frantic to get their fish, which they had worked so hard to catch, counted in and get themselves out of the dories. This was the day I learned about another hazardous part of the idlers' job.

It was tough enough to try to keep the dories centered on the fishports in that sea. The fishermen cursed us as occasionally the dories drifted aft beyond the ports when the surge of the sea dropped them into a trough and we simply couldn't hold them where they belonged. Then it was a muscle-wrenching job to haul them forward again, trying to maintain a footing on that glass-slick running board. With the top of the ship's rail hitting us just below our knees, an idler could be jerked off his feet and over the side if he hung onto the mooring line with too much tenacity. I had heard stories of men falling overboard in the Bering Sea, with the tide running, and swept away before anything could be done to save them. It had happened in relatively calm weather. With the sea that was running now I knew for certain it would be the end of me if I ever went over the side.

Still those dories had to be counted in. Roy was counting in Skys'l Sam at the aft port as Paul Myers, the last dory to come in and with a heavy load for these conditions, came moving slowly through the heavy seas toward the ship. He was shouting above the increasing howl of the wind for an idler to grab his bow line. There was no help for it. I was the nearest idler to the forward port. Working as cautiously as possible, ignoring his imprecations to hurry, I got him secured.

This time I didn't worry whether he hit me with a flying fish. From one end of the running board to the other I slid, clutching the mooring line desperately as it pulled me first in one direction, then the other, letting it run through my hands when I must, trying to keep an accurate count of the codfish that Paul Myers was pughing aboard like a man obsessed.

He was just about empty as his dory dropped suddenly fifteen feet below me. With a brief surge of relief I realized as I looked down that there couldn't have been more than ten fish left on the bottom of his boat. Then, as if a giant hand had grasped the dory, it was suddenly rising vertically up, directly opposite me.

I could hear Frank Simmons cry out, "Watch it, Russ!" at the same instant that I realized the dory was being carried higher than the ship's rail. It would be thrown directly aboard by that monstrous wave, I was right in its path, and it would crush me like an insect.

I knew better than to try to escape inboard. My only hope was to move fore or aft. I was facing slightly forward at that moment and started to move forward—too fast. Both feet shot out from under me. For an awful instant, frozen in time, I lay on my right side on the running board. I could see the flat bottom of the dory, the green translucent wave suspending it above me, with a white, foaming crest running off its stern. The bottom was about sixteen feet fore to aft. To my terrified eyes it looked like the sky itself had focused into that flat, hard surface about to crush me into oblivion.

Then, as suddenly as it had appeared above me, it plummeted straight down the side of the ship. Some miraculous fluke of the wind, or the configuration of that wave, stopped the dory from being swept aboard. When it started to drop it was moved outboard from the rail of the ship at the same instant so that it didn't hit the top of the rail. This would surely have spilled Paul Myers into the churning sea. We were both still alive.

I felt someone grabbing me under the arms, pulling me forward and off the running board. It was Chris Olsen.

"Yesus, Roos, dat vas close!"

My heart was pounding as I leaned against the deckhouse trying to quiet my trembling legs. I couldn't speak. I looked dumbly at Chris and nodded. This time it hadn't been my fault. This was simply part of codfishing in the Bering Sea. I had stared death in the face for a terrifying instant and this time had come away unscathed.

By then four men, two fishermen and two of the portside idlers, were fighting the bow and stern lines of Paul Myers' dory. I could see him balanced amidship in his dory and as

117

another wave, not as large as the one that had come close to finishing me, carried it up, he rolled out of the dory and over the rail of the ship.

Finally all the dories were in and hoisted on their davits.

Other than Chris Olsen's brief exclamation, no one said a word about my incident, and I went back to work. However, even though I was doing the best I could, I realized I was working more slowly than usual. I did notice that Frank Simmons didn't say anything to me about my slow pace.

Finally the day's catch was dressed and salted. I saw Frank standing by the splitting table as Jack Anderson hosed it down.

I went over to talk to him. "Frank, you ever see a dory washed aboard up here?"

He nodded. "Yeah, a couple of times."

"What happened to the idlers?"

He didn't answer my question. He just shook his head with a grimace on his face. Then he looked out to sea. "Looks like we'll have at least a day off, anyway. They won't be going out tomorrow for sure. You'll get a chance to rest."

I knew that in his own way Frank Simmons was trying to be comforting. But he hadn't answered my question because there was no answer except to acknowledge the obvious. Accidents—fatal ones—happened on codfishing schooners.

I was grateful that I was still alive, still a bit sick to my stomach, and aware of a growing determination that by God I was not going to be killed up here. Going aloft in the leeward rigging had been stupid and my fault. This near-miss today was just one of those things that could happen. But I vowed it would never happen to me again. One hand for the ship, one hand for myself. I would not forget.

25

The next morning I awoke to a feeling of total relaxation.

There was a stir in the fo'c'sle, and I could hear the sounds of food being served in the mess above, but I knew we would not be working this day. The motion of the ship told me it was really blowing. There would be no fish to dress, I could sleep the whole day if I felt like it, and feel like it I did. But first there was breakfast. This was the only meal of the day I could count on not seeing codfish on the mess table, and I didn't want to miss it. After breakfast I was in my bunk again half sleeping, half drowsing, and thinking sleepily of all the whorehouses in San Francisco; at two dollars a visit I could make up for lost time with the payoff from this voyage no matter what the total catch turned out to be.

It was during the afternoon of this first real blow in the cod-fish grounds that I became aware of a feeling that was almost palpable in the fo'c'sle. It stopped short of tension, but it was there. Then I realized that this was literally the first time since the first night at anchor off Belvedere that the entire crew was in the fo'c'sle at the same time. It was too cold and uncomfortable on deck, one third of the hands were not out on watch, and the fishermen were not sleeping in a drunken stupor, as they were when they first came aboard. I never considered the fo'c'sle of the *Smith* as the most ample accommodations I had ever seen, but I had never realized before just how cramped these quarters really were.

There simply wasn't enough room below for thirty-five work-hardened, now well-rested, men with nothing to do to occupy their time. I noticed it that first day, and when I realized just what was nagging me I decided to go up on deck regardless of the weather. I put on my pea coat, struggled into my oilskins, as much for warmth as for any other reason, and went topside. I took my pencil and one of my writing tablets with me and found a shelter under the foredeck and a seat on one of the coils of line. The head was directly opposite me, and as I glanced at that one-holer with the chute running down to the waterline I remembered the first time I had used it. Attempted to use it would be a more accurate description. We were sailing on a starboard tack, and just as I seated myself, braced against the roll of the ship, a gust drove the schooner over to port and a surge of cold Pacific water shot up the chute, drenched and chilled my cold posterior, and ended my first and last attempt to use the sanitary facilities provided by the *William H. Smith.*

Frank Simmons had been standing by the port foremast shrouds looking out to sea when I came stumbling out from under the forepeak, my pants at half mast. By the amused look on his face I could tell he knew exactly what had happened.

"What's the matter, Russ, you get a cold douche?"

I nodded. "What're you supposed to do on this ship?"

Frank grinned, not unsympathetically. "Hang your ass over the side. Just make sure you're to leeward and hold on tight to the stays if we're hard on the wind."

Necessity overcame my youthful modesty and, in due course, I managed to accommodate my bodily requirements to the exigencies of life on the *Smith.*

By unstated protocol the mates, Sparks, the cook, and Frank Simmons had the use of the after section of the quarterdeck rail for these purposes. That rail was low enough and narrow enough to make a very comfortable seat compared to the wide bulwarks of the *Smith* which the rest of us used.

The captain, as befitted his rank and dignity, had his personal head in a small closet in his cabin with a chute spilling aft into the sea.

There were two urinal chutes abeam of the foremast rigging, one port and one starboard. When the decks were awash, which was most of the time when we were sailing, we urinated wherever and whenever suited us. When we were becalmed and the decks were dry, the urinal chutes were used or we climbed up on the foredeck to let go over the side if we were so inclined.

As I sat under the forepeak thinking back over my life on the *Smith* thus far it seemed to me that I had learned a great deal, but not really a hell of a lot that would have much application in my future life.

I made my usual abbreviated entries in my diary and was just finishing when I became aware that Roy Brewer was standing there looking at me curiously.

"What are you doing, Russ?"

For some reason I was self-conscious about keeping a diary on the *Smith*, and I *had* finished my current entry.

"Trying to figure out how many fish an hour we dress."

Roy was immediately interested.

"That right? What have you got figured out?"

"Well, I'm just starting. It takes us about twelve hours to dress down ten thousand, doesn't it?"

Roy nodded. "Seems like about twice that long, but I guess you're right."

By then I had a fresh page of my writing tablet turned over and Roy sat down on the deck with his back against the coil of line.

"With Frank splitting I know damn well we put more fish into the hold than the starboard side does, Roy, but let's call it even and work it out from there."

Laboriously we did the arithmetic. If our portside dress gang took care of 5,000 fish in twelve hours we were dressing over 416 cod per hour. That meant that we were putting a split, boned, and fileted codfish into the splitting tank just about every eight or nine seconds. I thought of Frank's dexterous slashes with his razor-sharp boning knife and then his yanking out the backbone with one strong pull.

Neither one of us had really thought of it in those terms before, and we were both impressed.

Roy shook his head. "You know when those damn fish are coming aboard we don't have time to watch him, but I have noticed he goes like a machine at that splitting table."

I nodded my head. "That's right. When you think about it High Pockets is getting good, but he'll never go as fast as Frank. Frank's probably splitting and boning a fish every eight seconds or less."

Roy's thoughts turned to something else. Without any preamble he voiced his curiosity. "How in the name of God did Harry Williams get signed on this vessel?"

I shook my head. "Beats me. Maybe he knows somebody in the Union Fish Company." Then I grinned. "Maybe someone in the company knows him and wants to get even!"

It was inexplicable. Harry kept totally to himself. I could not recall ever exchanging a word with him since I had been on the ship. Moreover, I had never seen him talk to anyone else.

It was difficult to tell how old he was, but he was in his middle years. He could have been as old as Doggy Anderson, but once Doggy recovered from the DTs he was a good hand. Due to his age Doggy didn't come close to pulling in the fish that Paul Myers did, for example, but there weren't many fishermen aboard who did. The point was that Doggy was alert, aware, and for his age remarkably agile.

Harry, on the other hand, moved slowly and rather awkwardly. As we were approaching the Bering Sea I began to wonder just where Frank would put him to work.

His mind still on Harry Williams, Roy asked me another question: "You ever hear of codfish tongues before?"

"Hell, no! When I heard that Harry was going to be cutting out codfish tongues, I thought it was a joke."

Roy nodded. "Me too, but at least he's out of the way there in that corner of the checker. Can you imagine Harry as an idler?"

I thought of the maelstrom of frantic action when the dories were coming in, the fish flying aboard. I shook my head. "I still can't figure out how he got aboard, Roy, or why, but at least he's out of the way."

Despite my original suspicious belief that someone was putting me on when I first heard about codfish tongues, they were a very real part of the fish, and the fishermen considered the codfish tongue the ultimate delicacy. For once I agreed. Boiled briefly to tenderize them and then fried, they had somewhat the consistency and flavor of scallops.

I remembered Chris Olsen asking me to save a dozen codfish heads for him when we were first in the grounds.

"What in the hell for, Chris?"

"Ya find out. Yust sav' dem for me."

I told Frank that Chris wanted twelve codfish heads, and Frank simply nodded.

On that particular day, after his second trip, Chris got out his sheath knife and skillfully cut out the twelve codfish tongues.

"Tonight, Roos, after de galley squared away, I cook ya some good chow." He nodded vigorously, as he often did to emphasize a point.

Chris, as usual, was right. The tongues were delicious and, for some reason I couldn't understand, simply did not carry the aroma and taste of cooked cod, which by now would almost turn my stomach.

The tongues that Harry cut out were washed and packed in small casks, salted down much as the filets of cod in the growing cinches belowdecks were. My understanding was that the tongues brought a good price in San Francisco. It took him so long to cut out a tongue that, on the one hand, Frank would not permit us to appropriate any part of Harry's laboriously accumulated store. On the other hand, there was an unlimited supply of codfish heads from which we could cut our own tongues and cook them in the galley when it was clear if we were so inclined.

I could not believe that Harry paid his way, as slowly and awkwardly as he worked, but day in and day out the small store of codfish tongues was growing. Harry Williams was and remained a mystery to me. He was there, on board the ship like the rest of us, but to me in a totally unaccountable way. I never did learn the answer.

It got too cold to stay out on deck, so Roy and I descended the steep ladder into the fo'c'sle. As I got to the bottom I saw Sam Culleson on his knees, a pack of cards on the deck at his side, three cards in a row face down before him. Johnny Tango was facing him, also on his knees. There was a small group of men standing in a circle around them.

I could see Johnny with a forefinger poised above one of the cards as Sam moved them around in front of him.

Johnny stabbed his finger at one of the cards as they came to rest in a row again. "Dat vun, dat's de kink!"

Sam had leaned back on his heels as Johnny made his selection. Now Sam leaned forward and flipped the card over. The king it was. "Damn, Johnny, you gettin' too good at this. That's fifty fish I owe you."

Tango nodded with a self-satisfied expression on his face.

There was no rule against gambling on the ship, but there was relatively little of it. The only medium of exchange was codfish, and it was as if the fish caught by hard work and at the risk of life simply shouldn't be gambled away. Sparks was rather accommodating about making tally transfers on his sheets with both parties signing, but it didn't happen too often. Among the dress gang we sometimes bet small numbers of fish on anything that came to mind, such as which dory would be first in that day. It usually occurred when we were fishing off the side, and the transfer could be made right there on deck, from one group of fish to the winner's catch.

I heard Sam talking.

"Tell you what: Let's bet double what I owe you on the next pick. You win, I pay you a hundred fish. If you don't pick the right card, you pay me fifty fish."

My thoughts flashed back to the day we got our heads shaved. I remembered that look in Sam's eyes. He had Johnny Tango set up. I knew it. Then I could really feel the atmosphere in the fo'c'sle. It was electric with tension. A hundred fish often represented a good average day's catch for a fisherman in a dory. It was about ten dollars, a significant amount of money in 1937.

About half the crew were gathered around in a circle now.

Johnny looked at Sam with a grin. "Das goot, Sam. Let's go."

Sam laid the three cards on the deck face up in front of him, king, queen, and jack. Then he turned them face down. Johnny stared intently at the three cards.

"I pick de kink again."

Sam nodded and slowly, or so it seemed, started to move the cards around in the row before him. Johnny's forefinger hovered over the king, face down on the deck as Sam moved it in and out of the row. Finally he stopped and leaned back on his heels.

"OK, which one is the king?"

Immediately and unerringly Johnny's finger stabbed the middle card in the row.

Sam flipped the card over. The red queen stared unblinkingly up at Johnny Tango's incredulous expression.

"But, but . . ."

Sam was sympathetic as he started to gather up the cards. "That's too bad, Johnny, you know—" He never finished the sentence.

From where I was standing I could see the red creeping up Johnny's neck. With a bellow he shot out a beefy right hand, grabbing at Sam's shirtfront. "You cheat, dat's cruuket! I know dat kink is dere!"

Sam avoided the right hand with the instincts of a trained boxer, was on his feet and racing for the fo'c'sle ladder, shouldering me out of the way as he went flying up it, Johnny Tango on his feet a split second later and in hot pursuit.

Halfway up, Johnny slipped on one of the narrow steps, came down hard on his chest, and went rapidly bumping back down the ladder to the fo'c'sle deck. The jolt was severe, and he sat on the deck at the bottom of the ladder for a little while, shaking his head.

All of us knew that he was a former professional fighter, but with his habitual good humor and childlike ingenuousness it was easy enough to forget. When I saw that explosion I was really surprised, and fearful for Sam. I had the feeling that Johnny Tango could do a lot of damage if he put his mind to it.

As he got slowly to his feet I was staring at him and he saw the expression in my eyes.

"Don' vorry, I not 'urt 'im." He shook his head again and looked at his large hands. I had heard somewhere that it was a felony for a professional fighter to use his fists outside the ring. There was no law of organized society on the *Smith*, but Johnny obviously remembered how lethal those hands of his could be. The shock of his fall off the ladder had snapped him out of his rage.

He looked at me again. "Go tell 'im iss h'OK. I not 'urt 'im."

I climbed the ladder and went out on deck looking for Sam. I found him crouching behind the after deckhouse. There wasn't a trace of fear on his face. He reminded me of an alley cat backed into a corner, all steel and sinew and ready to spring.

I called out as I got near him. "It's all right, Sam. Johnny slipped on the ladder and got a pretty good jolt. It seemed to snap him out of it."

Sam took a deep breath. "Thank Christ! I don't want to tangle with no heavyweight like him." Then he grinned. "What in the hell does he think three-card monte is? I believe you, Russ, but I'm going to stay out on deck for a while and make sure he's cooled off."

Within the delicate and complex structure of acceptable male behavior in this closed society of ours on the *Smith*, no one questioned Sam's courage. No one on the ship would have willingly stood up to Johnny Tango. With his usual good humor it had come as a shock to see his rage explode when he realized he had been conned. As far as we were concerned, Sam had acted with commendable good sense.

Sam, however, was hypersensitive about the incident. He considered that he and Johnny were the fighters on the ship, they could take anyone in a fair fight. It just was not good sense to do battle with another fighter who outweighed him by at least forty pounds. Still, he didn't want anyone misreading his hurried flight.

126

As Sam descended into the fo'c'sle Trotsky happened to look up from where he was sitting on the bench by the stove. The sight of Sam flying up that ladder, Johnny Tango charging after him, had been funny. Trotsky grinned.

Sam strode over snorting his breath through his nostrils. "What's so goddamned funny, Trotsky?"

Like many large men, I am sure Trotsky had had his share of bantam challengers. I am equally sure that normally he would have passed it off one way or another. The problem was that Sam's belligerent tone in that fo'c'sle could not be ignored—not with the whole crew looking on.

"Seeing your ass disappearing up that ladder, Sam, that's what's so funny!" Trotsky's tone was equally truculent.

I thought, here we go again. I liked both Sam and Trotsky, I really didn't want them fighting each other, but I did feel an anticipatory thrill at the idea of their battling it out.

Sam had turned pale. In a controlled way he was as enraged as Johnny Tango had been earlier.

"Trotsky, come out on deck with me and we'll see how funny I am."

There was no turning back now. The gauntlet had been flung down. I thought of the fights I had had in my grammar school in the Mission District in San Francisco—ritualistically commenced with a wooden chip knocked off a shoulder. Just as surely now, these two had to fight it out.

Trotsky's reply was terse: "Suits me." Within minutes the fo'c'sle had just about emptied. Harry Williams, lost in whatever world he lived in, and a few members of the crew who had slept through it all were the only ones left below.

Topside the wind was screaming, but the deck was fairly dry. There wasn't too much deck space available, but the crew ringed the area inboard of the forward fishport. It was a space roughly twelve feet square.

They faced each other, moving warily at first, and it was immediately apparent that Sam was in his element. He was giving away at least sixty pounds in weight and probably six inches in height, but he could move.

He flicked out a left jab and left a red welt under Trotsky's right eye. Then Sam shot two jabs in a row, both landing. I could hear the sharp crack of the bare-fisted blows on Trotsky's face. Sam followed up with a hard straight right to the stomach. He was well coordinated, a skillful boxer, and his punches had plenty of body weight behind them. I heard Trotsky grunt as the right to the body sunk home. There was blood trickling from his nose now.

The ship was straining on her anchor chain, but the pitching motion was relatively gentle and there wasn't much roll. They were both keeping a solid footing.

Trotsky stood his ground with Sam circling him carefully, then darting in quickly to throw a punch. Suddenly I realized Trotsky knew what he was doing also. He didn't have the experience or skills Sam had, but he wasn't flailing out blindly. He faced Sam with his arms raised in an orthodox stance, his elbows in. He threw a left hook which Sam ducked easily.

As much as I loved fighting, it suddenly came through to me that this was crazy. They were fighting over nothing with bare fists, with hard surfaces and corners all around them, and on that moving deck someone could get hurt bad.

The crew was silent, watching them intently. We could hear Sam and Trotsky breathing hard now. The work had toughened their bodies, but they weren't in condition for this sort of action. Trotsky threw another left hook, and this time Sam didn't quite duck cleanly. It caught the top of his head, and he fell off to his left. Trotsky didn't press his advantage, but Sam moved back out of range. All of the time Sam was exhaling through his nostrils with a brisk, sibilant sound. I could see in his eyes a growing respect for Trotsky. This wasn't going to be all that easy.

I glanced around at the faces of the crew. Their eyes were locked on the fighters. I noticed a slightly puzzled look on High Pockets' face and the faces of a few of the fishermen. I couldn't figure it out at first, and then it came to me. These particular individuals fought rough and tumble when they fought; no boxing matches for them. Rough and tumble, anything-goes fighting meant taking advantage any way you could get it. Knees to the groin, biting, gouging, fighting sometimes to the death was their style. It was self-evident that with Trotsky's advantage in size and weight he could have smothered Sam in a bear hug, wrestled him to the deck, and killed him if he chose. Instead he was fighting fair, taking a beating doing it, but abiding by the unwritten rules of his background. This was how males settled their differences in the San Francisco of those days.

The fight continued, Sam scoring with hard, sharp blows to the face mainly, Trotsky trying hard but not doing much damage.

Suddenly Sam feinted a left jab, Trotsky rolled back to his right, and Sam moved in with another right to the stomach. Trotsky was waiting for him this time. As Sam drove for the body Trotsky rolled back toward him and shot a short, straight right that caught Sam just above the left eye. The thwack of fist on head sounded like Trotsky could have broken his hand. Sam hung upright long enough for Trotsky to connect with a left hook to his jaw, and Sam was down. Trotsky stood above him, the blood streaming down his face.

Then Sam was on his knees, shaking his head to clear it, and I saw to my horror that he was struggling to get up. He was going to the end. There was no referee to stop this one, and it seemed to me that someone, most probably Sam, was going to be killed if this went on.

I wondered what would happen to me if I interfered. My God, honor had been served. This was enough.

Trotsky was looking a little sick. He knew, despite the beating he had taken, that he had to finish Sam, and it was obvious that he could do it now.

Just as Sam forced himself upright and squared off facing Trotsky again, we all heard the roar from the quarterdeck: "All right, men, belay that! You've been playing long enough. Knock it off!"

It was Captain Thomas's voice. I had been so absorbed in the battle I hadn't even noticed he was up there on the quarterdeck watching the fight from his elevated vantage point. With a sure instinct he took command at just the right moment, and there was no way his orders were going to be disobeyed.

Uncertainly, both Trotsky and Sam looked aft. The captain did not repeat his order. He simply stared at them. They dropped their hands then and looked at each other.

Trotsky had the good sense to speak first. With a smile that must have hurt his swollen and battered lips, he stared at him. "I've had enough, Sam. How about you?"

It probably was about the only thing he could have said that permitted Sam to withdraw gracefully. Slowly Sam smiled too. His face was almost unmarked except for the red abrasion over his left eye, which now was dripping blood, but he knew what could have happened. "Yeah, I reckon so, Trots. That's one hell of a punch you have."

It was even colder now than it had been earlier, and most of the crew had gone below. Roy and I stood there with our shipmates, not saying anything.

There was an unmistakable warmth and camaraderie between them now. The challenge had been given and accepted. Both of them had acquitted themselves with courage and honor.

Roy dipped a bucket of cold, brackish water out of the rain barrel to wash off the blood. Unnoticed, Johnny Tango had joined us, holding one of his own towels.

Expertly he examined Sam's forehead. "Iss h'OK, Sam, no bad cut."

Then, gently but effectively, he sponged off the blood on Trotsky's face.

We were all there together on the deck and, as dangerously as I knew I was living, I couldn't resist it.

"Sam," my expression was serious, "do you want me to have Sparks tally those fifty fish Johnny owes you?"

For a second there was a stunned silence, then we all broke up at once, Johnny Tango laughing harder than anyone.

As far as I know, Sam never did collect those fish.

130

Jack Davis looking into the mouth of a halibut about as long as he is tall and considerably wider.

Jim Bewla and part of the third watch on deck studying tops'ls in a blow.

View from the topmast crosstrees with codfish on deck during dressing operations, port and starboard sides.

View of the *Smith*, anchored, sails down, waiting for the fishing dories to return.

Author sitting on the anchor just above the waterline, calm sea.

Portside dress gang including Jack Anderson, center rear; his right hand is on the pugh stick. Cowboy and Bob Henderson, *to the left*, were not members of the portside dress gang and were hamming it up for the camera.

26

The wind dropped during the night, and at 0500 or there-
abouts I could hear the muffled, small roar of the outboards as the fishermen shoved off the next morning.

I had fished off the side during the blows which kept the
dories in and, while my personal catch was slowly growing, the
cod just didn't seem to grab the hooks during stormy weather as
they did when the sea was calmer. I took advantage of the calm
and caught another twenty fish that morning.

The first dories were late coming in, and none of them had
heavy loads.

We started dressing down about a thousand, and it was obvious that this was not going to be a ten-thousand-fish day. We
worked steadily but without the pressure that frequently kept the
whole operation in an organized state of intense, rapid movement.

Frank Simmons genuinely liked me, I thought, and other
than Roy Brewer, in whom I had confided, no one aboard knew
my true age. Still, I think Frank suspected that the eighteen
years entered on my seaman's papers probably stretched it a bit.
I don't think he was really as psychic as he sometimes seemed to
me to be, but he had an uncanny facility for saying something
that seemed to echo my most private thoughts.

I was working near the splitting table pughing fish into the
heading box when he called out, "Hey, Russ, try some of this
liver! It'll put hair on your chest!"

I had noticed that Frank and some of the other old-timers
occasionally sliced off a good-sized piece of the pinkish cod liver
and chomped it down raw with just as much apparent relish as
they ate the cooked cod. For me, other than the tongues, they
could have the rest of the codfish.

But this time, for no reason other than that Frank chose to make his offer when the whole portside dress gang could hear him, I felt constrained to eat the liver.

What made the blood rush to my face (unapparent, I hoped, under the wind and sunburn) was that I *had* been worrying about when I was going to start growing hair on my chest. Most of the men in my family had hairy chests, the hard work on the *Smith* was developing my muscles, I was exhibiting every bodily characteristic of manhood, but my chest remained as devoid of hair as a newborn babe's.

Frank had a chunk of cod liver on the point of his splitting knife after a quick swirl through the splitting tank to wash off the blood. He extended the liver toward me.

"Cod is not my favorite food, but I guess I might as well try it," I said. I reached for the piece of liver and saw Frank grinning at me.

"Go on, Russ." I thought for a minute he was going to make another remark about the hair on my chest, but he didn't. It seemed as if once Frank Simmons had looked into my brain with his uncanny ability he left it there and didn't do anything further to embarrass me.

Actually, the raw liver was relatively tasteless. Like the codfish tongue, it didn't seem to carry the basic taste and smell of codfish. The chunk of liver went down like an oyster—and another small, new experience had been added to my education.

We worked steadily that day, and by 1800 hours the last dressed cod had been pughed into the hold for salting. Our catch for the day was just over seven thousand fish.

After dinner I went out on deck, found my spot under the forepeak and leafed through a volume of collected poetry that I had found in a crate of books stowed in the fo'c'sle. The light below just wasn't good enough for reading comfortably, and I was a bit self-conscious about reading poetry, anyway. I had very little exposure to that form of written expression, and it wasn't my first choice of reading material. It just seemed to me that if someone had taken the trouble to print this hardcover edition of verse it probably was worthwhile for me to read it. I had the instinctive feeling that with no formal guidance it was probably best to read this book in small segments. Doing so, over a period of time, I found I was developing a real enjoyment of poetry. It struck me that these poets, about whom I knew next to nothing except for the short biographical sketches in the book, had a most eloquent way of expressing themselves on subjects I often thought about but never really discussed. The vastness of the universe, the immortality of the soul, the meaning of life—these were frequently touched upon in a graceful, speculative style that at least made me feel I was not all that strange for concerning myself sometimes with thoughts such as these.

I looked at the inside cover of the book. The Seaman's Mission of San Francisco stamp had obliterated the original owner's name. The collection had been published in 1912, and I thought of the chain of events that had brought that book to the first owner's hands, later donated to the mission, and finally to the forepeak of the *Smith* for my pleasure. I particularly enjoyed Walt Whitman and Robert Browning. I thought of Whitman speaking from a Civil War hospital to an individual like myself on this lonely schooner in the Bering Sea.

The next morning I went out on deck at about 0600 and saw the fishermen still aboard standing in small groups staring out to sea and talking quietly.

I looked at the hard, metallic-gray sky merging into the gray sea. The weather was not unusual and I couldn't really tell any difference, but it was apparent that the fishermen could.

Then I heard Paul Myers talking. "Yah, it may blow, but ve up here to fish. I'm goin' out!"

He moved purposefully to his dory slung on the davits.

With that two of the fishermen moved to the fore and aft davit lines, and his dory started down to the sea.

Captain Thomas used a speaking trumpet from the quarterdeck.

"The glass is holding steady, men, but mind you, keep the vessel in sight."

Soon all of the fishermen were dropping their dories down to the surface and one by one fanning out from the ship.

This was the first time I had observed this type of concern before a day's fishing. Without knowing why exactly—perhaps it was no more than seeing the fishermen's obvious caution about shoving off—I felt a troubling premonition about this day.

The first dories were in about 1000, and the day's dress down began. Before shoving off for their second trips I saw the fishermen studying the sea and sky carefully once more. Then they went out again.

As nearly as I could tell, the sea and the sky remained the same, but still, looking at the fishermen quietly staring out to sea, I had an ominous feeling. These damned codfish were not worth risking their lives for.

We finished dressing the morning's catch, had our midday meal, and I was back out on deck when I suddenly heard Frank Simmons exclaim, "My God, look at that!" He was pointing over the port rail toward the west. What had not been visible on the horizon when we had gone into the mess for our meal was now a dark cloud stretching for miles. The sea was still calm where the *Smith* was anchored, but I could see the whitecaps in the distance and the storm front driving toward us.

Frank turned to me. "Russ, get the whole dress gang on deck—*now!*" He barked out the last word.

Since the salters and salt passers were the last ones to go to work when the fish started coming aboard, they often went back down into the fo'c'sle for a brief nap after the midday meal before returning to the cargo hold.

All four of them and a couple of the starboard dress gang were below when I went scrambling down the ladder.

"Frank wants everyone on deck, *now!*" I repeated the last word sounding as much like Frank as I could.

Oscar Quarten turned over sleepily in his bunk, then looked at me.

"Vhat's goin' on?"

"I don't know for sure, Oscar, but there's a squall heading right for us."

134

He came full awake then, swung his feet out of his bunk, and started pulling his boots on. His tone was serious. "Yesus, dat means all de dories comin' in at vunce."

The entire dress gang was gathered on the deck, portside forward. Frank had to raise his voice above the increasing moan of the wind.

"Men, I got a feeling we're going to be seeing every one of the dories about the same time. I don't know whether they're going to have fish aboard or not, but don't worry about it. Main thing is I want all of you standing by to handle their lines and get the fishermen aboard."

Roy Brewer spoke up. "Do you want us to count 'em in if they got fish?"

Frank's voice was somber. "I don't think they'll be wanting to count in. And I don't think there'll be too many fish to worry about. If there are, leave 'em in the dories. We can pugh them out later when they're on the davits."

I looked aft. Captain Thomas was balanced on the quarter-deck, scanning the horizon through his binoculars.

Frank finished his orders. "Spread out on both rails. Let the idlers handle the bow lines. They're more used to it." He looked straight at me. "For God's sake, be careful. Stay out of the way of those dories if the sea is running like I think it will be."

I shuddered as I remembered my near-miss with Paul Myers' dory. At least we didn't have to worry about keeping them abeam of the fishports.

We didn't have long to wait. About five minutes after we had stationed ourselves on the port and starboard running boards I could hear Captain Thomas from the quarterdeck.

"I've got the first one in sight." There was a brief pause as he studied the sea over the stern quarter, still staring hard through his binoculars. He dropped his glasses and turned to us, raising his voice to make himself heard over the wind. "Looks like he'll be coming in port side. Look alive, men. They'll be counting on you."

Then the weather hit us with a force that momentarily rolled the *Smith* over, and then once more she swung into the wind on the anchor chain.

I was standing on the running board, clutching the foremast rigging, and staring down at the sea. It was now a boiling fury. How in the name of God are we going to get them out of that? I thought. And then there wasn't time to think.

The first dory in was Skys'l Sam's, and he headed portside forward. I grabbed his bow line flying toward me and took a turn through the rigging to give me some leverage. Trotsky had caught the stern line, so we had basic control of the small boat now surging violently up and down by the ship's side. I could see Skys'l Sam's face. His expression was grim, but his shouted directions were calm, calmer than mine would have been, I thought, if I were in that dory. "Not too hard on dat bow line! Don't yerk dis dory! Easy now." Suddenly the rail of the dory was even with the top of the *Smith*'s rail and he was diving over. Frank Simmons and Oscar Quarten appeared out of nowhere on the running board, had Skys'l Sam under the arms, and were pulling him aboard.

Other dories were converging on us now. I could hear shouts and curses from the starboard side as the dress gang struggled with the dories there. Frank called out to Trotsky and me, "Drift that dory astern and secure it good!" By the time we had done so it looked as if just about all of our fishermen were either tied in or standing by to come in.

Now we were working frantically on a dory secured fore and aft by the fisherman's lines, keeping enough tension on the lines to give him a chance to get aboard but not so much as to jerk the dory into a capsize. It was Doggy Anderson. Despite his years he went over the rail and aboard with agility at just the right instant. As he was pulled in I looked over the rail and saw Chris Olsen keeping the bow of his dory headed into the wind, bucking in that sea like a live thing. He was about twenty-five yards off our beam. I prayed that his outboard wouldn't fail him now.

The expression on his face was much like Skys'l Sam's ear-

136

lier. There was grim concern but no panic. It would take every resource of seamanship and skill he had to get that dory in. There simply was no time for fear.

Chris watched us clear Doggy Anderson's dory from our mooring station, then slowly and carefully Chris powered forward through the raging sea until his dory was parallel to the ship and forward of our position. Then he drifted back down, and just as he came abeam, he tossed his bow line. It was expertly thrown, but as the line came sailing through the air, his dory dropped below us in a trough. He was throwing that line to me. Chris Olsen was depending on me. For a terrifying instant I thought it was going back over the side, but I managed to catch the last few inches of the end of it before it went over. I dreaded to think of Chris having to repeat that whole process in this sea. I dropped to my knees on the running board and leaned over the ship's rail clinging to that line, quite literally now Chris Olsen's lifeline. For an instant time stood still for me. There was no way I could control that dory from my position with just the bitter end of that bow line. Then, after what seemed an eternity, the dory was coming back up, I was hauling in the line and scrambling forward to get a turn around the rigging. Trotsky had his stern line now and we played the dory like a giant fish, slacking when necessary, hauling in for control when we could. The swells were breaking and combing away toward the stern. The delay caused when I almost lost Chris's bow line kept him in that wildly pitching dory for a lot longer than I wanted him to be there, but there was no help for it. Once more the dory dropped below us, and when it rose that time there was too much distance between it and the ship for Chris to try to come aboard.

The third time he started up I could hear him call out, strongly but with no trace of fear in his voice, "Hold her in snug, Roos, I'm comin' aboard!"

I followed his direction, hauling in on the line as his dory rose on a swell, and then he was rolling aboard.

Frank was shouting to my ear, "That's the last one on this

side! Leave her tied up there! We're going to have to get them on the davits anyway!" I made Chris's bow line fast to the rigging with a rolling hitch and sank down to a seat on the running board.

Then I was aware of Chris Olsen standing in front of me, a slow smile spreading across his face.

"Dat's a goot yob ya do, Roos, catchin' dat bow line of mine."

"Thanks, Chris. I'm glad you didn't have to come in again."

His expression now was somber. "Me too!"

It looked as if all of the dories were in. Now all hands turned to to get them hoisted on the davits. They wouldn't last through the night in that sea if we didn't get them aboard.

It was another hour of dangerous, backbreaking work, the fishermen in charge now, as one by one we got the davit hooks on and hauled on the lines. The dories slowly lifted out of the sea and were secured on the davits. All of the dories had some fish aboard, but not too many had been caught before the squall struck. We would get them out of the dories later.

I was working at a port midship davit with Chris, another fisherman, and Roy when I heard it. Someone, I never knew who, said, "Karl Miller's not in."

Chris and I were hauling on the forward davit line when we heard it. I could see his jaw muscles tighten, and I remembered what Chris had told me about his friendship with Karl Miller. He never stopped hauling until we had the dory snugged up. When it was secure he turned abruptly away and strode forward.

The last fisherman had come aboard more than an hour earlier. I looked out to sea. If anything, it was blowing harder now. I looked aft. Captain Thomas was standing on the quarterdeck and was braced against the motion of the ship. Binoculars raised, he methodically scanned each quadrant of the sea.

I could feel the presence of death on this vessel. If Karl Miller had not returned by now he would never return. The captain, and then the mates in turn, would spend the remaining long hours of daylight scanning the sea with those binoculars. But they knew, as did the rest of us, that our second mate was lost.

Sometime after the last dory was secured on its davits we ate a silent meal in the mess. One by one, after a last long look seaward, the men went below to the fo'c'sle.

I went up on deck once, at about 2200 hours. The wind was screaming through the rigging, blowing the spindrift off the rolling combers sweeping by the *Smith*, which was plunging on the anchor chain.

Daylight was fading from the gray sky, and I looked aft. There was no longer anyone searching the horizon for the missing dory.

I looked toward the bow and I saw Chris Olsen standing all the way forward, his left hand braced on a belaying pin thrust in its hole in the bulwark. He was staring out to sea, and tears were streaming down his face. I knew I could not talk to him. There was nothing to say.

As I turned to go below I saw him suddenly raise his clenched right fist and shake it wildly and impotently at the raging sea. The wind carried the sound to me of a choked Scandinavian oath wrung out of his very being.

It was the only eulogy Karl Miller ever had.

27

The next day was June 13, 1937. The wind was blowing almost at gale force. I went up on deck and stared at the stormracked sea.

I tried not to think about Karl Miller, but I couldn't help thinking of him. I wondered how it had happened, what had been his last thoughts as he was enfolded by the icy embrace of the Bering Sea.

Skys'l Sam was standing next to me, and we stared silently out at the desolate expanse of gray, wild water.

He spoke quietly. "Ve be movin' de anchorage vhen she lightens up."

"Why . . ." Then I stopped. At that point no one even spoke Karl's name, and instinctively I knew the answer to my unasked question. Regardless of how the fish were running, as meaningless as it might be to move the anchorage from one spot to another in this godforsaken sea, when a man was lost, the ship was moved. The next time those dories went out it would be from a new anchorage, not from the one where a shipmate had made his last voyage.

"How far will we go, Sam?"

He shrugged. "Not too far, yust somevhere else."

The day wore on, and the wind started to lighten about midday. About midafternoon it had dropped to twenty-five knots or so, and Captain Thomas gave the order to start hauling the anchor.

It was about four bells on the afternoon watch, so Paul Myers' watch would work the ship.

Even with the deck engine winching in that anchor chain, it was a long process.

I could hear the chain clanking into the chain locker forward of the fo'c'sle up in the bow at about the waterline. Then I heard Paul Myers' shouted orders, "Belay haulin' de chain!"

I looked around in surprise as the deck engine was throttled down and the clanking stopped.

Then I saw Sam Culleson and Trotsky pointing at something to starboard. Dimly at first, then more clearly I made out the gray shape of a steamship bearing straight for us. It looked something like the Coast Guard cutter which had taken off Johnny Gunderson. I was puzzled because we usually got the word from Sparks well in advance that a cutter was coming, in order to get our letters home ready for mailing. There was no word this time.

I joined Sam at the rail. "Is that a cutter coming, Sam?"

"No, it's a Jap survey ship. They've got our number-two dory." He spoke in a subdued voice.

"How do you know?"

"Sparks put out the word just a minute ago."

Of course; the wireless. As little help as it had been for our lost shipmate, Sparks would have been on the ship's radio just as soon as the captain knew that the fishermen were in trouble. All vessels would be asked to be on the lookout for our fishermen.

This Japanese ship had not found Karl Miller, but his dory had been found, and it was being returned to the mother ship.

The gray Japanese ship chugged into position, bow into the wind about two hundred yards off our starboard beam.

I had not really known Karl Miller, since I was not on his watch. But the quiet, assured manner in which he officered the second watch, and his friendship with Chris had made more of an impression on me than I had realized.

As I watched the Japanese seamen expertly drop a large power launch into the still turbulent sea, followed shortly after by the number-two dory taken in tow, I felt a sudden rush of bitterness. Why in the hell should anyone salvage that dory, which had caused the death of a good man?

Then I thought, more calmly, that it wasn't the dory, it was the sea. These men knew what they were up against when they shipped on a voyage like this. Still, an impotent residue of anger and bitterness remained. It just didn't seem right for anyone to be concerned with that dory.

Then the Japanese were alongside. They were as expert as our Coast Guardsmen, but there were no grins or shouts this time. They knew as well as we that the sea had claimed one of our men. They wasted no time, simply coming into position paralleling the *Smith*, expertly casting off the dory, and tossing its bow line to Johnny Tango standing by at the rail to receive it. Then with a brief wave from the helmsman they went surging off to their own ship.

I looked over the side into the number-two dory. It obviously had been capsized and scrubbed clean by the wild sea. There was no residue of fish blood and gut now. There was nothing loose in the dory. It was immaculate and empty. As I stared at the dory I thought of references I had read to washing a corpse. I turned away as the davit lines were hooked on and the number-two dory came home.

28

The deck engine revved up again, and the monotonous clank of the anchor chain into the chain locker resumed. Paul Myers stood on the main deck. One of his watch, Ole Johansen, kneeled on the forepeak just aft of the butt of the jib boom and peered over the side to pass the signal when the anchor was in sight. The engine would be eased off as the anchor was snugged into place on the lower port bow just above the waterline.

Paul shouted his orders to his watch. "Fores'l halyard, start hoistin'! Stand by on the mizzen halyard." The *Smith* had plenty of sea room; we didn't have to worry about drifting ashore or anywhere else while the sails were going up, but they went up much easier with the bow into the wind while still held there by the anchor. The mate could make a practiced estimate at just about when the anchor would break clear. He wanted the foresail up and the halyard secured at just that moment, since this old schooner did not handle like a yacht, and it took experience to get her under way properly. There would be a period while we slowly bore off with the anchor free but still fathoms below the ship as the anchor continued to be hauled in. That didn't help her sailing qualities either, but it involved a compromise of all of the factors Paul Myers was automatically calculating.

I was standing amidship on the port side as I felt the ship heel to starboard when the anchor broke clear.

Paul Myers stood facing aft, his legs braced against the motion of the vessel. Cupping his hands around his mouth, he bellowed his orders: "Helmsman, hold her into de vind! Mizzens'l halyard, start hoistin!"

The *Smith* began to come alive now as the mizzensail went slowly up the mast. Then the halyard was secured, the foresheets and mizzensheets slacked off until we were moving at about five knots on a close reach. The anchor chain continued to clank into the locker.

A few minutes later I felt a thud against the port bow and simultaneously a metallic clang and the racing of the deck engine. An instant after that the engine throttled down and Jack Anderson was on deck, out of the engine house, and shouting at Paul Myers, now up on the forepeak. "What in the hell happened?"

Paul's voice was savage. "Dis lubber didn't pass signal in time!" I had raced forward myself and for a second I really thought the mate was going to club his man into the Bering Sea. Ole was a fisherman and one of the most experienced hands on the ship. For whatever reason—a momentary glance away, a few seconds of forgetfulness—he had not passed the signal to his watchmate standing on the main deck to pass the word to Jack Anderson to slow down. Far worse, as the anchor broke the surface it was only six feet from its nesting place against the hull, and the signal to cut power totally was never given. Not rapidly, but with inexorable force, the deck engine pulled the anchor into the port bow until the gear wheel meshing the hauling operation with the winch, just outside the engine deckhouse, broke with the strain it could no longer tolerate.

The whole crew was on deck now, and I could hear mutterings from the fishermen.

"Dis ship be yinxed!"

"Ve best head fer Frisco now!"

By then Captain Thomas was at the engine deckhouse, where Paul Myers joined him.

"Any damage to the hull, Mr. Myers?"

"No, sir, but ve don' haul dat anchor wit dis engine no more,

I tink." His voice was still choked with rage. This was a serious mishap, it had happened on his watch, and he felt the responsibility.

The captain turned to Jack. "What about it, Anderson? Any chance of repairing it?"

Jack shook his head. "No way, Cap'n. We don't have the tools, and we don't have a spare wheel."

Captain Thomas had heard the fishermen's muttered forebodings too. His job was to run this vessel, and there were times when that entailed more than navigation and seamanship.

Not once had Karl Miller's name been mentioned. Captain Thomas turned from his inspection of the broken wheel and raised his voice.

"All right, men, it could be worse. If that flywheel didn't break we could have been holed, and that would've been a real problem." A wintry smile briefly crossed his face. "All this means is that we'll be haulin' the hook by hand from now on. I haven't heard a capstan chantey in a long time. Be good for you!"

Abruptly he turned and strode aft to his quarters.

The captain's words were hardly cheering. Every job on the ship seemed to be physically arduous. Now, added to our normal toil, was the work of hauling the anchor by hand. But somehow or other Captain Thomas' words had an effect. It was basically the energizing force of his personality. No matter what happened, he was master of this vessel. The crew did not forget it.

We sailed a generally northeasterly course, which would take us closer to the Alaskan coast. With the anchor now secured, and under fore and mizzen only, the *Smith* heeled over, not quite with a bone in her teeth, but moving briskly.

I suddenly realized that I was feeling better. The sensation of this old ship coming alive, the canvas straining, the timbers creaking, the wind pouring over our port-bow quarter—it was like a tonic.

We sailed for about six hours, and at precisely 2030 on our

watch Captain Thomas gave the order to Jim Bewla to round up into the wind and drop the hook.

At about 2100 we had the fore- and mizzensails down, and the anchor was securely hooked into the bottom of the Bering Sea some fifteen fathoms down in this shallow water. The wind had almost died now, and we were sure we would be fishing tomorrow. My diary entry for June 13 was as terse as the usual conversation on the ship:

> Today one of the Jap survey ships brought back #2 dory from which Karl Miller, our Second Mate, was lost. Yesterday it was blowing and all the fishermen were in except Karl. Most of the old hands thought he was lost then and today has confirmed that belief.

This was Karl Miller's epitaph.

I don't know why Captain Thomas decided to drop the anchor where he did, but it turned out to be in the middle of the richest codfish grounds we were to fish the entire season. One ten-thousand-fish day followed another. Sometimes the day's catch mounted to eleven thousand, then to twelve thousand. It was as if the gods of the sea, having claimed one of our men, were now making amends by giving us fish and calm weather.

My diary entries for this period just about stopped entirely except for matters of importance. My entry for June 23, 1937, read:

> At 9:00 p.m. last night we found out that Joe Louis knocked out Braddock in the 8th round and became the

new heavyweight champ of the world. I won 5 fish from Trotsky on the fight.

Although Karl Miller's name never appeared in my diary again, his death continued to preoccupy me. Used to a society which, rightly or wrongly, commemorates the passing of an individual from this life with ceremonial functions, I could not get used to the apparent acceptance of Karl's death on this ship. I know that with a sailor's superstition each one of the men realized it was better not to voice his name. For the fishermen, going out in those dories day after day directly confronting the fate which had befallen our second mate, it was not only best not to speak of him, it was also the only way to preserve their resolution. Thus I also did not speak of Karl Miller, but my concluding entry for June 23 read as follows:

> I read a philosophy of Whitman's tonight that I thought was pretty good. "Did you think that life was so well provided for, and Death, the purport of all life, is not well provided for!"

Life on the *Smith* became for me a never-ending round of codfish flying aboard, moved along our human production line, finally fileted, drained, and pughed down into the hold, where the salters and the salt passers toiled.

One evening, as I wearily pulled off my shirt for a brackish-water wash under the forepeak, I happened to glance down at my chest. For an instant I couldn't believe my eyes. I dashed out from under the forepeak for better light, quickly scanned the deck—no one was topside—and then looked again. Sure enough, unmistakably, a few hairs were beginning to sprout on my chest. That damn Frank Simmons, I thought, right again! Ever since the day I had been given the raw liver by Frank I had surreptitiously been salvaging at least one cod liver a day and swallowed as much of it as I could—quite privately. And now I was rewarded!

146

Finally the fish count began to drop. My entry for July 4 read:

Well today is our great National Holiday at home but it's just another day up here. We celebrated by dressing down six thousand codfish.

We stayed at the anchorage for another two days after the Fourth of July, averaging less than five thousand fish per day.

Pete Sorensen, much like Paul Myers, consistently came in with good loads of cod in his dory no matter how the other fisherman did. On the morning of the last day before we moved on I was awakened by the sound of an argument from the fishermen's side of the fo'c'sle. I could hear Pete's voice.

"Ve stay here, by Yesus, ya vork hard enough ya get de fish!"

Ole Johansen's voice was menacing. "Most of de crew vant to move dis vessel. Vy de hell ve stay here yust because ya gettin' cod!"

It was a senseless argument. Ultimately it would be the captain's decision as to when we moved on, influenced to some extent by the collective wishes of the fishermen. But the long hours of grueling toil in those tossing dories, the unspoken realization that death was as close as the surface of the Bering Sea just inches below the dory gunwales—all this took its psychological toll. I could sense an explosion coming.

Then I heard Chris Olsen's voice, as soothing as he could make it. "Come on, Pete, Ole, ve move when de cap'n say so. . . ."

Pete's tone was low and threatening. "Stay out of dis, Chris!"

From where I was watching lying on my side in the bunk, I couldn't quite see what Ole did or hear what he said this time, but the effect on Pete was instantaneous.

With a tremendous roundhouse right, he swung at Ole. The sharp thwack of his fist on Ole's head resounded in the close quarters, and Ole dropped in his tracks.

Then all of the remaining fishermen in the fo'c'sle surrounded Pete and kept him separate from Ole, on his knees now groggily shaking his head. By their code, if two men had to fight it out, it was one on one to the end of it. But this time they knew without saying it how senseless this fight was. It was a product of frustration and weariness. It could not go on. Pete too seemed to realize this as he abruptly shouldered his way through the men surrounding him and made his way to the ladder.

Ole sat on the seatboard holding his head in his hands. I could hear Chris talking to him, his tone was conciliatory.

"Ole, ve all feelin' tired. Pete be good man, he yust blew up. Don' hold grudge."

Ole nodded, then he too got to his feet and headed for the ladder.

That night after dinner I was standing on deck talking to Chris.

"We only dressed down about four thousand today, Chris. When do you think we'll be moving?" It was obvious we weren't going to make our catch for the voyage at the rate of four thousand codfish per day.

"Tomorrow."

"How do you know?"

"Cap'n passed de vord. Secure de dories good, cause ve'll be sailing tomorrow."

I thought we'd be moving a fair distance this time, motivated only to find new codfish grounds now, not moving solely to avoid the shadow of death. I suddenly realized that we would probably be sailing the watches around, and no one had been selected to replace our second mate. It was uncanny on this ship at times. It may have been the close proximity in which we lived, but it was as if Chris Olsen directly answered my unspoken thoughts.

"Cap'n vanted me to tak' over mate's berth, but I be stayin' for'ard."

"Why not, Chris? Those aft quarters are one hell of a lot better than the fo'c'sle."

148

He shook his head somberly, and I knew he was thinking of Karl Miller, so I didn't press him.

"Who will be taking over as mate?"

"Pete Sorenson takin' over as mate of de tird vatch. Yim Bewla, he be takin' over de second vatch."

He looked at me then with sardonic amusement. "Dat Pete, he keep dis vatch in line."

I thought of the sight of Ole Johansen dropped with one blow of Pete's fist, and I nodded.

At 0600 the next morning I heard Jim Bewla's shout reverberate in the fo'c'sle.

"Second vatch on deck, ve be haulin' anchor!"

There were mutterings and grumblings, but the second watch began to stir. I lay in my bunk thinking of the job of work it was going to be hauling the anchor with the capstan bars. Then, as so often on this voyage, I thought this is something I've never seen. I also thought briefly of an old Marine Corps adage Frank Simmons had once, in a fatherly way, imparted to me early in the voyage.

"Russ, goddamnit, you keep your bowels open, your mouth shut, and don't volunteer!"

I knew, as sure as I was lying there warm in my bunk, if I got anywhere in sight of that capstan on the foredeck Jim Bewla would be drafting me into service.

I decided to stay in my bunk until all of the second watch were on deck. Then I would quietly get topside and watch the anchor hauled by the capstan.

Fifteen minutes later, the fo'c'sle was quiet again as the last of the second watch went topside.

I had just climbed out of my bunk and was pulling on my seaboots when I saw Jim Bewla descending into the fo'c'sle. Since my tier of bunks was just aft of the point where the bottom of the ladder joined the deck of the fo'c'sle, he couldn't miss me.

A large grin split his face. "Vy, Roos, ya miss me! Ya vant to bear a han' on my new vatch. Come on."

"Gee, Mr. Bewla, all I wanted to do was watch."

"Nay, ya need de exercise. Ya dress gang people yust loafin' on dis vessel anyway. I'm gettin Skys'l to give us a capstan chantey. Good for ya!"

He grinned again and crossed the fo'c'sle to Skys'l Sam's bunk. "Come on, Skys'l, ya be the only vun aboard know de ol' chanteys. I vant vun for my hands."

Skys'l protested. "No, too many years since I do dat!"

Jim Bewla was determined. "Dat's an order, Skys'l. Get ya gear on and get topside!"

Skys'l Sam protested again, but I thought I detected in his voice that indefinable but clearly perceptible something that told me he really wanted to lead a chantey. Modestly he just wanted to be urged.

Jim Bewla had us both. By the time we got topside the capstan bars had been inserted, projecting like four spokes from the round capstan head, and four men of the second watch had commenced their slow, straining circle on the foredeck. They were all leaning into the bars, and the slow, monotonous clank of the anchor chain dropping into the chain locker began.

I stood at the bottom of the starboard ladder leading to the foredeck as Skys'l Sam went up. He passed around the men straining at the capstan bars and stood on the jib boom, grasping the jib stay with one hand as he took a deep breath.

Then, with his unmistakable Scandinavian accent, he sang a sea chantey completely unfamiliar to me but wonderfully melodic. His voice was surprisingly true and the effect on the men toiling at the capstan bars was unmistakable. I remembered Captain Thomas' words, "I haven't heard a capstan chantey in a long time. Be good for you!"

The men didn't move any faster, but somehow they moved more effectively, more willingly. The muscle-straining labor of forcing those capstan bars around and around went far too slowly for the toiling hands to move in rhythm with the chantey. But this old song of the sea made more of a game of it. The men knew that the one singing the chantey realized how hard they were working and cared about them.

150

Skys'l Sam's voice rang out over the foredeck, "I'll go no more aroamin'!" The rest of the watch now roared back the capstan chantey chorus. "Aroamin', aroamin', that's always been my ru-i-in. Aroamin', aroamin', I'll go no more aroamin'!"

I suddenly realized how right Captain Thomas had been. This was good for the crew. Skys'l Sam was obviously enjoying himself immensely. I could tell by the satisfied look on Jim Bewla's face that he was pleased with his idea, and with the number of men on the watch to take turnabout on the capstan bars, they were enjoying it too.

With an impish grin on his face, just as he had the crew absolutely synchronized on the chorus, Skys'l Sam suddenly switched to Danish. The Scandinavians grinned then and bellowed out the chorus in a similar-sounding mix of Swedish, Norwegian, and Danish.

It came to me that I was seeing and hearing something that had just about disappeared from the sea. I wanted to be part of it and, as if reading my mind, Jim Bewla sang out. "Hofvendahl, bear a hand. Ve be hoistin' sail now." He grinned at me. "De hard vork over, anyvay."

I should have known! After the first half hour on that capstan, the anchor chain slack had come clanking aboard. Now, as I fell into step at the end of one of the capstan bars, Bob Henderson stepped out, and I strained in his place. The ship had been winched up until it was almost over the point where the anchor lay hooked into the bottom of the Bering Sea. It came to me that this was just about literally a backbreaking job. Still Skys'l Sam sang on, against the background sounds of Jim Bewla's shouted orders to the rest of the second watch hoisting sail. Bent over, leaning into that capstan bar, I could feel the sweat rolling down my arms as Sam broke into an exhilarating chantey, "Away You Rio!"

He was obviously in his element now. "Ve're bound for de Rio Grande!" Then he was leading us in the chorus, "Avay ya Rio! Avay ya Rio!" The crew bellowed back the chorus with a will.

The wind was brisk now, pouring over the foredeck, drying the sweat on my body as I toiled. Then, with the sound of the foresail slatting just aft of us, we strained mightily to the sound of Skys'l's chantey, and the anchor was free. That anchor and the remaining chain were heavy enough that our pace in the eternal circle did not accelerate, but it was perceptibly easier. I could feel the ship bear off on a port tack. As I faced aft in my straining circle on the foredeck I looked down the length of the schooner. All of the sails were set and drawing. We were under way again.

30

We sailed for a full twenty-four hours, watches around the clock, and then on through the next day. At 2300 hours of the second day Captain Thomas gave the order to round up into the wind and let go the anchor.

I could never figure out how the decision was made, but somehow there were always codfish to be caught where we anchored. One part of this gray sea looked just like another to me, but this time we were much closer to the Alaskan coast than we had ever been before. It was gray and overcast when we dropped the hook, and I didn't realize how close we were then, but the next morning I was awakened by the small roar of the fishermen's outboards as the dories fanned out from the schooner. I went topside to relieve myself and could hardly believe my eyes. It was a brilliantly sunny day, and in the far distance over the starboard beam I saw the first land I had seen since we had cleared Unimak Pass almost two months before. The Alaskan mountain range in the distance was completely, brilliantly white, etched against a cobalt sky. I shook my head as I stood there and realized how turned in on itself my world had become. As vast and apparently limitless as it was, as changeable in its moods, the sea simply did not offer the infinite variety of terrain and beauty as the land, which it seemed I had almost forgotten until I stared at that spectacular mountain range.

But the coast and the mountains had another effect on us too. Sudden violent squalls sprang up practically without warning. The fishermen came in with reasonably good catches that morning. Then the sky darkened, the wind blew up, and almost as soon as they had shoved off for their second runs, all of the dories at once were heading for the mother ship.

One by one we secured them, got the fishermen out and the dories on their davits. It was a repeat of the controlled, fiercely intense effort engendered by the entire complement of dories coming in, practically at the same time, standing by, heading into a pounding sea, and finally the idlers bringing all our fishermen safely aboard.

We dressed down three thousand codfish that day.

The next day was like the preceding one, but with a frightening difference.

The fishermen came in with about two thousand codfish in the morning, and I could hear mutterings as they stared at the distant mountains.

"Ve too close to dat range."

"De vind come fast off dat coast."

There were head shakings, and I knew that Karl Miller's fate weighed heavily on them.

Again, almost without warning, after the fishermen had left on their second runs, the wind was screaming and the dories were converging on the schooner.

With the intense, constant effort of getting all those dories in and secured on their davits in a relatively short time, it simply was not possible to know who was in and who wasn't. Finally, I dropped to a sitting position on the port running board to catch my breath. It seemed to me we were tempting Fate. Our fishermen could not always be that lucky.

Chris Olsen walked up to me. "Paddy's not in!" His tone was grim.

"You sure?"

Chris nodded and walked away.

I felt numb. Paddy was on the first watch, so I didn't see much of him when we were under way. But I had never forgotten the real courage he had shown in getting Doggy Anderson out of the rigging what seemed a lifetime ago now. I remembered the genuine warmth and compassion he had exhibited as Doggy fought off his personal demons.

Paddy Whelan was just as tough, just as much a seaman as the others. But there was a warmth about him that was different. It may have been the combination of his Irish brogue and the twinkle in his blue eyes, but it seemed as if every member of the crew was his friend.

Earlier, fighting for his life, getting his dory maneuvered into the rolling sides of the *Smith* in a blow, there could be no nonsense. But he had never lost his composure. He counted in portside, and even in the early days when we green idlers were not keeping his dory abreast of the fishport as we should, he was patient. He instructed us quietly. He didn't swear or fling a codfish at our heads the way the first mate and some of the others did. Basically Paddy Whelan was a gentleman.

It was over an hour now since the last dory was in. I looked out to sea, and I felt an empty feeling in my stomach. There was no sign of Paddy's dory.

Once again Captain Thomas was scanning the storm-tossed sea through his field glasses. Methodically, quadrant by quadrant, he steadied himself on the pitching quarterdeck and looked for his missing fisherman.

I knew it could happen. But somehow it seemed to me that we had already paid the price. This should not happen again. It was much earlier in the day than when Karl Miller had failed to return. I tried to reassure myself with this thought. Then bitterly I had to tell myself, what the hell difference did that make? There was only so long a dory could live in those seas.

Another hour dragged by. The deck was deserted except for the captain on the quarterdeck and me still sitting on the running board.

I was just inboard and abeam of the mainmast rigging where Paddy Whelan had fearlessly clambered up to talk Doggy Anderson down, despite that wildly swinging belaying pin. I remembered that night as I glanced at the rigging. If I climbed about fifty feet up I would have some advantage of perspective, and it would be at least one more pair of eyes searching for a shipmate I knew now was lost. As useless as it was, it was the least I could do for Paddy.

I pulled my watch cap down over my ears, put on my gloves, and turned up the collar of my pea coat. Slowly and carefully, I climbed the rigging. With the *Smith* pitching to her anchor chain, it wasn't too difficult, as there wasn't much roll. Still, I had to be careful. Finally I was up where the rigging was still reasonably wide, but at least fifty feet above the deck. I braided one leg through the cross brace, half sat on it, and commenced my vigil. Whenever I looked out over that wild sea, my heart sank. Still we didn't know for sure yet. Again I thought, this is the least I can do for Paddy, however useless it is. The wind brought tears to my eyes, and once in a while I would turn away to watch Captain Thomas on the quarterdeck. Patiently, methodically, he scanned the seas through those glasses. I don't know how long I was up there. It seemed like hours, but it could have been only twenty minutes. It had finally occurred to me, as little good as it was, that it was more logical for me to complement the captain's vigil rather than to duplicate his effort. Thus when he stared aft, I looked forward; when he was staring to starboard, I was looking to port.

I had just rested my eyes for a moment watching him below on the quarterdeck as he turned slowly to face across our starboard beam. I took a deep breath, shifted my seat on the cross brace, and stared out across the Bering Sea. Suddenly I caught a flash of yellow. Then it was gone in the trough of a rolling comber. I shook my head and thought, I've been up here too long. But I continued to stare in the same direction. This time it was unmistakable. It was yellow—it could only be the characteristic yellow of one of our dories. It was too far away for me to tell whether it was his capsized dory, or whether Paddy Whelan was still alive and battling his way in, but it was without a doubt our missing dory. I waited to catch one more glimpse of that yellow as it rose on a combing swell. Then I screamed down at the quarterdeck, "Captain!"

Captain Thomas visibly started, dropped his glasses, and looked up. He had been so intent that he had not even realized anyone was aloft. I am sure the sound of my voice just barely reached him. There was no point in trying to tell him what I saw. I pointed wildly, as accurately as possible, where I had last seen that flash of yellow. Captain Thomas swung about and focused his glasses in the direction I had indicated.

I stayed there for another look, and this time it was undoubtedly the yellow of one of our dories, but I still couldn't tell if it was capsized or upright.

Carefully I disentangled myself from my entwined position in the rigging and started down. As I was halfway down, it suddenly hit me: It had to be Paddy coming in! Every momentary glimpse I had had of that yellow chip out in the wild sea had been more visible than the last. If the dory had been capsized, it would have been drifting aft parallel to the length of the ship as we headed into the wind. I was elated, then immediately sobered at the thought of Paddy fighting his way broadside through those seas, but he had no choice.

I was on deck and racing aft as soon as I caught my balance. I called up to the captain, "Have you got him in sight, Cap'n? Is he going to make it?"

Captain Thomas lowered the glasses for a moment, looked down at me, and said, "I think so. Get a couple of idlers on deck to tie him in." He paused for a moment, then added, "That's good work, Hofvendahl. I appreciate it."

It didn't really matter. Whether I had seen the dory first, sooner, or later, he would have fixed him in his glasses. I think, more than anything else, my giving him the fix sooner impelled him to express his gratitude.

I raced forward as fast as my seaboots and the wet, heaving deck would permit. Leaning into the hole where the ladder de-

156

scended into the fo'c'sle, I shouted down, "Paddy's coming in!"

Almost as the last word was out of my mouth there was a man on the ladder heading topside. It was like a resurrection. There was no need to repeat the captain's order to get a couple of idlers on deck. Within minutes the entire crew gathered at the port rail. Now we could see him. Indeed, the number-eight dory was coming in, and Paddy Whelan was bringing her home with a skill born of a lifetime at sea.

Roy Brewer and I stood on the running board at the forward fishport as Paddy carefully turned his dory in a wide circle. I caught my breath as I saw a huge wave catch the dory broadside and he disappeared from sight. Then he emerged into view again. Now he was slowly bringing her into the wind, and the worst was almost over. Like all of these men at times such as this, his face showed no concern as he slowly powered up to where we waited for him. Then his bowline was flying through the air. I caught it and quickly secured it to the thimble on the mooring line as Roy handled his stern line. With both lines thus secured, we had the leverage and flexibility that the mooring line, rove through the blocks on each end, gave us. Working carefully in tandem, we maneuvered his dory opposite the fishport as Chris Olsen and Skys'l Sam climbed up on the running board and stood by. As Paddy's dory rose on a swell he called out, "Ready, lads, I'm coming aboard!" He was amidship in his dory, as close to his starboard side as he could get, and then he was rolling aboard with Chris and Skys'l swiftly grabbing an arm each and pulling him in.

A moment later he was standing on deck looking quizzically at the crew pressing around him. The humorous glint was back in his eyes.

"Now then, lads, were ye worried about Paddy Whelan? Sure now, takes more than a little blow like this to do an Irishman in!"

There was no sentimentality in these men, but the surge of relief and jubilation was almost palpable.

"Vhat happen, Paddy?" Sven Johnson called out.

"Ah, bloody engine stopped on me just as she started to blow up. Had to change a spark plug, that's all."

As casual as the words were, I had a mental image of Paddy alone in his dory, rolling and pitching in that sea, as he struggled to keep the engine dry with the cover off, get a spark plug out, and a new one in. As prosaic as it sounded, it took nerves of steel to do it right, not hurry, not lose a part irretrievably into the Bering Sea and with it the power which was the only thing that would permit him to survive and to reach the mother ship.

The fishermen clapped him on the shoulders as he started forward. Paddy should sleep well tonight, I thought.

Then with Chris and Skys'l standing by to help hoist the dory on its davits, I leaned over the rail to release the knot that secured the bow line to the thimble.

I don't think I was careless. It was another one of those things. The Bering Sea, cheated out of one member of this crew, seemed determined to get another.

Just as I grabbed the thimble with my left hand to untie the knot with my right, the dory dropped out from under me, and I did not react fast enough. I held on to that thimble just long enough for the weight of the dory to pull me half over the rail. For an agonizing instant I stared face down at those gray, breaking seas, balanced on my stomach on the rail. Then I felt the strong arms of Chris and Skys'l pulling me in.

Chris shook his head. "Roos, ya be a lubber lettin' yerself get yerked over de side lik' dat."

I nodded. I was in no mood to argue. I was still alive.

My diary entry for July 10 read:

> I thought for awhile we had lost Paddy Whelan because he didn't come in for a couple of hours after all of the other fishermen were in. There were some heavy swells and I almost got jerked overboard when I was taking his bow line out of the thimble.

31

The next morning, at about 0500, I heard the slow clank of the anchor chain into the chain locker just forward of the fo'c'sle. Then I was aware of the rhythmic tread of the men manning the capstan bars on the foredeck. I stretched out on my bunk, warm in my blankets. Jim Bewla was not going to draft me again! The second watch would hoist that anchor with no help from me.

As I lay there wide awake but luxuriating in the knowledge that another watch was doing the work, I thought of the previous day, when I almost went over the side because I had hung onto the forward thimble just an instant too long. I remembered all the near-misses I had survived on this vessel. Self-doubt began to gnaw at me. Was I really that careless, or was it some inexorable chain of circumstances that always seemed about to cast me in the role of victim?

As I was thinking, self-centered as only youth can be, I remembered Sam Culleson. If Johnny Tango had caught him that day when he had a fifty-fish bet, double or nothing, that could have been the end of Sam. Then I thought of the day Jack Anderson had almost pitched headfirst into the afterhatch. He had saved himself by letting go of that pugh stick with the load of cod on it—and almost harpooned Sam Culleson belowdecks. I thought of the day Trotsky had the wheel while we were running and the spanker had jibed. At five feet, ten inches, the spanker boom just cleared my head. At six feet, three inches, the boom could take off the top of Trotsky's head. He was standing at the wheel when someone shouted at the last instant as that heavy spanker boom came flying across. If Trotsky had not ducked at the last conceivable instant, it would have crushed his skull. And the fishermen. Probably every day, out in those dories by themselves, they slipped on the fish-gut slick of the dory bottoms, started to lose their balance, and then righted themselves—still alive.

Trying to consider the matter rationally, I finally concluded that I really wasn't all that careless. Codfishing in the Bering Sea was an inherently dangerous way of life. I had survived thus far and, by God, I would survive this voyage!

After what seemed a long time, I could feel the *William H. Smith* heel to port—we were sailing again.

Captain Thomas had decided that we were indeed too close to shore. No matter how potentially good the fishing was, it was not worth risking the effect of those lethal winds that swept down off the Alaskan mountain range almost without warning.

On occasion, Sparks would tack up a slip of paper with the total of codfish caught to date on the bulkhead just outside the mess.

His latest information was that we had 294,300 codfish salted down in the hold. That was quite a bit less than a good catch by this time of year, but it was not all that bad, either.

This time we sailed a day and a half out into the Bering Sea away from the Alaskan coast. We dropped the hook at about 1600 hours. Once again we would learn how good Captain Thomas' judgment was.

As usual, he was right. There were schools of cod out here, but the weather continued to plague us. At least the fishermen did not have to contend with the sudden, unpredictable blows that leaped at them from the coast. Still, if we got in two successive days of fishing, we were lucky.

It was about 1400 on the afternoon of Sunday, July 18. It had been blowing hard for two days. I came on deck to try some fishing. As little luck as I normally had on the blowing days, at least it was a reason to be topside and out of the fo'c'sle.

I had just baited and dropped my forward line and was facing aft, standing on the running board as I worked with my hooks and bait on my aft line. No one else was on deck, and I was surprised to see three persons emerge very carefully from the officers' stern quarters. As I stared at the slowly moving tableau, I knew that something was terribly wrong.

Frank Simmons was on his right side, and Jim Bewla was on his left. Jack Anderson was in the middle, being supported by both of them. As they neared me on the wet, slanting deck, I could see Jack's left arm in a sling and his left hand totally swathed in bandages. The sight that etched itself into my mind forevermore was the mask of his face. The blood was totally drained from his skin, his eyes stared straight ahead unseeing, and his features were frozen into a mask of pain such as I had never seen. They moved so slowly because Jack could hardly stand, and the other two were being extraordinarily careful with their footing on the wet, moving deck.

I admired and liked Jack Anderson as much as anyone on this ship. I felt as if I should do something, anything, but as I stood on the running board staring at them, my eyes locked on Frank's. He shook his head once, and I knew. There was nothing I could do.

I was waiting at the hatch when Frank and Jim returned topside. Their expressions were grim. Jim simply brushed by me, hurrying aft. Frank's expression softened as he looked at me. He knew that Jack and I were friends.

"My God, Frank, what happened to Jack?"

"Took off three fingers on his left hand in that bloody engine!"

My stomach gave a lurch. No wonder his face had looked like that."

"How?"

"I don't know for sure. We know he was tinkering with that damn engine and had it running. I think he slipped on the deck when she rolled, and he reached out without thinking. Probably grabbed the drive belt, and it took his hand right into the wheel."

For a moment I thought I was going to be sick. Then I spoke to Frank again.

"Is he going to be OK?"

"I don't know, Russ. I helped the Old Man." He looked at me bleakly. "You know, the Union Fish Company didn't give us much of a sick bay on this goddamned scow"

"What did you do?"

"The cap'n did it all. I just held Jack's left arm for him. Damn little he could do. He taped the forefinger to what's left of his hand. I hope to Christ he saved that finger, but I don't know. Used pure Lysol on the stumps to sear them."

"Pure Lysol!"

Frank's tone was savage. "Yes, goddamnit, pure Lysol! Don't know what else it'll do, but it seemed to stop the bleeding. He sure as hell won't get an infection."

"Will the Coast Guard cutter be taking him off?"

"They will."

"When?"

"I don't know. Sparks raised them while the cap'n was working on Jack. We're pretty far north now. Probably sometime tomorrow."

"Did the captain have any pain-killer, Frank?"

Again his tone was savage. He fairly spat out the word: "aspirin!"

I shook my head. "What can I do, Frank?"

"You might try prayin' for him, Russ. Pray that cutter gets here sooner, not later. Pray that he'll keep what's left of that hand."

Then his voice softened again. "I know Jack thinks a lot of you, Russ." He smiled briefly. "You're a real pain in the ass the way you charge around this vessel, but it's always sort of tickled Jack. He's told me. Anyway, we got him in his bunk, but there's no way he's going to get out of it now until the cutter gets here." He paused again and then continued, "You know, Russ, he's a hell of a guy. I really can't imagine what that hand feels like, but he didn't say a word when Jim and me were easin' him into that bunk. Anyway, he's going to have to piss once in a while, and I think he'd rather have you help him than anyone else on the ship."

"What'll I do?"

"Get the cook to find you an empty can and just give Jack a hand when he needs it. For God's sake, be careful. Don't touch that left arm of his anywhere."

"I'll be careful, Frank."

"I know you will, Russ. I don't think he's going to feel much like eating, but I have a hunch it would be good for him to get some food down. Don't push him on it but try to get him to eat something."

I nodded and then turned away abruptly. I walked over to the starboard rail and stared out at the stormracked sea as Frank walked aft, rolling with the motion of the ship.

It was just over a month since Karl Miller had been lost. Now this calamity. Maybe the fishermen were right and the *Smith* was jinxed.

I went into the galley and got an empty coffee can from the cook. Then I went below. It was quieter in the fo'c'sle than I could ever remember.

Thus began the longest hours I spent during the entire voyage.

I stood on the seat that projected from the inboard side of the bottom bunk. This put my head above the level of the top bunk so I was looking slightly down on Jack lying on his back in his bunk, rigid, and with tears running down his cheeks. They were purely and simply the involuntary expression of a pain that was almost beyond bearing.

Nothing in my life, or anything I had ever read, had prepared me for this. Somehow, instinctively, I knew that any expression of sympathy simply was not called for. As matter-of-factly as I could, I spoke to him in a low voice.

"Jack, I'm going to stand by. My bunk's right here anyway."

Slowly he turned his head and looked at me. I almost wept. With a barely perceptible movement of his head, he nodded.

"I got a coffee can for you if you have to piss. Just let me know if you need some help and I'll empty it for you."

At least the frightful, engraved expression of pain on his face seemed to be relaxing. I thought for sure I would weep when I saw him trying to smile at me. His voice was barely a whisper.

"That's nice of you, Russ. I'll let you know."

I had to say something. "I'll get you something to eat too, Jack."

He just barely shook his head, and I remembered what Frank had told me. "Only if you want it."

This time he did barely manage a smile, and I had to turn away hurriedly.

Then I climbed into my bunk, and the vigil began.

Hour after countless hour I wondered if that Coast Guard cutter would ever get to us.

The fo'c'sle remained quiet except for the never-ending creak of the ship's timbers as the schooner pitched at the end of the anchor chain. No one came near our corner of the fo'c'sle except the men who bunked there.

Periodically I would help Jack with the coffee can, then go topside to empty it.

Whatever bodily mechanism took over, it seemed as if the pain had stabilized to a barely tolerable level. I knew nothing of the outward manifestation of shock, but I guessed that something was happening to Jack Anderson that was permitting him to survive with his sanity intact.

Still, it was a terrible torment he suffered. At about 1900, after the crew had eaten, the cook prepared some broth from a can of corned beef that I suspect came out of his private stores.

I took it down to Jack's bunk. "I got something pretty good for you. Let's get your head braced up on the headboard so you can get it down."

His voice was barely audible. "OK, Russ, I'll try it."

Pushing with his right hand, he got himself into a semi-upright position. As he did so he accidentally moved his left arm, and my blood ran cold as a sudden strangled half sob, half gasp burst from his lips.

I realized that my hands were shaking, and Jack Anderson did not need that now. "Jack, I'm going to sit here for a minute and

164

make sure this is cool enough for you." I slipped down to the seat by the bottom bunk, holding the can of broth. After a few minutes I could feel my body steadying. Making my voice as matter-of-fact as I could, I stood on the seat, again holding the broth and with my head about level with his where he was propped up in the bunk.

Very carefully now I spooned the broth into his mouth. I think it was the distraction of simply doing something besides lying in that bunk suffering, as much as the food value, but it seemed to me that it helped. When he had finished the last drop he very carefully eased himself down into a supine position again and looked at me.

"Thanks, Russ."

I simply nodded.

At about 2200 hours I was up on deck emptying the coffee can when I looked aft and saw Sparks standing at the rail, staring out to sea. I walked down the deck and stood there with him for a moment.

"Do you know when they'll get here, Sparks?"

"About 1100 tomorrow—that's the latest word."

"Jesus, that poor guy's hurting. Can't they make it any faster than that?"

"They're doing the best they can, Russ. You ever think what it'd be like up here if we didn't have the Coast Guard to help us out?"

There was no arguing with that. I nodded, then moved forward and back down below.

I slept intermittently. Twice Jack asked me to help him with the coffee can.

Once, I don't know what time it was, I was awakened by his gasping, "God, my arm's on fire." I thought of that undiluted Lysol applied directly to the stumps of his amputated fingers and shuddered.

Much later during that endless night I had dozed off and was awakened by his soft moaning. The only light in the fo'c'sle came from a faint flickering of the burning coal through the grate of the potbellied stove, anchored forward and amidship.

I turned on my left side and peered anxiously at him. I could hear him whisper to me, "I'm sorry, Russ. I know I woke you up. I just can't help it."

"It's OK, Jack." I turned away as the tears ran down my face.

With the hatch into the deckhouse secured because of the weather, the only way I finally knew the night was ending was when I heard the sounds of the cook and the messman working in the galley.

Then time started to move again for me. I left Jack long enough to have breakfast in the mess. I sought out Frank Simmons after he had eaten. He gave me a long look.

"You look like you had a pretty rough night, Russ."

I nodded. "You could say that, but it wasn't anything to what poor Jack's gone through. Any word on the cutter yet?"

Frank nodded. "Looks like about 1000 now."

"They'll have something in their sick bay to give him, won't they?"

"You better believe. Once he's aboard that cutter he'll be in good hands."

"Frank, I want to help, but I just don't dare try to get Jack out of that bunk. I haven't fouled up yet, but . . ."

He nodded sympathetically. "Don't worry, me and Jim Bewla will handle it."

I knew that Frank and Jim were two of the strongest men on the ship. If anybody could do it right, they could.

I went below and rejoined my stricken shipmate.

At about 0950 I heard the shout on deck, "There she is!" I leaned over Jack's bunk.

"I'm going to get Frank and Jim. The sooner they get you on that cutter the better. It won't be long now, Jack, they'll be taking good care of you."

He seemed visibly to relax on his bunk then and spoke to me, turning his head to the left and looking into my eyes. His voice was still just barely audible, but somehow it seemed stronger than it had been. "Russ, I want you to know how much I appreciate what you've done for me."

166

I couldn't say anything. I just looked at him and nodded my head. He went on talking.

"I'm going to meet you in Frisco when you get in." This time he did manage a smile. "Don't worry about me, Russ. I'll make it."

Those were the last words Jack Anderson spoke to me on the schooner *William H. Smith*.

When I got topside Frank and Jim were already heading forward to get Jack out of the fo'c'sle.

To our port beam, hove to in the turbulent sea, was a Coast Guard cutter. The lines of these cutters were lovely in any event. Bow into those seas in her coat of glistening white—I had never seen anything more beautiful in my life.

As I watched I could see the power launch dropping off the davits into the sea. I tried not to think of what it was going to be like for Jack getting him out of that fo'c'sle, topside, and then off the *Smith* and into that launch. It was alongside now. Roy Brewer had secured the bow line, and Sam Culleson had their stern line. To my relief I saw that there were seven Coast Guardsmen in the launch in addition to the coxswain. If manpower could prevent further suffering for our shipmate, this would do it.

Jack and I had said our good-byes. I walked aft and up on to the quarterdeck, where I hoped I wouldn't hear him if something jostled that mutilated hand.

The expressions on the faces of the Coast Guardsmen were serious—much like the Japanese seamen who had returned our number-two dory.

I watched from the quarterdeck as Frank and Jim carefully placed Jack Anderson in a sitting position on the ship's rail with his feet dangling toward the sea and held him there.

Then, with incredible seamanship, skill, and gentleness, these saviors in dungarees simply plucked Jack off the rail at the precise instant their launch rose on a swell to his level, sat him swiftly on a thwart, and went churning powerfully off to the cutter.

I watched while the davit lines were hooked onto the launch

and it rose from the sea. Even that seemed gently and carefully accomplished. Then in a powerful and graceful arc, the cutter steamed off in a long turn to port. As her stern came into view I could see *Daphne* boldly lettered across the sparkling white of her hull.

Thus ended the longest span of time in my young life.

My diary entry was somewhat longer than usual. For July 19, 1937, I had written,

> Yesterday Jack Anderson, our deck engineer, while in the engine house, slipped when the vessel rolled, and attempted to right himself by grabbing the drive belt. The engine was going and the belt took his hand into the wheel. It took off three fingers and mangled his hand badly. Last night he suffered a great deal. I didn't get a lot of sleep because I bunk right across from him and was up a few times to help him. Today the cutter came and took him to Unalaska and from there he will go back home. He took it in a philosophical vein, but it is very pitiful because he's just a young fellow and that will be a great handicap.

The duty officer for the *Daphne* had tersely logged this particular mercy errand of the cutter for July 19, 1937:

> Injured man J. L. Anderson, American merchant seaman, came on board from schooner Wm. H. Smith for transportation to hospital in Unalaska. Position of schooner Wm. H. Smith Lat. 57-18-00 N. Long, 158-50-00 w.

The *Daphne*'s log for July 20, 1937, contained the final reference to Jack Anderson.

> Injured man J. L. Anderson departed for Bureau of Indian Affairs Hospital, Unalaska, for treatment of injured hand.

168

32

The next day it was still blowing, and Captain Thomas gave the order for our watch to haul anchor and hoist the sails.

We sailed for eight hours due north and then dropped the hook again. As tragic as Jack's accident had been, it seemed to me that this move was made as much to break the tension produced in the *Smith*'s fo'c'sle by the enforced idleness of the stormy days aboard as for any other reason.

Or perhaps, with his seemingly infallible instinct, Captain Thomas believed there would be better fishing weather to the north. To some extent he was right. It was calm the next day and remained that way for nine days running.

The calms farther north produced large, smooth, gently undulating swells through which the dories powered back from the fishing runs to unload.

The pace was less intense now. The fish were not running as heavily in their schools as they had earlier in the summer. It was now the fourth week of July 1937. We were more than three months out of San Francisco, more than two months in the codfishing grounds of the Bering Sea.

We were dressing down between four thousand and forty-five hundred fish on an average day, and it gave the dress gang plenty of time to fish off the side.

Perhaps it was my aversion to codfish as food that jinxed my efforts, but my personal catch seemed to grow very slowly. I had almost four hundred now on Sparks' tally sheet, but Trotsky, who really worked at it, had almost double that.

On those days when we fished for longer periods of time, one factor that frequently ended my efforts was the unbelievable tides of the Bering Sea. Little by little I would see my lines angle up from the bottom until, if I had kept at it, my six-pound weights would have literally been strung out on the surface carried there by the tide. I had noticed the phenomenon of the tides once or twice earlier in the summer but hadn't given it much thought.

Now, with much more time to fish off the side, the tide was thwarting me more frequently.

One morning I was fishing at my starboard location and Oscar Quarten was fishing just forward of my station.

Finally, after I had caught nine fish, I could see that the tide was carrying my weights far enough off the bottom that there was no point in continuing to fish. Cod are bottom fish, and there would be no bites at the distance my weights and hooks were off the bottom now.

I noticed that Oscar had already reeled in and secured his gear when I started to reel in my first line. As I started to pull in the line the thought occurred to me that not once during the voyage had I heard the fishermen even mention the tides, much less complain of them.

Oscar had climbed down off the running board when I called out to him. "Hey Oscar, I want to ask you something."

"Yah, vhat?"

"How do the fishermen keep fishing all the time when the tide takes our lines off the bottom?"

Oscar gave me a look that was almost incredulous, and my heart sank. I knew immediately I had asked another stupid question.

With his walrus moustache and habit of opening his eyes wide when he was particularly emphatic in his speech, Oscar's appearance frequently amused me far more than I ever let on to him. I didn't dare even grin now. I knew Oscar was about to let me have it.

"Yesus, Roos, ya be serious?"

"Yes, Oscar, I'm serious. Why doesn't the tide stop the fishermen the way it does us?"

He shook his head resignedly. "Vell, it's dis vay. Dis vessel be anchored . . ." As soon as he said the word "anchored" I knew how stupid my question was. Oscar continued, ". . . and dose dories not be anchored. Dey move vit de tide, der lines hang down alla time. Ve stay one spot, de tide tak our lines."

He looked at the ship's idiot carefully to make sure I wasn't pulling his leg. Then he walked off, shaking his head. I continued to reel in my line against the tide.

One day Walter Jensen came powering in and there, perched on his load of fish in the midship well, was one of the most winsome creatures I had ever seen. It was a baby seal about two feet long—pure white with beautiful coal-black eyes peering at the ship and the men lining the rail and turning its head quickly from side to side as it took in the scene.

At that moment for me it epitomized all the tail-wagging, furry puppies I had ever seen with their front feet braced up on a pet store window, ears cocked forward expectantly. It was absolutely lovable.

The word spread magically, as it seemed to when anything out of the ordinary happened.

I think the sight of that baby seal had the same effect on the rest of the crew as it did on me. This tough, hard-bitten collection of seamen were suddenly acting like schoolboys.

There were shouted suggestions about rigging a sling to get the infant seal aboard. Someone wanted us to ease it through the fishport.

Then the authoritative voice of Captain Thomas rang out from the quarterdeck, "All right, Jensen, belay that. We don't need that animal on this vessel." The captain—our realistic, stern father figure. We could not bring the puppy home.

There were mutterings and oaths I could hear there on the main deck, but they were not loud enough to carry aft to where Captain Thomas stood staring at Walter Jensen in his dory and then at the rest of us lining the starboard rail. For an instant I thought Walter was going to say something as I saw his mouth open, looking up to where the captain stood. While this was not a naval vessel, the force of the captain's supreme authority aboard his ship was still there. Then Walter Jensen clamped his mouth shut, turned abruptly away and, as gently as a mother guiding her unsteady infant, carefully eased the baby seal off the load of cod and back into the Bering Sea. It gave us one last bewildered look over its shoulder and then went swimming briskly away.

Captain Thomas was right, of course. None of us gave any thought to how we would maintain that wild creature on this vessel with the intense activity generated by the occasional heavy runs of fish, and the storms while we were under way. It was undoubtedly better off in its natural environment. Still, it was some time before the resentment aroused by the captain's summary dismissal of this beautiful little anticipated ship's pet subsided.

Although I didn't think of it in those terms then, the Bering Sea was a teeming source of sea life.

From time to time one of the fishermen would come in with an Alaskan king crab sprawled across his load. The legs of this gigantic crustacean sometimes measured six feet from the tip of one leg across the body to the end of another leg.

There never were enough at one time to feed the entire crew. Thus, by unspoken protocol, the fisherman who had landed the crab would cook it up in one of the cook's large cauldrons as those few of us invited to dine would stoke the coal-burning stove in the galley after the evening meal. Then we would sit down in the mess to enjoy the repast. It tasted better to me than any of the cracked crab I had enjoyed at Fisherman's Wharf back home in San Francisco. I don't really know if it was better than our California crab. At the time any change of diet seemed incredibly delicious to me.

Chris Olsen came in with one such large delicacy on his second run toward the end of July, and he invited Trotsky, Roy, and me to join him for a crab feast that night.

We had tubs of butter aboard that seemed to stay as fresh as the eggs down in the hold of the *Smith*. Although there was strict water discipline enforced on the *Smith* with our limited supply of fresh drinking water, we could eat as much as we wanted of the ship's food stores.

172

I cracked a leg and dipped a large chunk of crabmeat into a pot of melted butter.

"This is great, Chris, I really appreciate it!"

He gave me a puzzled look. "How come, Roos, ya lik' dis crab so much, and don' lik' dat goot cod?"

It puzzled me too when I thought about it. But somehow for me, while they all came from the sea, the crab I loved, and the codfish just about turned my stomach.

The fishermen did not go out of their way to catch halibut, since this was not a commercial fish for this vessel except for its use as bait. But consistently, again with no apparent direction or orders, there were always enough halibut caught to keep the entire crew supplied with bait, cut in about two-inch squares from the tough white bottom hide. I had always thought of halibut as a small flounderlike fish bought in a fish store at home for an evening meal. The size of the halibut up here, and their weight, were astonishing to me. It was not uncommon for one of the fishermen to bring in a specimen measuring almost six feet in length and about half that across. They were so heavy that we would rig a block and tackle to get them aboard.

The whales were everywhere. And the killer boats. These were not the romantic, and deadly, dangerous whaling long-boats of the old-time New England whalers, pursuing their prey by sail, heart, and muscle at the oars, pursuing desperately until finally the harpooner's lance sunk home and they took off on the wild Nantucket sleigh ride. What I saw were power craft with the harpooner's cannon mounted on the very tip of the bow, with the gunner braced there in the bow pulpit. These whale hunts frequently occurred far enough from the *Smith* to give us a perspective on what was happening but close enough to view it in detail. Once the killer boat had a whale in its sights we could see it throwing out a wake, charging on its prey, and then the puff of smoke from the cannon. An instant later the sound of the report would reach us.

I really didn't know quite how it all worked then, but it was obviously far different from what I had read in *Moby Dick*.

As apparently unfeeling as my shipmates were, I was occasionally surprised by something I heard.

One evening, just after we had washed down and secured for the day, I was standing at the rail with Frank Simmons.

It was about 1900 and there would be at least another three hours of daylight. In the far distance we could barely discern the faint outlines of the whaler factory ship.

Nearer to us, and on a line more or less parallel to the fore and aft line of the *Smith*, we saw a killer boat cruising slowly. Suddenly it leaped ahead, the bow wave foaming up almost to the deck. Like a cat stalking its prey, it curved one way, then another. Abruptly I saw the telltale puff of smoke from the bow, and a second later I heard the report.

"Poor bastard, doesn't have a chance against that killer boat!"

Surprised, I looked at Frank. He was standing there, legs spread, hands thrust into his hip pockets. He was slowly shaking his head. There was an odd look on his face, almost a sadness.

"What's the difference between them killing whales and us killing cod, Frank?"

He looked at me for a long moment. "You may have something there, Russ. I don't really know. It's just that they're so big, and really easylike the way they move through the water." He paused a moment, still staring at the killer boat, which had slowed now, approaching its victim. "I've spent a lot of years at sea, had plenty of seagoin' time in the Marine Corps. Seen whales all over the world. They're just different than codfish, that's all. You seen one up close yet?"

I nodded. "Fairly close, maybe a hundred yards or so off our beam, I've seen them spouting. I know what you mean, Frank. They just seem more important than codfish. What kind of whales are they?"

"Grays and humpbacks mostly. Don't know how long they'll last the way they're getting them now. One thing about it, those bloody bombs finish them fast. At least they don't drown in their own blood the way they did in the old days."

"What's the difference now?"

174

"That harpooner's lance has a bomb on the end of it. Goes off about three seconds after it hits. Kills most of them right now."

We both stood there quietly. We could see the killer boat methodically winching the huge carcass up and to the side of the craft. Slowly it turned in a wide arc, heading for the factory ship, the inert carcass which had been such a miraculous, gigantic mass of life and energy just moments before lashed to its side.

I felt the same sense of regret and sadness that Frank Simmons seemed to feel.

On August 1 a Coast Guard cutter arrived with mail. Efficiently as always, the power launch from the cutter was alongside, passing up our mail sack, accepting our sack of homeward-bound mail in return, and then surging back to the cutter.

As usual there was a letter from my twelve-year-old sister Lois. Living with other relatives in the Sunset District of San Francisco, having no conceivable idea of what her brother's life on this ship was, she wrote faithfully. It had been years since we had lived together in our own family unit. Although we were separated by distance, gender, age, and a totally different environment, her letters were still immensely important to me. They were tangible links with home.

That night after dinner I referred to my diary and counted up the number of times a Coast Guard cutter had delivered us mail and provided succor. They had taken Johnny Gunderson off when we first sailed into the Bering Sea. Then on June 21 and June 30 a cutter had arrived with mail. I knew from the irregular timing of the mail deliveries that these Coast Guard cutters were on their regular patrols and the delivery of mail to the schooner *William H. Smith* was only incidental to their basic mission of providing help to all who needed it in this lonely sea. Still they did bring us mail from home, and at times when it was no mean feat simply to launch a boat into the turbulent waters of the Bering Sea. I thought with profound gratitude of their rescue of Jack Anderson. I remembered Sparks' words to me the night before they took Jack off: "You ever think what it'd be like up here if we didn't have the Coast Guard to help us out?" He was so right. I didn't know it at the time, but there was one remaining bounty the United States Coast Guard would confer on this old windjammer. None of us would ever forget it.

That night at about 2200 hours I went up on the foredeck to relieve myself over the side.

In calm weather like this, with the dark swells slowly moving aft below the sheer of the bow, it gave me some type of primitive satisfaction to arc my water into the surface of the Bering Sea. It wasn't quite like writing your name in the snow, as I had heard from some of my shipmates who had lived in colder climes than San Francisco. Still, it was something akin to that—a peculiarly male pleasure.

Thus occupied, I stood on the butt of the jib boom, my left arm crooked around the inner jib stay. There wasn't too much motion to the vessel, but I never stood or sat anywhere on the *Smith* where there was nothing between me and the sea without a secure hold on some part of the ship.

I was idly watching my stream splatter on the swells when suddenly a huge black surface rose vertically directly under me. Up and up it came. It was so totally unexpected that I was stunned rather than frightened—choked off in midstream. I could not comprehend what was happening to the Bering Sea on a calm evening like this. Then, an instant later, I heard the sibilant whish of a whale's spout just forward of the jib boom. I became aware that this great mass just a few feet below me was moving forward in a graceful, arching glide, and I knew that I had seen a whale closer than I ever had before and undoubtedly ever would again.

My arm had involuntarily locked onto the jib stay in a reflex action. I was welded to that stay in the crook of my elbow as I watched the gigantic animal slide slowly forward and disappear beneath the surface.

I stood there for quite a while. It took me a long time to

176

reengage my internal gears and complete what I had gone up on the bow to do.

Finally I was through. Thoughtfully I moved aft, descended to the main deck, down into the fo'c'sle, and climbed up into my bunk. The Bering Sea seemed always to have something new and different for me.

33

Then the weather began to blow up on us again. The sea gods had been kind to us long enough. Now, with the crew confined below by the weather, the accumulated tensions produced by day after day of hard work and the physical proximity we shared in the fo'c'sle began to surface.

Bob Henderson and Cowboy had joined the ship together. As with many of my shipmates, if they were not on my watch or didn't work with me, I learned surprisingly little about their lives. Bob and Cowboy were probably both about twenty years old; I knew they were from Southern California, but that is about all I knew.

On this particular day they were both stretched out on Bob's bunk. It was the lowest fore-and-aft bunk in its tier, fairly commodious because unnarrowed by the sheer of the vessel. High Pockets had the bunk just above Bob's. High Pockets and Bob were on the second watch; High Pockets was the starboard splitter, and Bob was a starboard idler. Consequently they saw a good deal of each other, and both were as friendly and easygoing as anyone on the ship.

But this day High Pockets was trying to sleep, and Bob and Cowboy were talking and laughing loudly. The first time he hung his upper body over his bunk and talked rather quietly to them.

"For Christ's sake, hold it down, will ya? I'm trying to sleep."

I was stretched out on my port-to-starboard bunk reading and I couldn't hear exactly what Cowboy's response was, but I recognized his voice.

For a while they talked quietly, and then their voices grew louder again.

Once more High Pockets asked them to keep it down, and this time I heard Cowboy's voice clearly.

"You're not the only one in this fo'c'sle, High Pockets. Anyway, you shouldn't be sleeping this time of day."

High Pockets lay back on his bunk, and I looked over at him. He was lying on his back, his hands clasped under his head, staring at the bottom of the bunk above him. I could see his jaw muscles working.

Once again, for a while, their voices dropped. Then Bob let out a peal of laughter at something Cowboy said. I was lying on my left side watching, and I saw High Pockets swing his feet over his bunk and drop down to the deck of the fo'c'sle. His jaw was set, but somewhat to my surprise I saw him start up the ladder topside.

I went back to reading until I heard the sudden roar of the wind a second time as the hatch to the forward house was opened and closed again. Puzzled now, I looked up to the top of the ladder and saw High Pockets carefully making his way down the ladder, the handle of a large bucket of seawater tightly clasped in his hand.

Jesus, I thought, he's going to douse them with that water. This was deadly serious. The damp pervaded everything in the fo'c'sle anyway, but if a man's blankets were drenched they could be a long time drying out.

Bob and Cowboy were again so engrossed that they didn't even see him coming.

I think I was the only one in the fo'c'sle who had watched the unfolding drama from the beginning. One thing I had long since learned on this ship was to keep my nose out of someone else's business. Because both Bob and High Pockets were such pleasant, decent types, I really hated to see what I knew was coming. But I was not about to get involved.

178

I watched as High Pockets reached the fo'c'sle deck, moved to a point just opposite Bob's bunk, crouched there with the bucket held in both hands now, and then flung the icy seawater squarely and thoroughly onto the bunk. There was a sputtering bellow of rage, and then Bob Henderson came rolling out of that bunk, swinging at High Pockets like a man possessed. Cowboy was right behind him, but I could see that it didn't look as if he was going to get involved either, even though it had been his taunting remarks that had really enraged High Pockets.

Bob caught High Pockets one glancing blow to the side of his jaw, and I saw to my surprise that High Pockets was not using his fists. Rather, he was fending off the blows with his arms and simultaneously trying to grab Bob. My mind flashed back to the puzzled expression I had noticed on his face when Sam Culleson and Trotsky had battled it out topside with their bare fists. Then it hit me: He was going at it rough and tumble. My blood ran cold. I remembered one such rough-and-tumble battle I had seen in a pool hall in the Mission District. I didn't want to see another.

At just that instant I heard the messman sing out, "Chow down!" It was time for the noon meal.

Bob and High Pockets had jostled into the area just amidships from where the ladder was bolted to the deck.

Most of the dress gang had gathered just forward of where they were battling each other. I saw Jack Davis in the front of the group. Jack was a bit older than most of us in the dress gang, probably close to thirty. He had spent a good many years in merchant vessels. He worked as the header on the starboard-side dress gang and was on the second watch. Consequently I had had very little to do with him. Just as the messman's call rang out, Jack suddenly turned his head toward the members of the dress gang and hollered, "Chow, men!" and made a sudden move into Bob and High Pockets with the rest of the dress gang surging behind him, automatically reacting to the mess call.

The press of bodies immediately smothered the fight between Bob and High Pockets and effectively separated them.

Then I heard Jack's voice: "Sorry, guys, but I'm hungry!"

I was staring at the milling group of men at the bottom of the ladder. Bob had been forced back to my tier of bunks, High Pockets was now about ten feet from him on the fishermen's side of the fo'c'sle, separated by at least six or eight members of the dress gang charging for the ladder and that food topside. As Jack swung onto the ladder he looked up at me and winked, his expression quite serious. All of a sudden I realized that Jack Davis didn't care for rough and tumble any more than I did. He had probably seen more of it in his years at sea than I ever would. He could not appear to interfere in this fight, but by quick thinking he had effectively broken it up.

All we could hope for now was that two basically decent men would cool off and forget it.

I watched as Bob moved around the ladder to his bunk and began to remove the wet blankets. High Pockets stared at him warily for a moment and then went topside to join the first sitting. I heaved a sigh of relief. Good, honest, bare-fisted fighting was one thing. The ferocious, maiming rough and tumble was distinctly another.

It was now too late for me to join the first sitting, so I went back to my reading.

All through the first sitting Bob worked methodically trying to get the water out of his bunk, going topside to weave his blankets through the rigging. It wasn't raining, and the force of that wind would do something toward drying them out.

By the time the mess was ready for the second sitting, I was feeling relaxed again and swung my legs over my bunk. Bob Henderson had finished doing all he could do and was simply sitting on the seatboard, staring straight ahead.

I looked at the expression on his face. It was almost exactly the same look I had seen on High Pockets' face just before he had gone topside for the seawater. I had an ominous feeling we had not seen the last of this.

By one means or another Bob Henderson and High Pockets avoided direct contact with one another for the next hour or so, and after I had eaten, Bob sitting at the same mess table with me in stony silence chewing his food, I was back in my bunk, reading.

Once, early in the afternoon, I glanced over to their bunks. High Pockets was stretched out on his bunk, his hands clasped under his head—a rather grim look on his face. Bob was nowhere to be seen.

At 1400 hours I heard the roar of the wind as the hatch topside opened, and a moment later it stopped as the hatch closed. I felt an emptiness in my stomach. I knew what was about to happen.

Bob Henderson was descending the ladder, a bucket of seawater suspended from the handle in *his* hand.

I looked over at High Pockets. He was staring intently now as Bob made his way carefully down the ladder. I saw him bring his right arm out from under his head, and his right hand seemed to reach for something, but I couldn't tell what it was.

Inexorably, deliberately, neither saying a word, like two gunmen of the Old West, these two moved inevitably to their confrontation. High Pockets knew what was coming as surely as Bob Henderson knew what he was going to do. I watched the scene unfold, my heart in my mouth, but I was not about to say a word.

Bob reached the bottom of the ladder, turned to his left, took two steps to a point directly abeam of High Pockets' bunk, and let the seawater fly just as hard and as carefully as High Pockets had earlier.

Almost before the last drop had hit him, High Pockets was springing out of his bunk like some sinewy mountain lion. I saw to my horror that he was clutching a belaying pin in his right hand. This was lethal.

Bob stepped back, his fists raised, and then he saw the belaying pin as High Pockets raised it high in the air, bringing it whistling down, aimed directly for Bob's skull. Bob was stocky and strong, High Pockets was tall and sinewy. In strength they were about evenly matched. The difference was that High Pockets, with his mountaineering background, intended to kill his adversary. Bob was merely fighting as honor dictated.

When he saw that belaying pin aimed at his skull, he knew what he was in for. With a quick move to his right he ducked away and the weight of the pin with all of High Pockets' considerable strength behind it carried him forward until he was almost sprawled on the deck. Bob seized the pin and flung it clattering across the fo'c'sle deck. He snarled at his shipmate, "Fight fair, you sonofabitch!"

There wasn't a sound from High Pockets as he was on his feet like a cat, again circling, not trying to hit but warding off Bob's punches as best he could and groping for him. Bob was doing some damage, but nothing I feared to compare with what High Pockets would do if he ever closed with him.

They were battling near our tier of bunks. Trotsky in the bunk to midship of mine was sitting with his legs hanging over the side, watching intently.

Then, just as it seemed that Bob might land one punch that would at least stun the killer he was battling, the ship rolled to port as Bob's feet hit a place on the deck where some of his seawater had spilled. He lost his balance for a split second. High Pockets lunged at him at that instant and Bob was on his back, the sinewy frame of High Pockets pinning him there as the powerful hands groped for his throat.

Bob knew he was fighting for his life now. With his last breath before those hands closed around his throat he screamed out, "Cowboy, help me!"

The fishermen had gathered in a silent, intent semicircle on their side of the fo'c'sle, staring at the struggle.

Cowboy, who had been standing forward on the port side of the fo'c'sle, moved toward the figures struggling on the deck and stopped in his tracks as a low, ominous, animallike growl came from the fishermen's side of the fo'c'sle. They would watch a man killed before their eyes, but by God it would be one on one. I prayed for the courage to do something, but that dangerous growl had me stopped too. I looked at Trotsky. He was the biggest man on the ship, still really a boy only a year or two older than I, but large and strong. He was staring intently at the now silent struggling figures directly below us.

I looked back down. Bob's face was beet red, his eyes staring, his mouth open, his tongue protruding. Horrified, I saw High Pockets' thumbs reaching up Bob's cheeks toward his eyes. At the same instant, out of the corner of my eye, I saw Trotsky leaping off his bunk. I was right behind him.

Trotsky hit High Pockets' back with such force that it would have stopped any man in his right mind. I landed on the left side of his back. I grabbed High Pockets' left arm as Trotsky grabbed his right. The strength in that arm was unbelievable. Alone I'm not sure I could have even stopped that hand with the thumb groping for Bob's eye. I was able to hold his arm where it was, and then Trotsky's strength asserted itself. Little by little he was pulling High Pockets' right arm back, and abruptly I felt his left arm relax. It was over.

Only then did I think about the fishermen again. I looked apprehensively at them on their side of the fo'c'sle. Thank God nothing perceptible was happening. Chris Olsen was standing nearest where we lay sprawled out on the deck. I caught his eye. He nodded once, almost imperceptibly. I knew then that it was all right. When they had warned off Cowboy they were telling him that Bob's friend was not going to gang up two on one. When Trotsky and I both jumped High Pockets at the same time they knew we were just trying to stop it, and I am sure they would've preferred not to have Bob's eyes gouged out either. In fairness, what was about to happen may not have been as apparent to them as it was to Trotsky and me directly above.

Finally we were disentangled and standing there—all four of us breathing hard. Then Bob Henderson did the bravest thing I ever saw on that ship. He had come within a hairbreadth of being killed by that belaying pin, he had been only seconds away from losing both of his eyes to those groping thumbs and he knew it.

But he stood there, tears of rage rolling down his cheeks, and yelled at High Pockets, "You dirty, yellow bastard! You don't fight fair . . ." Choking sobs stopped him. High Pockets just stared at him for a moment, then shook his head like a man coming out of a daze and turned away.

We were then more than a month and a half away from the end of this voyage in San Francisco Bay. These two men were on the same watch. They both worked on the starboard-side dress gang together. One's bunk was directly above the other's. I never saw them speak a single word to each other again. It was as if each of them had disappeared from the other's world.

The day after the fight between Bob and High Pockets, August 4, the weather was calm enough for the dories to go out. Then for another six days the weather held but the catch was down to almost nothing. We were averaging less than fifteen hundred fish a day.

Although the wind didn't spring up on us, the fog started to hamper us almost as much as the blows. For the fishermen it could be as deadly. The schooner was a small speck in that expanse of sea if you were a fisherman alone in a dory five miles away and the fog had closed in.

Whenever the fog descended and there were fishermen out, the idlers took turn about, thirty minutes at a stretch, pumping our hand-operated foghorn. This was simply a rectangular box with a lever on one side. I didn't know anything about how the acoustical gear inside that box worked, but by moving the lever vigorously forward and back we generated a surprisingly penetrating, discordant low note-high note sound. Even when I was kneeling behind the box working the lever, aiming the foghorn systematically around the compass, it didn't sound all that loud to me. Yet more than one of the fishermen told me it had provided the homing sound for them sometimes from as far out as a half mile away by their reckoning.

This was a bleak time for me on the *Smith*. I had on at least two occasions awakened from a horrible nightmare—feeling thumbs groping for my eyes, waking in an almost pitch-black fo'c'sle and not knowing whether I had been permanently blinded or not.

Consciously I couldn't get that last scene out of my mind. I asked myself if I would have moved if Trotsky hadn't leaped off his bunk first. There was no way of knowing, but what was shaming and depressing me was the thought that maybe I would not have made the move. There was no way to be sure now.

I struggled with the idea of courage as an abstract considera-tion. If there was one man in that fo'c'sle who should have literally been on High Pockets' back, it was Cowboy. Not only had his verbalizing precipitated the first fight between Bob and High Pockets, Bob was his friend, and he was crying out for help. But Cowboy had been stopped by that ominous growl from the other side of the fo'c'sle and had been more concerned with his own welfare than his friend's. Then, as I felt a rush of contempt for Cowboy, I thought of his work aloft. It still took all the resolution I could muster to climb that rigging and clam-ber into the crosstrees to handle the tops'ls. For Cowboy it was just as high and just as dangerous, yet he seemed absolutely fearless up there.

I remembered the last blow before we raced through Unimak Pass. Someone on the first watch lost the mizzen tops'l halyard as that particular sail was dropped, and the knotted end of the line flew up to the block at the very tip of the mizzen topmast. The topmasts were bare, smooth poles, not even stayed.

When the halyard was lost there was no attempt to recover it on that watch because of the storm.

But the next afternoon I vividly remembered coming out on deck to see every member of the crew then on deck staring aloft at the mizzen topmast. I followed the collective gaze and felt my stomach turn over as I recognized Cowboy two thirds of the way up that bare pole. We were sailing briskly at the time, heeled over to starboard, and rolling rather gently down at deck level. But up there where Cowboy was, the topmast was describing great swinging arcs against the gray sky. As we watched, little by little he inched his way up. Finally he was at the very top, hanging on tightly with his left arm with his flexed legs glued to that bare pole. Carefully he reached up with his right hand, retrieved the end of the halyard at the block where the knot had stopped it, tucked it into his belt, and came sliding down the topmast to the crosstrees.

I shook my head at his courage. Quite literally, if my life had depended on it, there was no way I could have forced myself out of the relative security of the crosstrees and shinnied up that topmast the way Cowboy had.

Then I was back to thinking about what I considered his absolutely shameful failure to act in the fo'c'sle. Philosophically it was getting to be too much for me to resolve in my mind.

Finally I forced myself to think of the fact that Trotsky mainly, with some help from me, had ended that terrible struggle. If I wasn't as courageous as I would have preferred—so be it.

For the first time in my life I considered the male instinct which seemed to be an integral part of me and of all the men I knew. To settle a difference physically—that was acceptable. But more and more I questioned the logic. Just what did it prove?

I thought back to that first night at the wheel when Chris Olsen had pushed me away, and Jim Bewla had decked him. For a moment I smiled wryly. "Decking" someone was a common colloquialism in my environment back home. On the *Smith* it acquired a very special literal meaning. It seemed to me that the third mate had dealt with that situation in just about the only way he could. He wasn't trying to prove anything; he simply solved a problem directly and effectively.

On the other hand, what did these shipboard fights prove? As sickened as I had been by High Pockets' fighting tactics, it began to occur to me that his view of it made at least as much sense as mine. No matter who you were, Joe Louis himself, a small piece of metal propelled explosively from a gun could more than equalize any fight. And what did *that* prove?

186

I didn't quite realize it at the time, but one of the factors making me feel so low was that just when life aboard the *Smith* had settled into a comfortable routine for me, something totally traumatic blasted me out of it.

I hadn't come close to killing myself for days now, the hair was sprouting on my chest most satisfactorily, I knew my work, and I did it well. While I would never dream of saying it out loud, I had basically come to enjoy life on this schooner—except for the expectation now that something terrible could be lying in wait the next day or the next week. Finally I forced myself to stop worrying. What would be would be. We had well over three hundred thousand fish salted down in the hold now. It might not be too long before we would be sailing home. Maybe we had had our share of bad luck.

After we had dressed down our meager catch on August 10, I sought out Frank Simmons.

"Frank, how come the captain isn't moving the anchorage? We're sure not getting any fish here."

Frank gave me an amused look. "You really like this Bering Sea, Russ, don't you?"

I had the feeling I had asked another stupid question, but Frank treated me more kindly than I had reason to expect aboard this ship. He continued speaking.

"We've got our catch now—not outstanding, but it's enough, over 320,000 cod. We're just waiting for the right wind, as I see it." He turned away and walked aft to the stern quarters down the rather narrow passageway on the deck between the checkers on the outboard side and the hatches and engine deckhouse on the inboard side.

His words sunk in slowly. I had adjusted to life aboard the *Smith* more than I realized. Instead of a sudden rush of jubilation, it was a dawning realization: One of these days we would be sailing south for home.

August 11 was a red-letter day on the schooner. The *Hale*, a Union Fish Company steamship that serviced the salmon canneries on the Alaskan coast, hove to off our port beam. Paul Myers took Roy Brewer with him in his dory and powered over to trade codfish for fresh meat—at least meat that had been fresh at some point in its distant past before being consigned to the freezer. The first mate returned to the *Smith* with a dory-load of frozen pork chops. We would go through them, three meals a day, in two days, but I had never tasted anything more delicious in my life than those tired pork chops.

After the sacks of pork chops had been hauled aboard, Paul Myers went aft. He returned forward in about half an hour to where a group of us were standing outside the forward deckhouse. It was still an hour before the night meal. I don't know what was happening to the rest of the crew, but I know I was actually salivating just thinking about the feast to come.

Paul strode up to us. "De cap'n say ve sail fer home soon's ve get a norderly." That was all; there were no shouts or cheers from the crew, but now it was official.

The next day we caught a fair wind and fairly flew to the south, heading for Unimak Pass. Since Captain Thomas knew, probably better than anyone else on this old windjammer, that our passage was not to be reckoned until we were through the pass, the fish checkers, splitting tank, and all the other dressing fixtures remained solidly in place on deck. If the wind did disappear on us the fishermen would go out again, we would dress down codfish again, and undoubtedly it would be psychologically better for this crew than simply standing by on a becalmed schooner praying for a wind.

My diary entries, which had been almost nonexistent during long stretches in the grounds when the cod were running, resumed on almost a daily basis.

For August 12 I had written:

Today at noon we started heaving anchor and at 1:30 had all the chain in. Half an hour later we had all sails set and were heading for the pass with a fair wind.

We won't tear down the checkers etc., I think, until we get in the Pacific, but the dories probably won't go out again. I'm sure hoping for a decent wind through the pass because once in the Pacific we're assured of a fairly good passage home because of the Northerly winds prevailing along the coast.

Without ever being specifically conscious of the reason for it, my spirits seemed to soar with those driving sails when we sailed like this. The sound of the ship's timbers in the fo'c'sle literally never stopped. Even on the calmest of days there was always movement under me wherever I was on this ship. But when the wind came and the sheets trimmed the sails for maximum drive, it was different. Then it seemed to me this old ship came alive like a seabird soaring over the swells. Now the ship's timbers had a steady, rhythmic sound; the motion was stronger but consistent and purposeful. I felt alive and glad to be so—particularly given the direction in which we were sailing.

We were back on watches now. I had gone down into the fo'c'sle on an errand after a midmorning wheel turn on Friday, August 13, 1937.

As I reached the bottom of the ladder I could see Paul Myers standing in the center of a group of fishermen.

"Ve goin' to secure de dories, men. Cap'n's orders."

There were mutterings and grumblings that I couldn't really distinguish, and then I saw the mate's usually dour expression disappear as a grin split his face.

"Vhat ya say if I tell ya I yust be yokin'? Ve goin' to drop de hook and go fishin' dis afternoon!"

This time there was nothing but startled silence.

Chuckling, Paul Myers shook his head and started for the ladder. "Dis gottdamn crew, no matter vhat I say first, ya don' lik!" Still shaking his head, he climbed the ladder.

Then I noticed that Frank Simmons was standing forward in the fo'c'sle on the port side. He had been watching the first mate and the fishermen and he was grinning too. Then he spoke to the dress gang. "You heard him, men. If the fishermen ain't goin' out, no sense in us leaving our gear in place." He

189

looked around and raised his eyebrows. There was absolutely no argument from the dress gang. Just about every man there had a grin on his face to match Frank's.

"You lazy bastards! Thought someone might want to do a little work on this vessel." Frank shook his head. "Been a bloody vacation this summer, that's what. Wish I'd had you on the *Louise* two years ago. Would have snapped you in, by God."

Frank was in his element. He really was a superb administrator. As I listened to him I thought back over the first light days, and then the heavy runs of cod. I couldn't remember just how or when we had shaken down, but somehow Frank Simmons, while performing his key splitting function with maximum efficiency on the port side, had managed to turn the port and starboard dress gang into the most efficient working operations I had ever seen.

Frank knew it, the men knew it, and they also knew that this was as close to letting his men know that he appreciated their hard work as he would ever come. He turned away then. "Tomorrow we'll knock down the checkers and the rest of the gear." As he reached the ladder and started up, he saw me reaching into my bunk.

"Hey, Russ, I want to talk to you." He backed down the ladder to the fo'c'sle deck and waited for me. There was something in his voice that reminded me of the day Jim Bewla had dragooned me into capstan duty. But Frank's look was serious when I spoke to him.

"Yes, Frank, what do you want?"

"Remember when Eric Johnson took over the messman's job when we found out Johnny Gunderson was clapped up?"

I was suspicious. "Yeah, I remember. So what?"

Frank did smile then. "Don't you wish you'd been able to keep that job when Johnny Gunderson took it away?"

"Christ no, Frank. Working in that galley—with that cook!"

As much as we appreciated the cook's efforts—and he really was effective with the ship's stores he had to work with—his temper was horrendous and known to everyone aboard.

I literally shuddered when I thought of what my life on this ship would have been like if Johnny Gunderson hadn't snatched that job away from me, to be succeeded by Eric Johnson—both hungry for the extra compensation produced by the messman's higher pay per ton of fish salted down below.

From the day we shoved off on this voyage to the day we dropped the hook for the last time in San Francisco Bay, the cook and the messman were up at 0400 every single morning. Every day of the voyage that stove had been stoked with coal, and the entire crew had been fed three times a day. Every dirty plate, utensil, and pot had been washed in salt water after every one of those six servings. The confinement in that cramped galley with the evil-tempered cook was a purgatory I had escaped without even appreciating my good fortune at the time.

As usual, Frank Simmons read my mind, and once again he displayed the capacity to do justice and keep his area of responsibility on this ship functioning smoothly. It was his born administrator's instinct which made him so effective.

"You're a good kid, Russ. You know as well as I do that if they gave Johnson the whole goddamned catch it wouldn't be enough to pay him for what he's been through. I'm going to give him a break. For two weeks apiece you and Roy'll be pearl divin' in the galley. He's going to have plenty to do anyway, but at least we'll get that off his back."

My tone was anguished. "Why us, Frank? Jesus, we've worked just as hard as anybody else on this voyage!"

Frank nodded. "I know." He dropped his voice to a conspiratorial whisper. "You two are the only ones I've got in the dress gang who stand a chance of gettin' along with that goddamned cook. You've got to help me out."

I didn't think of it at the time, but the force of Frank Simmons' personality, in his own way, was just as strong as Captain Thomas' in his. Even though it wasn't couched in those terms, Frank was giving me an order. It didn't even occur to me to disobey it.

191

Frank continued to read my mind. "'Course, we'll take you off watch. It won't be too bad."

"I *like* standing watch, Frank. I like the sail handling and standing a wheel turn."

Frank could have cut it off there, but I think he genuinely liked me, and he did want me to accept the inevitable as willingly as possible.

"Look, Russ, if this wind holds we could be through the pass and home in three weeks. Why don't you draw straws with Roy? The second one of you may not have more than a week's duty in the galley."

"OK, Frank, but you tell Roy. I don't want to tell him!"

Frank grinned again and started back up the ladder. "That's just what I was about to do."

Disconsolately I finished what I was doing and went topside again.

About ten minutes later I saw Roy sitting on the running board, starboard side aft, staring glumly at nothing. I knew that Frank had already given him the bad news.

I made my way down the deck, through the narrow passageway by the side of the checkers.

"Frank talk to you, Roy?"

He nodded. "He said we ought to draw straws to see who goes first. That OK with you?"

I nodded in my turn.

Roy then went forward to the galley, broke off two pieces of the straws from the galley broom, and returned to where I was sitting on the running board.

He held them in the palm of his left hand. "I'll break them off so there'll really be a difference. Short straw draws the first two weeks' duty, OK?"

"Guess that's about as fair as anything else, Roy. Go ahead."

Very carefully he broke one straw into a piece about four inches long, the other into a piece about two inches long. Then, with his hands behind his back, he positioned the straws firmly in his left hand, the ends projecting about the same distance above the pocket formed between thumb and index finger as he extended his left hand toward me.

"Go ahead."

I stared at the two projecting straws. Roy had done a good job of concealment. There was no way to tell which was the short straw.

With a shrug I reached for the straw to my right as I faced him.

With his work-hardened hands I don't think Roy knew, any more than I did, where each straw was located.

I grasped the end of the straw between my thumb and forefinger and started to pull. In a second I realized I was pulling the long straw. Roy Brewer had the first two weeks' duty in the galley.

35

On Saturday, August 14, 1937, I came up on deck to find the *Smith* heeled over to port, driving hard on the wind for Unimak Pass. As usual it was a gray, overcast day, but my spirits soared with the flying movement of the ship.

After breakfast I was out on deck with the rest of the third watch when Frank Simmons sounded off.

"All right, men, I want the whole dress gang on deck. We're knockin' down the checkers. Let's move!"

It was surprising to me how hard and effectively the men on the *Smith* had worked on this voyage. Now we were like schoolboys liberated at the end of the academic year. With shouts and oaths we tore into the deck structures like men possessed. I found myself working with Trotsky levering one of the heavy thwartship planks out of the wooden deck where it had been toenailed with heavy nails.

The sweat was running down his face, but he was grinning.

"Damn, I haven't enjoyed anything this much the whole voyage!"

The sweat was running down my face too. I simply nodded as we strained on our crowbars and the plank slowly rose with a protesting groan and then flopped over on the deck.

The heavy redwood planking comprising the checkers, running boards, and other dress-down gear could withstand the most violent attack with hammer and crowbar with no apparent damage. It was reused, voyage after codfishing voyage.

With the entire dress gang attacking the checkers and other structures, in about an hour and a half there was simply a jumbled mass of lumber on both the port and starboard sides where there had been an orderly set of structures for dressing codfish.

Then we turned to with hard-bristled, long-handled scrub brushes. There were times when I wondered at my own lack of observation, and this was one of them. For days obviously the messman had been saving ashes from the cook's stove and I hadn't noticed a thing. There were two good-sized barrels of ashes available to us now, one for each side of the deck.

The accumulation of dried fish blood and guts under the checkers, between the running boards, and on the ship's bulwarks, in what seemed like every seam and cranny on the vessel, was unbelievable. Every day during the season we had washed down with a will—I had thought—and now this.

This was hard, monotonous scrubbing. It was not the exhilarating work of demolition that knocking down the checkers had been. Still there was a growing feeling of satisfaction as we started forward on each side and slowly worked our way aft. The salt water and ashes, with vigorous scrubbing, began to transform the schooner. The *Smith* would never look like a yacht, but slowly the original white of the inboard sides of the bulwarks began to emerge. Then the unsightly ridges of dried fish blood and guts defining the checker planks where they had been nailed to the deck began to disappear.

By two bells on the second watch all of the lumber had been

scrubbed and stowed below on the cinches of cod. The deck was clean, the bulwarks were white again, and the seawater swept through the port scuppers and swirled aft unobstructed as we surged through the gray sea.

It was almost dinnertime, I was tired, but I experienced a deep feeling of satisfaction as I turned and took a last look down the clear expanse of deck before going below.

That night on our watch I found myself pacing the starboard side of the deck with Chris Olsen, rolling with the motion of the ship as we made our way aft, then turning and walking forward.

"Man, it feels good to have room to walk again, doesn't it, Chris!"

He chuckled quietly and looked sideways at me. "Seems dat I 'member ya t'ought ve crazy, valkin', valkin' all de time on deck."

I started to protest, then I had to grin. "I didn't exactly think you were crazy, Chris, but . . ." My voice trailed off.

Chris simply nodded. "I tol' ya den. Ya go to sea long enough, ya be doin' it too!"

Whatever, it was good to have room to walk as the *Smith* drove through the sea, heading home.

We sailed steadily, and at times under fore and mizzen only as the blows hit us—always driving us in the right direction, but sometimes with a force that absolutely required us to shorten sail.

On August 18 word emanated from the captain's quarters, where the charts were spread out on his chart table, that we should be somewhere near Unimak Pass by the next day.

We were, and then began for us the most frustrating period of the entire voyage. Day after day we would sail into the northern end of the pass, and then the wind would die on us completely, or head us so that we had no choice but to bear off back into the Bering Sea.

The tide ran through the pass like a millrace, but it never coincided with the wind that would have brought us out into the broad reaches of the Pacific, with all the sea room this old schooner would ever need.

I began to wonder if the Bering Sea would ever let us go, whether we were doomed to sail forever in these northern latitudes like some latter-day *Flying Dutchman*.

These were perilous waters, and the fogs that enclosed us regularly added to the problems now afflicting the schooner *William H. Smith*.

I could feel the tension growing in the crew, but aside from an occasional outburst of temper, there were no fights.

My diary entries mirrored my frustration:

Aug. 19   Today we got practically to the pass but are becalmed outside and can't get through.

Aug. 20   Still becalmed. I thought we were going through for awhile this afternoon but the wind died out again.

Aug. 21   And we're still becalmed. A little breeze sprang up this afternoon and we set the tops'ls. But again it died out and the fog really came rolling in. You can hardly see your hand in front of your face. I'll sure be glad when we get a good wind. This waiting around is getting me.

Aug. 22   Still calm, still foggy, and still nothing to do or write about.

Aug. 23˙   Today is the same as yesterday. Days are so exactly alike up here you lose count of them.

Aug. 24   Today started out the same as the preceding ones. But about 11:00 a.m. a breeze sprang up. This is a pretty good wind and it may put us through the pass sometime tonight. I'm sure a-praying.

Aug. 25   Naturally the wind died out again and we drifted back into the Bering Sea. As I write this we have a good wind through the pass but I don't expect to get through.

I was so right. Halfway through a passage that we had cleared in no more than three hours on the way into the Bering Sea the wind died, the fog rolled in, and we drifted back into the Bering Sea.

Now the superstitions of the old sailors began to assert themselves again. Once more I heard the mutterings.

"Dis ship be yinxed. Ve never get out!"

Even Paddy Whelan's Irish humor couldn't josh them out of it.

I had, with extreme care, never once even come close to asking Chris Olsen when he thought we would make it through. But the topic of this seemingly impossible passage out into the Pacific was always there.

We were pacing the deck the night of August 25 on our watch.

"Chris, what's the longest it's taken a sailing vessel to get through?"

His tone was gentler than usual. "Dey don' keep dose records, Roos. Ya know, ve all vant to get out, but for de Ol' Man"—he jerked his head aft, toward the stern quarters—"he has de vorry. Startin' to get late in de season up here. Ve could get some real blows. Vater may be gettin' short, too. Glad I be for'ard in de fo'c'sle, not hav' vorries like he has."

I started rather guiltily. All my thoughts had been focused on my own boredom, my own frustration. I really hadn't given a moment's consideration to how this might be weighing on Captain Thomas. It was so bloody maddening. We had completed this part of the voyage with a reasonably good catch. As tragic as Karl Miller's loss and Jack Anderson's accident were, I knew by now that the loss of one or two men from a schooner fishing the Bering Sea each season was not unusual. For the captain to have all this behind him, to have his crew healthy and the hold full of salt cod—it all meant nothing if we could not get

197

through Unimak Pass, back out into the Pacific, and run for home.

Then, just as we came on watch the morning of August 26, the wind came out of the west with a steady feel. It meant that we had to sail close hauled on a starboard tack, we might have to tack once or twice, but it did feel as if we were finally on our course through the pass.

I had the second wheel turn that morning, and as two bells on the third watch struck, 9:00 A.M. ashore, I stepped to the helm. Skys'l Sam gave me the course: "195. Hol'er steady, Roos."

"Course 195." I repeated the compass direction.

Skys'l paused for a moment. "Looks like ve hav plenty sea room, but de fog . . ." He pointed off our starboard bow. Some distance away I could see a thick bank of fog lying low on the water. Our present course would take us south of it, but those fogbanks shifted up here. I prayed to myself. Maybe this time we would get through.

Captain Thomas was invariably on deck now when we were sailing. He seemed to sleep only when we were becalmed.

Restlessly he paced fore and aft on the starboard, weather side of the quarterdeck. Pipe clenched in his teeth, skipper's cap jammed square on his head, the intent blue eyes always scanning the visible horizon, he was totally in command. Then I remembered Chris Olsen's comments about what the captain had to worry about. I felt a surge of sympathy for this middle-aged man with the weight of responsibility squarely on his shoulders for this old windjammer and its crew.

I had long since learned to steer a true course, and I particularly enjoyed the wheel turns when we were sailing on a beat close hauled. The schooner seemed more alive to me then, easier to hold on course, and easier to bring back if she wandered off a point or two.

Regardless of the weather, there was always someone from the duty watch on the bow standing lookout during this seemingly endless attempt to get through the pass. I think that Captain Thomas was more tired and frustrated than perhaps even he realized, and this may have been what brought us so close to disaster. As difficult as it was for him to get a precise fix on our specific location, he must have believed that we were going to make it this time if we could just hold our course.

Then the fog closed in on us and we were in the middle of a fogbank. I saw Captain Thomas take the pipe out of his mouth, jam it into his jacket pocket, and I heard him speak to Pete Sorenson. "Sorenson, go forward. Make sure that lookout keeps a sharp eye. Have your watch standing by on the sheets."

"Aye, aye, sir!" Pete was gone, down on the main deck now positioning the watch, calling up to the man on the bow to look sharp.

On we sailed through the fog, not quite as briskly as before, but still moving well. I was holding course 195 steady on.

The stillness was shattered by the lookout's scream, "Land ahead!"

Just at that instant we broke out of the fogbank and I recognized the ugly, low-lying silhouette of Ugamak Island dead ahead. Then to my horror I realized we had sailed dead into a broad indentation on the island's shore. I could see the surf pounding the rocky shoreline in every direction I looked. I kept my course—someone had to do something right now—but until I got the order, the course was still 195. One look over the starboard rail and I knew there simply was not room for this 170-foot schooner to come about through the eye of the wind and clear that terrifying shoreline. On we surged, really driving now, heading directly for our doom.

For an instant Captain Thomas stared directly ahead. Then he was shouting orders: "Bear off, helmsman!" Shouting forward to the third watch on deck: "Ease off those sheets. Stand by to jibe!"

As I turned the wheel to port, the sheets were being simultaneously eased on deck. Captain Thomas was personally handling the spanker sheet, slacking it off with a half turn around the belaying pin.

I could feel the *Smith* driving even harder now. Then I saw, as we bore off on a reach, that we were blocked to port. There was no way we could bear off on a run that would clear that arm of the bay we had sailed into.

It was all happening so fast that I didn't have time to feel any more than a primeval surge of terror at the prospect of being pounded to death in the icy surf.

Then I heard Captain Thomas' roar as he took a turn on the belaying pin with the spanker sheet.

"Hard aport, helmsman! Jibe ship!"

I exerted all my strength and saw the bow start to swing to port. We were so close to the breakers now that I could see the black, glistening surface of the rocks between waves.

The wheel turned two spokes fairly easily and then I couldn't move it farther. The force of that beam wind on the hull, and all the canvas the *Smith* could carry, were just too much. I could not bring the rudder through and force the stern around in a jibe.

Locked onto that now immovable wheel, I pulled directly athwartship, my legs braced on deck and straddling the wheel. As I was gasping with the effort, seeing that terrible graveyard of a surf pounding, rocky shoreline drawing ever, inexorably closer, Pete Sorenson came leaping up the starboard ladder to the quarterdeck, racing to the starboard side of the wheel. He was a powerful man and without a second's lost motion he had planted himself on deck astride the wheel facing me and grasped the lowest spoke on the wheel on his side. I could see the veins on his forehead bulge as he heaved upward with all his strength. There was no time or need for orders. I pulled down as Pete pulled up, and suddenly I felt the wheel start to turn.

Pete was breathing hard now. "Vatch dat vheel vhen she com' tru', Roos. She kick. I help ya. Get behind it!"

Then the wheel was spinning fast now, as we stood shoulder to shoulder trying to control it and slow down the spin. With a tremendous crashing of blocks, lines, and sails, the schooner finally jibed, turned almost in place, and started back out of the trap. For an instant she almost ran up into the wind on us, but we managed to steady her on course, and then we were sailing out. I had taken one terrified look aft as the stern slewed across the wind. We were so close to the rocks at that instant that the spume from the surf crashing on them drenched the afterend of the quarterdeck.

I didn't think of it at the moment, but Captain Thomas had to wonder if these old spars could stand an intentional jibe in that wind and pray that they would. But there was no choice. His instant right decision and the seamanship of the third watch had gotten us out.

We were heading away from Ugamak Island, bearing north-easterly back into the Bering Sea. Frustrated again in our attempt to escape into the Pacific, at least we were still alive. I looked back at Ugamak Island and the waves crashing ashore in a seeming fury now. Thank God the deep water ran right up to those terrible rocks. If it had shoaled out at all we would have grounded for sure, as close as we had been when the ship finally jibed. It was certain that none of us would have survived a grounding on that godforsaken shore in those seas.

Captain Thomas half sat on the skylight above his cabin, took off his cap, and wiped his forehead with his left coat sleeve. It was the only time during the entire voyage that he ever seemed as human to me as the rest of us. He looked at the third mate.

"That was close, Sorenson. Glad we didn't take the sticks out of her on that jibe."

About five minutes later my wheel turn was over. The new course was 180 degrees in the opposite direction. I gave my relief the new compass direction: "course 15." "Course 15," he repeated, and I went down to the main deck. I stood at the port rail watching Ugamak Island recede astern. As I stood there I noticed that my legs were trembling almost uncontrollably. I made my way over to the afterhatch and sat down staring at the deck. I wasn't sure whether I was going to be sick.

Then I was aware of Frank Simmons standing in front of me, balancing with the movement of the vessel.

"You feelin' OK, Russ?"

"Not too good, Frank."

He smiled slightly. "This crew's born to be hung, son. Always have said that. This proves it!" I simply nodded, too spent to talk.

My diary entry for August 26 read as follows:

> This morning I had the 9-10 wheel and we had a wind right through the pass. All of a sudden the lookout hollered land ahead! The Skipper let go the spanker and I put the wheel hard over to port. The rest of the watch clewed up the tops'ls and jibed ship. We finally got around all right but we were that close to the rocks we got wet from the breakers. That was plenty close enough for me.

The next day, August 27, was Roy's last day as pearl diver in the galley. The day after that, I would start. I thought bitterly of Frank Simmons' advice to draw straws for the first turn. Roy Brewer had done his two weeks, and here we were still in the Bering Sea. I knew for sure that I would be doing my full measure of fourteen days also, and God only knew if by then we would be any closer to San Francisco than we were now.

On the morning of August 28 I took my place behind the small wooden sink attached to the outboard bulkhead of the galley.

As fellow sufferers Roy and I had only commiserated with each other. There was nothing funny about this, and there was no joshing between us. His advice to me as I prepared to assume my new duties was terse:

202

"Stay out of the way of that goddamned cook. He's crazy mean. Johnson's not much better. Been cooped up in that galley with the cook too long. Didn't even thank me for all those dirty dishes I done for him!"

What Frank Simmons had accomplished for Eric Johnson by drafting Roy and me as pearl divers was to relieve him of about five hours a day of the most miserable galley duty imaginable. It would have been difficult enough if there had been an ample supply of hot fresh water, and clean dish towels. What we had to work with was a limited supply of what very rapidly became lukewarm salt water, dish towels that never even started out dry and most of the time were as black as the large coal burning stove that ran completely athwart the forward end of the galley.

I was setting up for the night meal when I heard a shout on deck: "Cutter's coming!"

A day or so earlier I had decided it wouldn't be a bad idea to write a couple of letters home to my uncle Jerry and my sister, Lois. I wasn't sure whether there would be any more mail pickups this late in the season, but if there were, at least my relatives would know I was still alive, even if I was doomed to spend the rest of my life in the Bering Sea.

I stuck my head through the hatchway and saw the sleek lines of the Coast Guard cutter easing up on our port beam. The mail pickup made no allowances for personal delay. If you didn't get your mail aft to be stuffed into the mail sack in time, that was unfortunate—it didn't get aboard the cutter. I bounced down the ladder to the fo'c'sle, climbed up on my bunk, got my letters, and charged back topside. As I reached the deck I could see the Coast Guard power launch shoving off from the cutter, and I thought momentarily that there was something different-looking about this maneuver. I was concentrating so on getting my mail aft that I didn't think about it at the time. After I had handed my letters to Sparks and was assured that they would get into the mail sack, I went out on deck to watch the launch approach us.

Then I realized that it was moving much more slowly than it normally did. As expert seamen as they were, and as gentle and careful as they could be, the Coast Guard coxswains had a way of gunning their powerful launches across the space of sea that separated the two vessels and then coasting up to the *Smith's* side with consummate skill. As usual we were becalmed, and normally I would have expected to see the launch flying toward us, a bow wave spreading to port and starboard and feathering aft.

This time the launch was obviously moving very slowly and for some reason was gradually pulling away from the stern of the cutter.

Frank Simmons was standing at the rail staring intently at the launch. I walked up and stood beside him.

"How come they're moving so slow, Frank? They usually gun hell out of those launches."

He never took his eyes off the launch. "Can't you see what they're doing, Russ?"

"No. What're they doing?"

"They're bringing a hawser over. They're goin' to try to tow us through."

My heart gave a leap. "You mean right through the pass, Frank?"

"That's what I mean. But we got to get lucky. She's only 230 tons. We're 566 tons empty, and we're at least another 300 tons with the cod we've got below. I don't know if she can do it with the tides we'll be bucking."

"Do they do this every year for some of the schooners?"

Frank gave me an odd look. "You know, Russ, this is the tenth season for me. With some of the old-timers I've shipped with on codfishers I guess I've heard about most of what's happened up here since the codfishing schooners been coming into the Bering Sea. I never heard of a tow through the pass before."

"How come they're doing it for us?"

"Don't really know. Part of it probably because if we don't get through pretty soon we could be in real trouble. Be hittin' heavy weather up here any time. We don't have all that much fresh water left, either." He paused briefly. "Main thing I guess is the Coast Guard's here to help, and that Coast Guard skipper is one hell of a man. Don't really know if they can do it, but they're going to try."

By then I could clearly see the heavy hawser being paid off the stern of the cutter as the launch powered slowly toward our bow. I could see the ship's name, *Alert*, on her stern.

As I watched the light lead line being tossed onto our bow, I thought of those tides that carried my heavy fishing weights to the surface. I was a born optimist, but this last week or so was making a pessimist of me. Also, I had the utmost respect for any opinion of Frank Simmons. If he thought there was a real question about whether it could be done, that was enough to make me question it too.

I watched as three of our crew pulled the heavy bight of the eight-inch hawser up on our bow, draped it around the capstan, and then fed the hawser through our forward port chock. The Coast Guard coxswain gave a forward wave of his left arm to the cutter, and it slowly powered ahead to a position about two hundred feet directly forward of our jib boom, taking up the slack in the heavy line with a barely perceptible jerk. The launch circled back now, pausing amidship just long enough to catch our mail sack and toss the sack of incoming mail aboard. Then it sped off to rejoin the cutter.

Very slowly but steadily, we began to move forward in the wake of the cutter. The Coast Guard captain selected a course that would eventually bring us to the nearer side of Unimak Pass but would still leave us plenty of sea room if he had to cut the tow for any reason. I guessed that maybe the tidal effect was somewhat reduced closer to shore. I was elated as I saw that we were finally moving in the right direction through the slowly undulating swells in the direction of Unimak Pass. Then I was sobered by the realization of just how slowly we were moving—and the tide wasn't even against us yet. Still we were moving, and in the right direction at last. Maybe this time!

The hours passed slowly. Although it grew dark earlier now with the waning of summer, we still had daylight until about 2100 hours.

At about 2030 I climbed up on the foredeck to gauge our

progress. As I peered over the toerail, sprawled out on my stomach, to study the movement of the bow through the sea, my heart sank. It didn't look as if we were moving at all. Forward the cutter steamed valiantly, the hawser stretched out like a steel bar between the two vessels. I tried to study the pattern of the water at the cutter's stern. I couldn't detect anything, and land was too far off our port beam to measure any forward progress. Finally I got slowly to my feet and spit over the side. My spittle just barely drifted astern. We were lucky if we were making one knot an hour in a forward direction, and we were still a long way from the entrance to Unimak Pass. Sunk in a gloomy introspection, I was startled when I heard Chris Olsen call out to me from the main deck.

"Roos!" His tone was peremptory. "Get down here!"

Puzzled, I climbed down the ladder to the main deck.

"What's the matter, Chris?"

"Yesus, boy! Ya ever seen vun of dem big lines break?"

"No. Why?"

"Vy! Dey cut a man in half dey hit him right! Ya stay avay from dat line unless ya ordered dere. Ya hear me?"

"I hear you, Chris." Lord, I thought, is there anything that ever happens on this ship that doesn't threaten your life? Not ever having witnessed the kind of accident Chris was worried about, it was hard for me to grasp. Still, as I stood there with him on the main deck staring at the rigid line of the hawser connecting us to the Coast Guard cutter, I could begin to visualize what he meant. If that heavy line snapped near our bow, there would be no telling what damage it would do whipping back across our foredeck like a scythe. I shuddered as the mental picture came into focus, and I turned away.

All that night we inched forward. By the time I had finished the morning dishes on August 29 we had just entered the pass, and Unimak Island was a hazy blur off our port beam.

I spent the morning hours, before my noonday toil in the galley, pacing the deck.

The time crept by. I continued to walk up and down the deck. Most of the crew were topside. There was very little conversation, and none that I could hear concerning the topic that occupied the mind of every man on the vessel—would we finally get through the pass this time? From time to time I spit over the side. It seemed to me that my spittle drifted ever more slowly astern.

About an hour later I saw Frank Simmons standing at the starboard rail, just forward of the stern quarters, staring moodily out to sea. Most of the crew on deck were staring over the port rail trying to gauge our progress, if any, by the blur of land in the distance. I had long since given that up—it was too discouraging.

Frank looked at me as I stood beside him at the rail.

"Sparks just gave us the word, Russ. That Coast Guard skipper's going to give it another hour. If we don't start making more way by then, he's going to have to cut the tow."

My voice was anguished. "Why, Frank? Why can't they hang on till they get us through?"

"He's got his problems. Those cutters weren't built to be tugboats. Don't know how far from his base he is, and God only knows how much fuel he's burning on this tow."

"I know, Frank, but—"

He interrupted me in a surprisingly gentle tone. "Look, Russ, the man's really trying. There are a hell of a lot of uncharted rocks in these waters. He's got us as close to the Unimak side as he dares—trying to get out of that tide. Believe me, if he can do it, he'll do it, but he's got his own ship to worry about. If we don't start logging some distance over the bottom in an hour, it's his judgment that he's not going to make it. He'll have to cut us loose."

"What'll happen to us?"

Frank's tone was serious. "We'll drift back into the Bering Sea."

I could have wept. "Is Sparks talking to him?"

Frank smiled grimly. "You better believe! Never seen him working so hard on that key this whole voyage. Cold sober, too!"

I turned away and started pacing the deck. I heard six bells on the third watch strike. I didn't own a watch, and I could only estimate that it had been about a half hour since I had talked to Frank.

Now there were wind and heavy swells right on our nose. Occasionally a dense bank of fog would block the cutter from our sight. The Coast Guard skipper did not have the latter-day miracle of radar to warn him of a sudden, looming, uncharted navigational hazard. He could only pray that his navigational dead reckoning was accurate.

I recognized the truth of Frank's simple statement. The man had his ship and crew to worry about also. There was no point risking both vessels if it wasn't going to do any good. Still, the thought of cutting that lifeline, drifting perhaps without steerage way in that fog, relatively near the Unimak side, made me shiver. I remembered the sight of that hellish shoreline on Ugamak Island two days earlier, just as ugly as its name. Lord, I prayed, please get us through!

When it was close to an hour, I walked aft to where I had been talking to Frank earlier. The starboard hatch was open and I could hear the staccato clatter of Sparks' wireless.

Just before I had to resume my labor in the galley, I heard a shout from Sparks: "He's hanging on! We're logging two knots now! Says we're almost at the ebb of the tide!"

I could just barely distinguish the words through the intervening bulkheads, and there was no one else I could see on the starboard side of the deck. Yet, with the mysterious element of communication that seemed to exist on this vessel, at almost the same instant I heard a shout from the port side forward. "We're going through! We're going to make it!"

Then there were voices and shouts all over the deck. I couldn't quite believe it yet. I walked forward and stared at the bight of the hawser around our capstan. I could only follow the line for a few feet forward along the jib boom before I lost it in the fog that momentarily enclosed us. But it was unmistakable. The line was stretched forward as rigidly as before. We were still being towed. It was impossible for me to see anything on the surface of the sea; there was no way I could judge our forward progress by spitting over the side.

Somehow I felt as if I had to stay on deck just to make sure nothing changed. Then I thought of those mounds of dirty dishes, pots, pans, and God knows what that were waiting for me, and I went to work in the galley.

That afternoon I stretched out in my bunk and tried to interpret the sounds of the ship's timbers, but it was no good. I couldn't gauge our speed by that measure either. Worn out by nervous tension, I fell asleep.

About a half hour later I was awakened by shouts on deck. I listened for a moment and then I heard something else. It wasn't the sound or movement of the ship that informed me. It was the sound of the sea rhythmically dashing against the blow of the *Smith* that told me we were making knots.

Hurriedly I rolled out of my bunk and went topside. I could see the cutter forward still towing us. I spit over the side, and now my expectoration went swirling aft. I guessed that we were making about four knots. I walked aft and looked up to where Paul Myers paced the quarterdeck as mate of the first watch.

"Mr. Myers, are we through the pass?"

He looked down at me. For almost the first time on this entire voyage I saw a pleasant smile spreading across his face. "Yah, ve be tru."

"How long is he going to tow us?"

"Long time, maybe. Don't really know. Vants to mak' sure ve got plenty sea room. Looks lik' ve get some vind now too." He pointed to the northwest. I looked in that direction and could see the telltale rippling of the surface that foretold a wind coming. And a fair wind at that, coming from our stern quarter. The sky was overcast, the sea was a steel gray, but we were in the Pacific at last!

My diary entry for August 29 read:

> The miracle has come to pass! We are through the "hole" and once more in the Pacific. I sincerely hope I

have seen the last of the Bering Sea. The cutter is still towing us so that we will be beyond any danger of running aground when it blows. For awhile they didn't think they'd get us through because of the tide and head winds, but the cutter prevailed and we got safely through.

The cruise summary for the Coast Guard cutter *Alert* for August 28–30, 1937, reads as follows:

Saturday, 28 August, 1937:

ALERT departed Unalaska at 0915, with mail on board, to contact cod fishing schooners SMITH and LOUISE, reported to be in near vicinity of Unimak Pass, in Bering Sea. 1052, passed Priest Rock, abeam to starboard, distant 1.0 mile; commenced steering various courses standing toward reported position of schooner SMITH in latitude 54°30′ North, longitude 165°50′ West. 1610, hove to, maneuvered vessel as necessary to maintain position in near vicinity of schooner SMITH. Master of SMITH requested a tow to and through Unimak Pass having waited two weeks for favorable winds. Received information that schooner LOUISE now in vicinity of San Francisco. 1625, commenced maneuvering ALERT to windward side of SMITH. 1630, passed an eight inch towing hawser to schooner. 1637, ALERT commenced towing schooner, standing toward western entrance to Unimak Pass; set course 120° psc, and speed, 350 r.p.m. 2130, change course to 115° psc.

Sunday, 29 August, 1937:

Underway, as before, having schooner SMITH in tow. 0205, commenced steering various courses, using fathometer at frequent intervals because of fog. 0910, entering Unimak Pass. During morning and afternoon encountered strong southeasterly winds and large swells, latter coming from eastward through Pass. 1420, passed Scotch Cap abeam to port, distant five miles. 1444, standing out of Pass, set course 129° true, 118° psc, 2340, commenced preparations for discontinuing tow.

Monday, 30 August, 1937:

Underway as before. 0005, hove to, crew on board schooner cast off towing hawser. 0015, hauled in hawser, aboard standard speed and set course 287° psc, returning to Unalaska, via Unimak Pass. 1140, Priest Rock abeam to port, distant 1.0 miles, entering Unalaska Bay. 1245, moored to Alaska Commercial Company wharf, Unalaska, Alaska.

Miles cruised——277 miles
Hours underway—— 51 hours and 30 minutes
Vessels towed——one; hours towed, 31 hours and
　　　　　　　　　28 minutes

37

For the four months I had been on this schooner I had waited my turn for the mess sitting three times a day every day of the voyage, just outside the galley. During the night watches I had, at least once on every watch, poured myself a cup of coffee in the galley to accompany the mug-up prepared from the slabs of salt pork or corn beef and roughly sliced bread that were always spread on platters on the mess tables for the night watches.

I had watched the cook grimly laboring at the large, black, coal-burning stove. I had watched Eric Johnson sullenly peeling potatoes, seemingly by the bushel, on numerous occasions.

Yet, when I stepped into that galley as chief pearl diver, it was like Alice stepping through the looking-glass. I now saw this integral part of the ship's function from the inside out. I again marveled at how much I had looked at on this voyage and, at times, how little I had really seen.

I was scrubbing the last of the breakfast plates my third morning in the galley when I felt the ship coming about onto a port tack. Then I heard a bellow from the cook, "Gott in himmel! Dis no-good sonofabitchin' vindyammer!"

I could hear the sudden crash of a large pot against the sea rails on the stove. It was something the cook was preparing for the midday meal. I looked up, startled, and saw that about half the contents had slopped over the edge and were running down the side of the stove.

The cook was a beefy German, with a powerful, stocky build running to corpulence in his middle years.

Now he stood braced in the narrow galley area just aft of the stove facing astern about seven feet from where I toiled. He held a glistening cleaver in his right hand, his fist holding the cleaver jammed against the port bulkhead. His left hand was planted against the midship partition that separated that part of the galley from the mess.

It had never previously occurred to me what the ship's motion did to the cook in that tiny galley trying to prepare food for this entire crew three times a day, day in and day out, without respite.

Now he stood there, his head hanging down, a steady stream of the most vituperative invective I had heard on the ship snarling out of his very being.

I started to say something, to commiserate. Then he looked up and I thought better of it. His eyes were absolutely wild as he continued to curse. I thought for a minute he was going to split my skull with the cleaver. Then I realized he was looking right through me. It was his fate on this bloody sailing ship he was cursing.

As I stared at the powerful arms spread out, bracing him thwartship there, I saw the burns on the underside of both forearms below the short-sleeved shirt he wore. There were scars of old burns, and there were fresh burns.

On and on he cursed as we slowly came through the wind and bore off on our new tack.

Finally, with a resigned sigh, he stopped and turned back to the stove. As fast as possible I finished the dishes and got out of the galley.

Since Frank Simmons had consigned me to this purgatory, the least he could do was tell me what ailed the cook. I found Frank on deck that morning and fell into step beside him as we paced the weather deck.

"Frank, I think that cook's crazy. What's wrong with him?"

Frank Simmons could be authoritative, and he could be caustic. However, more and more I was appreciating his capacity to understand and empathize with a fellow human being.

"Russ, this is Mueller's first berth on a windjammer." I realized that this was the first time I had heard the cook's name on this voyage. He was invariably referred to by the crew as "Cook" or "Cookie," nothing else.

"What'd he sign on for?"

"He's a sea cook—that's how he makes his living. Poor bastard just didn't realize what it'd be like trying to cook on a coal-burning stove on a windjammer."

I had totally forgotten my own original lack of any information about this voyage—the fact that I was almost aboard the ship before I even knew it was a sailing vessel.

"Well, Jesus, Frank, he's aboard now—he did sign on."

"You mean he asked for it?"

I looked puzzled.

Frank paused in his walking for a moment and looked at me. "You know, Russ, the Marine Corps has always been an all-volunteer outfit—always. So no matter how rough, tough, or miserable it got, the bastards always had one answer for us: 'You asked for it!'"

"I see what you mean, Frank."

"Trouble is, for Cookie this isn't the Marine Corps. He didn't really ask for what he got himself into. I do think someone conned him about what his galley would be like. He's used to cooking on merchant vessels where he's got a cook's helper—at least he can get a day off."

It was finally beginning to penetrate for me. "You mean he knew he was shipping on a sailing vessel, but he just didn't really know what the conditions would be."

"That's right. Shipping's tough these days. I think Mueller needed a berth, but I kinda doubt if he'd have taken this one if he knew then what he knows now." Frank stopped talking for a moment as we rounded up at the forward end of the deck, then started pacing aft. We were sailing at about five knots close hauled. We had every reason to expect strong winds out of the northwest this time of year—winds that would fly us home on a broad reach. Instead the wind had shifted to west by southwest and even more to the south. We found ourselves beating home, and it wasn't making the cook's life in the galley any easier.

Frank continued talking. "You know, if there was anyone on this ship who could cook anything but a pot of coffee I'd sure give that poor bastard a rest, but there's not." He looked at me and grinned. "You remember that pleasure cruise my dress gang had up in the grounds?"

I grinned back, remembering the ten-thousand-fish days. "Yeah, I remember, Frank. I just didn't know how soft it was going to be on this voyage."

"Well, you just think about it. What time do you think the cook rolled out to feed the fishermen when we were fishing?"

"I never really thought about it."

"At least by 0400. That's every day that we were fishing." Frank's tone became sarcastic. "Life got real easy for him when it was blowin'. Might not have to roll out of his bunk till 0415. You've got to admit, Russ, you lazy bastards had a lot of time off when it was blowin'."

"That's right."

"You may have, but the cook and Johnson sure as hell didn't.

214

You ever think what'd it be like to work every bloody day in that galley without one single day off in over four months?"

Chastened, I had to admit that I hadn't.

"Anyway, Russ, that's why our poor goddamned cook seems half crazy. He's got pretty good reason. On the other hand, that Johnson's such a miserable bastard the only reason I wanted to spell him was to get him out of the galley as much as possible before the cook killed him."

"I was wondering about that. That's not quite what you said when you told me and Roy we had to go pearl diving for two weeks apiece."

Frank smiled briefly. We were both remembering his appeal to my humane instincts, his then expressed wish to give Johnson some relief from his burdensome duties.

"Johnson really did ask for it. After Johnny Gunderson found out he had a dose of clap, Johnson was really on me to take over for him. He should have known what the job was, but all he could see was the higher share. Been pestering me ever since last July to get him out of the galley."

I thought once again admiringly of Frank Simmons running this diverse group of men and keeping everything under control. Wonderingly, I thought of one more potentially serious conflict on this ship, in our galley, that I had been totally unaware of until Frank had enlightened me.

Much as Chris Olsen's reference to the load of responsibility Captain Thomas carried on his shoulders had opened my eyes in that connection, Frank's words opened my eyes as far as the ship's cook was concerned.

Other than being acutely worried about my own physical safety in the galley when the cook took off on one of his tirades, I had not really run afoul of him.

Now, seeing him in a far more sympathetic perspective, my unspoken commiseration for his plight seemed to communicate itself. With Johnson out of the galley a good portion of the time, the cook's general attitude tended more toward resignation than futile rage.

Doggedly I faced that damned sink, washing dishes, knives,

215

forks, and spoons by the countless hundreds in the hard, luke-warm salt water.

There was one unanticipated small bonus attached to this duty: I learned something about Captain Thomas that I hadn't known.

He was as stern a master as ever commanded a sailing vessel. But he also had an innate sense of fairness. He could have ordered his meals delivered aft to his quarters, but he didn't. Part of it, I am sure, was his belief that it was easier for him to walk the length of the vessel forward to the mess to take his meals with the cook, after the second sitting was cleared, than it would have been for the overworked messman to deliver those meals aft and then return for the dirty dishes.

The larger part of it, I learned, was the fascination he and the cook shared in arguing the most abstract philosophical questions.

Particularly after the noonday meal, I would sometimes steal a look at the captain as he leaned back in the far corner of the outboard mess table, light up his pipe, and start out with the cook.

"When we see a falling star, Cook, are we lookin' at something that happened a couple of hundred years ago?"

The cook was a changed man then. It began to dawn on me that these private talks and arguments with Captain Thomas may have been just about all that preserved his sanity.

Then I would hear him respond, "I don' really know, Cap'n. Dat Einstein, I know he got somethin', but I not really sure vhat."

I couldn't eavesdrop too obviously, but when I knew they were going to start one of their sessions I would try to work as close to the midship bulkhead as possible to hear everything I could. It also was making me feel a bit more normal. I had heard so little, if any, abstract discussion on this ship that at times I wondered if I might not be a little bit strange with my occasional preoccupation with first causes, how the universe was created, and the like.

216

I gathered that Captain Thomas' religious opinions were on the positive side of agnosticism, but he had a savage contempt for the views of organized religion.

The cook, on the other hand, appeared to be a devout German Catholic.

They spent hours hammering at each other. I thought wryly, on occasion, of something I had once heard that one should not argue religion. What a void it would have left in the lives of our captain and our cook if they had avoided that subject!

One early afternoon, toward the end of my stint in the galley, I heard Captain Thomas open up in his usual abrupt fashion.

"Cook, how in the hell can you swallow that nonsense about the virgin birth?"

"Vell, Cap'n, ya must have faith, of course, but I see it dis vay." He went on for some time with a conventional Catholic explanation of the miracle. From time to time Captain Thomas would interject an objection to the cook's line of reasoning.

They were both obviously enjoying themselves immensely.

I was not particularly indoctrinated with fundamental theology, but the Lutheranism and Catholicism in my family had sufficiently affected me that I was careful not to insult the basic convictions of someone who did believe, at least if I could avoid doing so.

I could hear the cook speaking again. "De Holy Ghost—if ya could accept dat, Cap'n—"

Captain Thomas interrupted him with the tone of finality I had come to recognize as signaling the end of their daily discussions.

"Cook, I happen to think Jesus was one of the greatest men who ever lived. World would be a hell of a lot better place if people really followed his teaching. Fact that it's come down to us through all these years—that's somethin' of a miracle all by itself. But I tell you one thing: Somebody screwed his mother, and it wasn't with any ghost's prick!"

I was so startled I almost dropped the large pot I was scouring. I expected to hear an outraged bellow from the cook. I peered through the sliding port between the mess and the galley. Captain Thomas was knocking out his pipe with one hand, placing his skipper's cap on with the other. The cook rose with him, chuckling.

"Cap'n Thomas, ya not get to heaven talkin' dat vay!"

Then they both emerged from the mess—obviously content with their latest encounter.

As my galley duty drew to its end, I had been increasingly annoyed by the taunting I was getting from the men waiting for the second sitting. It was just one of those things that generated out of nowhere and was usually indulged in by different members of the crew.

As I labored over the dishes and eating utensils from the first sitting, the crew would gather for the second in the small area between my sink and the fo'c'sle ladder.

"Hey, Russ, you really doin' good now!"

"We goin' to talk to Frank about you keepin' this job till we hit Frisco!"

It wasn't particularly inspired, funny, or even ill-intentioned. But I was getting totally sick of that goddamned galley and the never-ending stream of dirty dishes, knives, forks, and spoons. I didn't need this kind of banter on top of it.

On the morning of the fourth day before my release I had deliberately left the dish towels as unwashed and black as they could get. The first breakfast sitting had finished and I was starting on that round of eating utensils as the men for the second sitting gathered.

I recognized the tone of voice.

"Hey, Russ . . ."

"Yeah, what's on your mind?"

I turned to face the men standing there watching me with grins on their faces. As they watched, I casually sloshed a handful of knives and forks through the lukewarm salt water. Then carefully, and holding them higher before me to make sure no one missed it, I wiped off the dirty knives and forks with the remnants of egg white, egg yolk, and the bacon grease on one of my coal-black, wet dish towels. It almost made *me* sick to see it. As soon as I wiped a knife or fork I carefully placed it in the box from which I would place it on the table for this sitting.

The grins slowly faded.

"Jesus Christ, Russ, you're supposed to be washin' them tools!"

My blood was up. "You think you can do it better, god-damnit, you're welcome!"

I heard the mutterings and grumblings, but there was no answer to my challenge, and they knew it.

I repeated the performance one more time, for the benefit of the midday second sitting, and then I knew I had made my point. There wasn't another word said for the remainder of my tour in the galley.

Once I knew I had put an end to the needling, I concentrated on keeping the salt dishwater as hot as I could stand it. I had, after the fact, become concerned about causing an outbreak of intestinal problems on this ship. Then it occurred to me that I had never felt healthier in my life. I thought back over the voyage and, despite the damp, the cold, sometimes the freezing, wet conditions, I hadn't even had a head cold the entire voyage. More interestingly, other than Johnny Gunderson and his dose of clap, I could not think of any member of this crew who had failed to work a single hour on this voyage because of illness.

I had some understanding now of what Eric Johnson had been through pearl diving in that galley. I suspected, and I couldn't really blame him, that his attention to our eating utensils had probably, on a day-in, day-out basis, been about equivalent to what I had deliberately done to get the crew off my back. Again, during the entire voyage, there had not been a single case of a stomach problem. Another of the *Smith*'s small, recurring miracles.

Our southerly progress during my two weeks in the galley had been a laborious beating, first on a starboard tack, then onto a port tack, and then back again. Always we were drawing closer to California, but far more slowly than we should have if the winds had just come out of the northwest, as we had every right to expect.

In much the same manner as I had, during our first days in the grounds, calculated just how long it took us to dress down a codfish, I now calculated how many of the ship's plates, utensils, etc., had passed through my hands.

My diary for September 10 read:

> I haven't written anything for the past 4 or 5 days because there was nothing to write. One day is just a prototype of another except today which is my last in the galley. At the conclusion of the last meal today I have washed and dried approximately 1,680 dirty plates, knives, forks and spoons; 1,260 cups, 420 bowls; 168 pots, platters and large bowls. A record which I hope I never have another chance to equal.

38

The last week on the schooner was a time of sheer spirit-lifting exuberance for me. It was not just that a hard voyage would soon be ended. It was not even my release from the ship's galley, although God knows that had plenty to do with it.

It was the wind, the weather—steady days of blessed sun now, the feel of a windjammer driving hard on a beam reach. Perhaps it was, more than anything else, the realization that I had survived this far and, God willing, would survive to see my beloved San Francisco once more.

When I reported on deck for my morning watch on September 11, 1937, the sky was a brilliant blue, the sea was a deeper blue flecked with the whitecaps of a thirty-five-knot westerly and we were flying—reaching southeasterly toward San Francisco and home.

I had the last wheel turn on the morning watch, and I never enjoyed a turn at the wheel more. The schooner rolled down the seas, carrying us toward home. She was easy to handle on this point of sailing, and I handled her well now.

Captain Thomas was on deck for the latter part of our watch, and I heard him talking to our mate.

"Think she may shift to the north, Sorenson. If she does another point or two, we'll break out the spinnaker."

"Aye, aye, sir."

The wind didn't shift on our watch, but toward the end of the next watch it veered to the north and I watched as the men of the second watch set the spinnaker on the pole secured to the foremast. This was the first time on the voyage that sail had been set, and it took some doing. This was not the colorful, rainbow-hued spinnaker of the sailing yachts. Our spinnaker's canvas was as worn and patched as the rest of the ship's sails. Still, like all of our sails, when it filled with the wind coming over our starboard stern quarter, it was a thing of beauty. I didn't know just how much speed it added to our passage, but it added something, and the *Smith* sailed on like a graceful seabird over the Pacific.

That night Roy and I were walking the deck again together for what seemed like the first time in a long time. During the relatively short passages from one anchorage to another up in the codfish grounds, and with the deck obstructed by the checkers, we simply didn't pace the deck as we had on the voyage up to the Bering Sea. Our four weeks in the galley had also served to deprive us of this companionship for that period of time.

In one sense I did not form any enduring friendships on the ship. There was no one aboard who, at my age, shared the community of background, ideas, and interests that had created such a strong bond of friendship between Herb Ainsworth and myself back home. I think that Jack Anderson, if the voyage had not ended so tragically for him, would have been the closest for

221

me, but with an eight-year age difference between us, that was not the same either.

On the other hand, there were certain ties of mutual interest I shared with different individuals that were quite strong. Basically the men comprising the crew of this ship, as tough and hard-bitten as life had made many of them, were decent, totally reliable individuals.

Without my ever being consciously aware of it, my social contacts with various members of the crew ran along narrow but rather strong lines. Chris Olsen had become my seafaring mentor. He had taught me more about my watch duties than anyone else on the ship. He had also, more than any of the other old hands, spun the yarns for me that were to him not even seagoing yarns—they were simply chapters out of his own hard life at sea.

What Roy and I shared was a youthful appetite for hedonistic pleasure, and a love of song. His voice was true, and it was a real pleasure to wile away some of the watch hours singing along with him. Once again we were singing "Abdullah Bulbul Amir," the bawdier verses of "Frankie and Johnny," and the current popular songs—at least current when we shoved off from San Francisco in April.

He had been asleep in his bunk the morning that Skys'l Sam chanteyed the anchor up from the bottom of the Bering Sea. I had told him about it and he had been fascinated, but there had never been an opportunity since to learn those chanteys from Skys'l.

Now as we paced aft down the deck we saw Skys'l, walking by himself, coming forward toward us.

Roy placed himself in front of him. "Hey, Skys'l, Russ told me about your capstan chanteys. He really liked that 'Away You Rio!' How 'bout teaching me that one?"

As usual, Skys'l Sam had to be coaxed. "Nay, Roy, vhat ya vant to learn dat ol' chantey fer? Not many sailin' vessels left."

I joined in. "Come on, Skys'l, I thought it was a hell of a song. You don't have to be hauling chain to sing it!" I looked at

222

Roy and winked. "Tell you what. You teach Roy the words and I'll whistle . . ."

Skys'l Sam whirled on me. "Ya vhat? Gottdamn, boy, look at da vind ve got . . ." Then he saw Roy and me grinning at each other, and he started to chuckle. "All right, I teach ya. At least ya can't be vhistlin' if ya be singin'."

So we three paced the deck together as Skys'l Sam taught us "Away You Rio!" With Roy's ear for a tune and his memory for verse he had soon mastered what has always seemed to me to be one of the great sea chanteys. I didn't have it down nearly as well as he did, but it sounded good to me. The three of us bellowed out the rollicking words as we paced fore and aft on the *Smith*'s weather deck, rolling with the ship's motion, the masts moving in steady arcs, silhouetted against the starry sky above us.

As preoccupied as I was with my own life on this vessel, it began to occur to me that before too long I would be parting company with my shipmates, and probably for all time. Without ever consciously acknowledging it to myself, I knew that deep down I would miss this ship and these men.

Four days from San Francisco, during the morning watch, I was walking the deck with Chris Olsen. It was probably the subconscious realization of how important this man had become to me that caused me to address him on a more personal level than I ever had before.

"Chris, what're you going to do after this voyage?"

Startled, he looked at me. "I . . . I . . . dunno. Ship out again, I guess, if I get a berth. Berths hard to come by dese days."

"Do you ever think about what you'd like to do?"

He laughed, rather bitterly. "Yah, Roos. Like evervun, I tink vhat I like to do. Fer men like me not much choice—not dese days."

I persisted. "You told me once that Karl Miller had his mate's ticket." I saw Chris wince as I spoke Karl's name. It was the first time I had done so, or to my knowledge anyone else had done

223

so, since the number-two dory had been returned to the ship. I ignored the expression on his face and plunged on. "Damnit, Chris, you're smarter than a lot of these guys. If you're goin' to go to sea, why not get your mate's ticket and get a decent berth for yourself?"

I could tell he was getting exasperated with me, but then I'm sure it was gratifying to have anyone demonstrate the interest that I obviously had in his life.

"Roos, ya yust don' know how tough shippin' be dese days. I got my able-bodied seaman's ticket—many year now—lucky if I get an AB's berth, let alone a mate's!"

As I started to open my mouth again he interrupted me hurriedly, I think as much to shut me up as for any other reason. "Ya know, dere's vun ting I like to do. Like to get back to Bergen, see my mutter vunce more. She old lady now."

The Scandinavians on the ship referred to themselves as Svenskas, Danskas, and Norskas, depending on their country of origin. Most of them were fair-skinned, blue-eyed types. A few, like Chris, were basically fair-complexioned but with dark brown eyes and brown or black hair. Among themselves Chris was known as a "black Norska."

I saw the expression in his brown eyes soften when he spoke of his mother.

"How much family you got, Chris?"

"Yust me mutter, really. Two brudders seagoin', but I ain't heard from dem in years."

What was really chewing on me, down deep, was the memory of Chris Olsen being dragged across the deck with the rest of those drunken seamen my first day aboard the ship. Now, as I walked with this strong, clear-eyed man on the deck of the schooner, I thought of all he had taught me. I might not have survived this voyage without his help and guidance. He *had* to focus on something besides those skid-row bars while waiting for a ship's berth that might never come.

I seized on what he had told me. "Why don't you ship out to Norway then, Chris?"

224

"Yesus Creest, Roos, ya yust don' unnerstand. Dere's more shippin' comin' out of Norvay den anyvhere. Ya yust can't find a berth *to* Norway." He paused a moment, then said almost to himself, "It be good to go back. Not been home to Norvay in tirty year."

We walked up and down the deck for a couple of turns, both of us silent now. Chris was lost in thought. I guessed that he was thinking of those northern fjords of his native Norway that he had not seen in so many years.

Then I had an idea. "Chris, you got a tally of better than eighteen thousand fish. That right?" While there was no reason for us to keep track of how many cod each fisherman caught, we were interested in who had the high counts. We all knew that Paul Myers, the first mate, had a count of over twenty thousand, which was the highest tally on the ship. We all knew that Chris Olsen's catch was next, at over eighteen thousand.

He nodded once. "Yah."

"You ever think of buying a passage home?"

He stopped in his tracks and stared at me incredulously. "Buy a passage! Me? Yesus!" The idea of a professional seaman paying his way instead of working a ship's passage was just too bizarre for him to grasp.

"Why not, Chris? I'll bet you could get a passage out of New York to Norway on a freighter for not more than a hundred dollars."

He was still protesting, but I could tell that the idea was taking hold. I pressed on.

"Your payoff on this voyage ought to be better than eighteen hundred dollars. If you just forget about shipping out, I'll bet you could take a bus to New York for fifty dollars and pay for a berth on a Norwegian freighter out of New York for a hundred dollars or so. You can do it if you really want to!"

We continued to walk in silence. Finally Chris said, "Let me tink about it." I decided to let well enough alone at this point and simply nodded.

That night I had the third wheel turn. With the number of

225

men on each watch the wheel turns were taken on a somewhat irregular basis and I rarely relieved, or was relieved by, the same man on my watch. This time Roy Brewer had relieved me. When he took over I found Chris on deck. "Come on, Chris, let's get a mug-up."

He nodded and followed me into the mess. None of the other members of the third watch were there. I wedged myself into the forward starboard corner after pouring myself a cup of coffee. This was the corner Captain Thomas occupied when he engaged in his discussions with the cook. I stretched out my legs on the bench, leaned my head back against the bulkhead, and listened to the satisfying sound of the schooner's bow sliding through the Pacific seas. We sat there for a long time in companionable silence. Somewhat surprisingly, it was Chris who spoke first.

"Ya know, Roos, I be tinkin' vhat ya say about buyin' a passage home to Norway." He paused and grinned. "Don' know vhat dese hands below tink 'bout Chris Olsen goin' home like a bloody passenger, but ya be right. I'm goin' to do it!"

I was surprised at the strength of my own feeling of relief and satisfaction that his words produced. Chris Olsen was a proud man. I knew better than to push it any farther. "I'm glad to hear that, Chris. It'll be good for you."

He nodded and we stayed there in the mess for another half hour or so. Eight bells sounded not too long after that, and I went below after taking one long, last look at the starry heavens above us. The nights were definitely cold out here, still far offshore, but so beautiful that I was reluctant to go below to my berth.

The word was that if the wind held, we would be in San Francisco Bay by September 16 or 17.

I know that I kept myself as clean on the *Smith* as the supply of rainwater and weather conditions permitted. However, in almost five months of diary entries, there is only one reference to a bath. My diary for September 13, 1937, read:

Nothing to write about. Washed a shoregoing shirt and
I'm going to take a bath tonight.

The excitement was beginning to build in me now, and the
remaining days before we would drop the hook in San Francisco Bay for the last time stretched ahead of me like an eternity. I tried to avoid thinking or talking about it too much, but
with a friend like Roy Brewer it wasn't easy.

We were pacing the deck the morning of September 15. The
blue sea sparkled, that blessed northwesterly continued to blow
with a steady force, the spinnaker billowed out, and the *Smith*
surged through the waves like a live thing.

I was too charged up to be described as content. I do know
that I was happy in a satisfied, anticipatory way that I had never
experienced before.

"Russ, what's the first thing you're goin' to do when you get
ashore?"

"Hadn't really thought about it."

Roy wasn't the slightest bit interested in my plans. He just
wanted an excuse to tell me about his. "First thing I'm going to
do is have my mom cook up a big T-bone steak. Then a whole
apple pie. I'm going to have her keep that warm in the oven
while I go through that steak. Then cover the whole damn pie
with about a quart of vanilla ice cream spread over it!"

He sure as hell had the power of description! I could feel
myself salivating as I thought of that juicy T-bone steak, and the
ice cream melting on the hot apple pie.

Roy went on. "Second thing!" He grinned at me wickedly.
Roy was two years older than I, good-looking with an engaging
personality. He did not brag about his conquests, but with the
natural exchange of confidences between two young men under
those circumstances, I had learned that he led a very active sex
life back home. He had been genuinely shocked to learn that I
had had my first sexual experience just before shoving off on
this voyage. I know he regarded me as somewhat socially re-

227

tarded, but he didn't lord his experience over me.

"The way I'm feeling now, Russ, I got to get myself taken care of in a hurry. But just as soon as I get squared away, I'm going to fix you up." His voice was ruminative as he thought out loud. "There's Midge, real sport. And Betty—"

I interrupted him. "Look, Roy, I really appreciate it, but my God, I'm feeling the same way you are. I can't wait to date one of those girls a few times and hope for the best. I'm going to take twenty dollars out of that first check and get myself laid ten times just as fast as I can."

Roy grinned appreciatively. "That's good thinking. Anyway, you'll be so goddamned horny when you get off this ship it probably wouldn't be safe to turn you loose on those girls I know until you can act halfway normal."

I grinned back. For some reason the number ten had fixed itself in my mind as an appropriate immediate goal. That seemed to me to be about what it would take before I could mingle in polite society without mentally undressing every female I looked at.

We continued pacing, each lost in our own dreams of going home.

On the morning of September 16 the wind began to lighten, but still it held out of the northwest. It was as if the sea gods were carrying this old schooner home to safety now, and with a predictable landfall waiting for us were going to drop her gently just off the Golden Gate.

I had the first wheel turn on our watch the night of September 16. Since Pete Sorenson had been in the fo'c'sle with the rest of us, I had never gotten used to calling him "Mister." He had an instinctive ability to command, and he didn't need the formal salutation to enforce his authority on the third watch.

It may have been our proximity to the California coast. It may have been simply the knowledge that for sure, by this time tomorrow night, I would be ashore. Whatever the reason, I was at peace. The sea, the sky, and the schooner, still driving through the rolling Pacific swells, never seemed more beautiful to me. As a parting gift, the water was alive with phosphorescence. I moved the wheel spokes only occasionally now as she practically sailed herself, well trimmed. Our course was 165, San Francisco not too far over the horizon. The bow wave flashed with the interior bluish incandescence of this magical seaborne phenomenon.

"Sure a pretty night, isn't it, Pete?"

"Yah, dat it be." He looked aloft with satisfaction. The tops'ls still billowed out against the night sky, the spinnaker still pulling us home.

"What time do you think we'll get in?"

"I tink ve be off de Gate 'bout 0900. Ve vill if dis vind hold."

"She feels steady to me. What if she drops anymore? Will we be able to sail in?"

"Nay, Roos, no matter vhat de vind, ve don' sail in."

This was a surprise to me. We had sailed out of the Golden Gate, and I had simply assumed we would sail back in the same way.

Pete saw the look on my face and chuckled. "Ve can't tak' any chance in de bay vit' dis ol' vindyammer, no power. Ve get a tow in vunce ve off de Gate."

"But we sailed out, Pete."

"Dat be different. Ve hav' goot vind dat day. Ve on same tack all de vay outside. Dis time can't tak' chance vit all de shippin' in de bay. Ve get tow!"

That relieved one worry. I *had* wondered just what in the hell we would do with this 170-foot schooner if we lost the wind inside the Gate and about halfway to Belvedere Island.

Chris Olsen relieved me at two bells on the third watch. I gave him the course: "165." He repeated, "165." I couldn't resist it. I spoke in a low voice. "Chris, it's OK if you take us back to San Francisco this time." He looked at me, startled for a moment, then grinned. Reminiscently he rubbed the right side of his head where Jim Bewla's punch had decked him the first night of the voyage. Neither one of us said any more. As I was climbing down the starboard ladder to the main deck I stopped once and looked back at Chris silhouetted faintly by the binnacle light. It struck me with a surprising pang that I had just stood my last wheel turn on the *William H. Smith*.

I had spent a part of the day getting my gear squared away and my seabag stowed. When my watch was over I went below to my bunk. I was no more nor less sleepy or tired than usual, but sleep simply would not come. I tossed and turned for hours. Faintly I heard two bells on the first watch strike, then four bells.

Finally I decided to go topside to see if I could walk myself into a mood for sleep. When I got up on deck I was surprised to find what seemed to be half the ship's company pacing the deck.

In the starry night I could pick out Frank Simmons leaning on the port rail staring out to sea. I joined him.

"What's going on, Frank? Looks like half the crew's up on deck."

He turned to me with a serious expression. "Channel fever, Russ. Damn near the whole crew's comin' down with it."

"Channel fever!"

Then he grinned. "That's right, boy. Don't care how long you been seagoin'. When you get close to the channel after a voyage like this, you come down with it."

I was obviously slow at this ungodly hour. "They going to be OK?"

Frank's laughter exploded. "Oh, Christ, Russ. Look out there." He pointed off our port bow. I followed his arm, and my heart gave a leap. Faintly, almost imperceptibly but unmistakably, there was the glow of what could only be the lights of San Francisco. "There's the channel. We're goin' to be there in hours now. When you get this close you get channel fever and you can't sleep. What're *you* doin' up here, anyway?"

"I couldn't sleep, Frank." My tone was sheepish.

"Don't worry about it. Soon as we hit that channel, the fever disappears like magic."

I shook my head and walked off. As usual, Frank Simmons

was right. It *was* like a fever. Finally, about 0400, as the second watch was relieving the first, I went below, rolled into my bunk, and finally went to sleep.

At 0900 on our watch on September 17, 1937, the schooner *William H. Smith* came ghosting in to a point about two miles off the newly completed Golden Gate Bridge.

I looked forward over our bow and I could see a tugboat churning out of the Golden Gate bearing directly for us. Then I heard Pete's bellowed order: "Third vatch, stand by to drop sail!"

I leaped to the foremast rigging. The wind had just about died now. One hand could secure the tops'l easily. Somehow, despite the fact that the topmast rigging still intimidated me, I wanted to do this one last time. I went scrambling up, thinking it didn't matter this calm and peaceful morning, but by God I was going up the weather side of the rigging.

When I got up to the crosstrees I shouted down to Chris Olsen standing by the fore-tops'l halyard on deck, "Lower away!"

Then the fore-tops'l was dropping into the crosstrees, and for the last time I was rolling it into a tight bundle, securing it with the gaskets.

When I was through I paused for breath, leaned back against the topmast, my legs securely braced, and stared across the water at San Francisco. September had to be the loveliest time of year in this most beautiful of cities. The morning fog had burned off early. I could see the dark, rich green of the Presidio—a lush background for the south tower of the bridge. In the far distance the white of Coit Tower was silhouetted on Telegraph Hill. There could be no other city in the world like my San Francisco!

Very carefully I climbed out of the crosstrees and descended to the deck.

Within the next fifteen minutes the tow was on and we were heading directly for the center span of the Golden Gate Bridge. We were almost there now.

As we passed between the headlands and then under the Gate, the crew began to assemble on the main deck with their seabags. I looked around at the faces of the dress gang. Sam Culleson, Bob Henderson separated from High Pockets still by half the width of the deck, Trotsky, Roy, and all the rest of them. We were dressed as heterogeneously as we had always been. I was wearing my recently washed shoregoing shirt, the Levi jeans that had survived the entire voyage, still durable, and my old Navy pea coat. Then I noticed the fishermen. Except for Johnny Tango, who had reached this vessel by a different route than these old-time seafaring men, it was as if the fishermen were dressed in a uniform. Except for Johnny, who had a turtleneck sweater and a watch cap on, every last one of them wore a well-worn, dark gray or blue suit, shiny but neat. Each one of them wore what passed for a dress shirt buttoned at the neck with no tie. Each one of them wore a peaked cap set squarely on his head. My mind went back to my first contact with these men. Then I saw a drink-sodden, disgusting mass of humanity. Now I recognized them for what they truly were—the last of the legendary iron men who sailed the wooden ships. Soon we would be parting forever.

It took the tug about half an hour to tow us in and drop us off Belvedere Island, where the anchor splashed down for the last time and the chain went rattling after it.

There was one last surprise for me. I had been thinking of that hike up to the top of Belvedere Island and wondering how the bus and ferry connections would work out to take me back to the city.

I was standing at the starboard rail with Chris Olsen. "When you goin' to be shovin' off for Norway, Chris?"

"Vell, Roos, I got to vait for de second check vhen dey get dis cargo of codfish weighed out. Den I'm on my vay." He broke off excitedly and pointed astern. "Dere she be!"

"What's that, Chris?"

"Dat's de launch vhat take us to Frisco!"

Sure enough, it was. We were going home the easy way.

232

The powerful Crowley launch, black-hulled with the raised long, rounded cover amidships, slid up to our starboard beam forward. The Jacob's ladder was flung over the side—the same ladder I had clambered up so clumsily what seemed a lifetime ago to me now. The launch was made fast fore and aft and a man in a business suit, clutching a portfolio in one hand, emerged from under the covered section of the launch and moved to the open stern section. I guessed that he was from the Union Fish Company. The way he climbed the ladder suggested to me that he had once been a seagoing man himself. He leaped nimbly off the rail down to the deck in the space we had made for him.

He sniffed once, shook his head with a grin, and then made his way aft to the quarterdeck, where Captain Thomas was waiting for him.

Then with shouts and laughs, four of the fishermen went rolling over the side and into the launch. In the usual unspoken, effective way of getting things done aboard this ship, the seabags were rapidly tossed over the side into the launch and passed forward to be stowed under cover. I worked with the men on deck passing the seabags up to the rail. In ten minutes they were all off the ship and on the launch. Then we poured over the side, finally the lines were cast off, and the launch was making a broad starboard turn for the run across the sparkling blue waters of the bay to the waterfront.

I was almost the last one aboard the launch, and I stood at the stern rail as we powered by the stern of the *William H. Smith*. Captain Thomas was standing there watching us. The company representative stood next to him. I was alone on the stern of the launch now. We were still close enough to the schooner that I could see the expression on the captain's face. I raised my right arm in a wave that I intended as a salute to one of the finest seamen who ever commanded a ship. To my surprise and pleasure, the captain smiled broadly at me and waved back. It was the last time I ever saw Captain Thomasen O. Thomas, master of sail and master of steam.

Then I shouldered my way through the crew until I found myself standing in the bow of the launch that the Union Fish Company had chartered to take its crew ashore in style. At that moment I forgave the company all of the codfish I had reluctantly forced down my gullet simply to fuel my bodily needs.

Balanced to the motion of the launch, heedless of the spray from the bow wave, I stared at the Ferry Building, which marked the point on the San Francisco Embarcadero where I would finally set foot on land after almost five months at sea.

I felt a lump in my throat, and my eyes misted over. It wasn't the bow wave from the launch that was clouding my vision. I was home at last!

39

On a Tuesday morning, a week and a half after our return, I was rattling down Mission Street on a Market Street railway car. I stood on the back platform, my left arm draped on the side of the platform section, feeling the breeze pouring through the opening between the side of the car and the ceiling. I took a deep breath as the strong Embarcadero smell of roasting coffee came wafting in.

My appreciation of simple things that I had taken for granted before had not yet been dulled.

I thought of my first steps on the Embarcadero ten days ago and how surprised I was to find what I thought was solid ground moving under me like the deck of the schooner. My sense of equilibrium for almost five months had been automatically adjusting my bodily movements to the unceasing motion of the ship. Now, with a solid, unmoving surface beneath my feet, the bodily mechanism simply went on functioning, and it took me almost a full day to regain my shore legs.

I smiled to myself as I remembered my ride out Mission Street the day I got home.

I had boarded this same numbered streetcar, tossed my seabag into the corner of the back platform, and fished in my pocket for a nickel to drop into the box. This was at the Embarcadero end of this particular line. There were a couple of people sitting forward in the car, but at that moment the conductor and I were by ourselves on the platform. He was busy with his trip book and didn't take any particular notice of me as I dropped my nickel in. Then he started suddenly and looked at me, staring hard, with his nose wrinkled.

"My God, son, don't you ever take a bath?"

I was insulted. "Damn right—just four days ago, as a matter of fact!"

"It didn't do much good."

By then I was standing, rather defensively, by my upright seabag.

The conductor studied me carefully, then he started to smile. "You off a codfisher by any chance?"

I nodded. "How did you know?"

"I know! I know! Every year about this time I get a couple of characters like you at this end of the line. Once in a while I get lucky and miss them. Someone else gets the benefit of that perfume." He was obviously more amused than anything else now. "Can't you smell yourself, son?"

I shook my head. "I'm sorry, I really can't. I thought I smelled pretty clean."

He shook his head resignedly. "How far you going?"

"Out to Fourteenth and Mission."

"Well, I tell you, just stand back there on the platform where we get some breeze. It'll be a long ride for me, but I've got to work here." He reached up and gave two sharp pulls on the signal cord. The streetcar lurched off.

About four times on the ride out Mission Street some man would get aboard intending to ride the back platform, sniff the air in a puzzled way, then stare long and hard at me. Finally he would go as far forward in the streetcar as he could get.

About the third time it happened I was getting downright embarrassed, but I could see that the conductor was becoming more and more amused.

As I swung off the rear step at Fourteenth and Mission, my seabag balanced on my shoulder, he called out. I stood on the street by the rear platform to hear him.

"Don't take offense now, but I want to make a suggestion. I realize it's kinda sudden, only four days since your last bath, but you might try another one—good and hot—when you get home."

He waved good-naturedly as the streetcar rattled off.

Then I was ringing the doorbell of our flat. It had never occurred to me that no one would be home. I hadn't bothered to telephone, of course. I could hear the brisk steps of my Uncle Jerry approaching the front door. He was home on a layover from the freight run he was working now.

He opened the door and, for a startled second, just stared at me. Then he grabbed me in a bear hug. I was surprised to see tears in his eyes as he finally held me at arm's length and just looked at me. Then I saw his nose start to wrinkle.

"Jesus H. Christ, Russ, you got any idea what you smell like?"

I simply nodded. "A little, Uncle Jerry. Guess I could use a bath."

For the past four days now I had been telephoning the Union Fish Company every morning to ascertain if the catch had been weighed out yet and our final payoff determined.

The dress gang had all received a fifty-dollar draw, a not inconsequential sum in 1937, against their individual shares. The fishermen had received a draw of about one third of what the company estimated they would receive finally, based on their individual tallies.

I had learned from the bookkeeper, over the telephone, that

236

after Johnson's Outfitters were paid off directly by the company, I had a check waiting for me in the sum of $152. My personal catch of 502 codfish accounted for about $50 of my total net pay for the voyage of slightly more than $200. What the hell, I thought, as we neared the end of the line, look at all that fresh air and good food I enjoyed on the schooner.

I walked the long block from Mission to Market Street breathing deeply of the smell of roasting coffee fragrant in the morning air, mingled now with the smell of the bay. It was a soft, sunny day. It felt wonderful to be alive.

I crossed the few short blocks to where Clay Street ran into the Embarcadero, thinking as I walked of the adjustment it had been for me when I had returned to high school. Although I had considered the hair sprouting on my chest rather copiously now as an obvious attribute of approaching manhood, the voyage had been a passage for me in another, deeper sense. It was not until I had returned to high school that I realized that my life on the schooner had matured me in a way I had not been aware of at the time. Those five months, more than any other experience of my life, had brought me swiftly through my remaining adolescence—if not to all the maturity and judgment of an adult, at least far closer to it than any of the high school students I knew, with the exception of Herb Ainsworth. He seemed to me to have been born an adult. For the rest of them I found myself impatient with what seemed to be the trivial concerns of their day-to-day lives. One evidence of my newfound maturity was that I didn't talk about the voyage except to Herb, who wanted to know about everything that had happened. The adjustment was not a serious problem for me, simply an unforeseen one.

As I walked toward the Union Fish Company I didn't know that the voyage had not quite stopped teaching me yet.

I opened the door of the Union Fish Company and I walked down the long, musty corridor to the bookkeeper's office. I collected my check and was halfway back to the door opening out to Clay Street when I saw Chris Olsen coming toward me.

I was really happy to see him—for an instant. Then I realized, as he came lurching down the hallway, that he didn't see me. He was, quite literally, blind drunk.

It hit me with an impact that was almost physical. I cried out, "Chris!"

I could have been talking to a wall. As he swayed near me I tried to step in front of him, but he pushed me aside with one powerful shove of his left hand and went swaying down the hall. I could see the heavy talcum powder of the barber's shave on his face, the dark eyes sunk in his head, and I got a whiff of bay rum and cheap booze as he moved by me. I started to go after him, and then I stopped. I knew, with a terrible finality, that this monkey would never be off Chris Olsen's back. I knew that he would never go home to Norway.

Shaken, I continued down the hall, and then I saw Oscar Quarten just starting to navigate the long passage, steadying himself with one hand braced against the wall.

"Oscar! What happened to Chris?"

He wasn't in quite as bad a shape as Chris Olsen, but he was feeling no pain.

"Vell, Roos, it be like dis. Ve hit a whorehouse on Turk Street de first night ashore." He smiled beatifically at the memory. "Nice girls, but dat Chris, he get mean drunk. Dey can't handle him. So dey had to mickey him. I go round dere next day to pick him up. He feelin' sick, by Yesus! Den he find out somevun roll him—lost all dat first pay."

"But that was only a third of what he had coming, Oscar. Can't you get him sobered up now?"

"Nay. Vhat for? Ve havin' goot time. 'Sides, Chris, he be drinkin' on de cuff half de bars on Howard Street. Now he got to pay dem off."

I thought bitterly that no matter what had been done to him, Chris would pay off those unconscionable bastards. Not just to keep on drinking, either, but because he was an honest man.

I knew that this was beyond any power of mine to affect. A human being, about whom I cared deeply, was spinning again into a frightening vortex of drunken hopelessness. There wasn't a damn thing I could do about it, and this, I thought, was the last lesson the voyage had to teach me. But there was one more.

Heartsick, I pushed through the doorway out onto Clay Street. I wanted to walk now and try to forget. I turned toward the hills in the same direction Herb and I had turned the day he had signed on the schooner. Just as on that day, the hills were etched against the sky, a softer autumn blue now, but just as lovely. And I was more miserable now, in a hopeless, despairing way, than I had been then, or ever before in my life.

I had taken only two steps when I heard my name called from across the narrow street. "Russ!" The voice was familiar, but I couldn't quite place it. When I turned toward the man who had called out, I was still puzzled. Then recognition dawned. It was Jack Anderson. No wonder I hadn't recognized him. He was dressed in a well-made suit, tastefully matching tie, shiny shoes, the very picture of the well-dressed man, circa 1937. I stood there immobile as he walked up to me and stuck out his right hand. I grasped it hard and, involuntarily, I looked down at his left hand.

He smiled easily. "It's OK, Russ. If anyone has a right to stare, you do. Look." He raised his left hand and made a pinching gesture with his left index finger and thumb. "The captain saved it for me, thank God. Damn near as good as a whole hand when you got that forefinger and thumb to work with."

"What're you doing now, Jack?"

"I'm majoring in accounting over at Cal. The company paid off enough for me to do finally what I've always wanted to do— go to college." He smiled again. "Of course, they weren't all that generous, but I've got a good part-time job in an accounting office in Oakland. I'm making it fine."

"How come you're down here today?"

"I wanted to see you. Been calling in almost every day. The bookkeeper told me you'd be picking your check up this morning." His expression became serious. "I was down at the corner when I saw you go in, and then I saw Chris and Oscar follow you in just a little while later."

"Oh, Christ, Jack, is there anything I can do?"

239

His expression was as sympathetic and understanding as a man's could be. "I'm afraid not, Russ. I knew that you were pretty close to Chris on the schooner. That's why I waited outside."

"But why, Jack?" My voice broke. "He told me he was going home to Norway. He could have stayed sober for ten days!"

"No, Russ, he couldn't. You just don't know. These poor bastards—they were treated like slaves when they were little kids on those windjammers out of the old country. Later, the boozing and whores ashore, that's all they've ever known."

"But Chris was different!"

"I'm not blaming him, Russ. I'm just trying to tell you that with what he's been through in his life, he can't help it"—he paused a moment, then lifted his left hand directly in front of my eyes—"any more than I can help this now. Come on, let's walk."

And walk we did, west on Clay Street, then over to Sacramento Street, up the steep hill to where the Fairmont Hotel stood and on past the lovely little park on the very top of Nob Hill. Always west, not saying much, just walking. Finally, though that last sight of Chris Olsen would be engraved on my memory forevermore, my mood began to lighten. I thought of the way Jack Anderson had handled that terrible pain all through that endless period on the schooner. I thought of how he had turned a disastrous accident into a brighter future for himself. This then was the last lesson the voyage had for me. Life was unsparing, it could be brutal, but it was up to me. I did not have the monkey on my back that Chris Olsen had. I did not have the physical handicap that Jack Anderson had. I did have my good health and a reasonable degree of intelligence. My life was mine to shape, my future was in my own hands.

EPILOGUE

Almost eight years to the day after my return to San Francisco on the *Smith*, I sailed into Nagasaki Harbor on a troop transport. The 2nd Marine Division was being deployed as the first occupation force in that part of Japan. I had served with the division two years, joining my battalion at Paekakariki in New Zealand. I had survived Tarawa, Saipan, Tinian, and Okinawa. Just short weeks before, we were scheduled to combat load from our divison camp on Saipan for the invasion of the home islands of Japan. The 2nd division, together with the other five Marine divisions in the Pacific, had been designated as the assault landing force on the island of Kyushu.

The psychological release for us, with the war's end, is beyond my power to describe. A voyage to what seemed to us would be a certain holocaust on those hostile beaches became, with the surrender of Japan, a pleasure cruise.

What I remember most vividly of that time is the trip up on the Navy transport. The weather was calm and balmy. For the first time during my years in the Pacific the ship did not batten down at darkness. The quarters were cool and comfortable at night—not stifling hot, as was so often the case when we had sailed before to an assault landing. The smoking lamp was always lit, and I could smoke on deck at night.

On occasion I would lean on the fantail rail at the very stern of the ship smoking my pipe, watching our wake streaming aft behind us under the star-studded heavens and thinking about how incredibly lucky I was. I was at peace with the world.

There was some understandable concern about how we would be received as the first occupation force in the history of Japan, and we went ashore combat ready. Still, it was not an assault landing. We were profoundly, deeply grateful for that.

During that voyage I thought often of the last week on the schooner and what a pleasure for me that time had been. Once again I had survived. That profound gratitude for simply having made it, the sheer joy of being alive—more than at any other time—these emotions take hold when I am at sea.

In the years following the Bering Sea voyage in 1937, and almost to the end of 1945, I spent about a year and a half of my life at sea.

On a Swedish freighter, on American merchant vessels, finally during World War II on a variety of naval ships from an aircraft carrier which transported us from San Diego to Nouméa, New Caledonia, to LST's and troop transports in between, always my pulse quickened when the mooring lines were cast off and I was aboard a ship—on my way.

For those who do not feel this excitement, there is nothing I can really say that can explain it. For those who do feel it, no explanation is necessary. John Masefield's poem "Sea Fever," as romanticized as the lines may be, states the case as well as it has ever been expressed.

Despite the living conditions and the hard work, undoubtedly sea fever infected me on the schooner, and I have never recovered from it. During my years as a practicing lawyer my seagoing has been mainly on sailing yachts, but there have been other memorable cruises as well. My wife and I sailed on a luxury liner, the *Aquarius*, in the Aegean Sea with a wonderfully friendly and efficient Greek crew—visiting the magical islands of those ancient waters.

I remember the *Yankee Clipper*, a trim one-hundred-foot schooner which carried us and forty other passengers to less-frequented islands in the Caribbean. My lovely (and long-suffering) wife, Beverly, did not seem to enjoy that sailing vessel as I did, but the years fell away for me when I handled the wheel of the *Yankee Clipper* as we surged through the blue Caribbean with a thirty-knot wind on our beam.

Beverly did not enjoy the S.S. *Benicia* as I did, either. There *were* cockroaches aboard.

But I shall never forget our departure from Papeete one starry tropical night. The skipper permitted me to stand on the bridge with him as he carefully conned the old steamer through the lagoon on our way to Raiatea, Huahine, and Bora-Bora.

For me—at sea—the beginning of it all was as a member of the crew of the schooner *William H. Smith.*

Herb Ainsworth made it to the United States Naval Academy the hard way—by competitive examination. We had one brief reunion, in Annapolis, just after I had been commissioned a second lieutenant in the Marine Corps at Quantico, Virginia. Herb was then completing his last year at the Academy in one of the war-accelerated classes.

Again, in early 1946, we saw each other briefly in San Francisco when he stopped en route to a duty station change. I learned then that our lives had briefly intersected during the war, although neither of us knew it at the time. Herb had been aboard the U.S.S. *Santa Fe* participating in the pre-assault naval bombardment of Tarawa while I was aboard the U.S.S. *Bell* in the transport fleet.

We lost track of each other then for many years. In 1973 I opened the local paper to see the handsome face of Rear Admiral Herbert S. Ainsworth looking out at me from the front page. He was, as Commander Fleet Air Wings, United States Pacific Fleet, conducting an official inquiry into a tragic air collision at Moffett Field, where his headquarters were based. That is just fifteen miles from my law office in San Jose. We resumed a friendship which has always been most meaningful for me. Herb retired from a distinguished naval career in 1974. He now lives not too far from my home in Los Gatos, and our friendship continues.

Of all of my shipmates on the *Smith*, I have seen only Trotsky again. One day, while working on the book, the thought occurred to me that few native San Franciscans ever settle very far from the city. I looked in the telephone directory and found an "A. Kalnin." I knew at once that it could only be my friend Trotsky, and it was. He is a successful businessman now living on the San Francisco peninsula, and his business cards today bear the name "Trot Kalnin." It has seemed to me that it required a good deal of moral fortitude to insist on that nickname all of his life and throughout the unlamented McCarthy era.

Like mine, Trotsky's family is grown now. He is in good shape and, happily enough, we recognized each other immediately when we finally met again after forty-four years.

I had the advantage of the diary and we found, as Trotsky conceded, that my memory of the voyage was more accurate than his. He remembered, for example, that we had lost two fishermen in the Bering Sea. We agreed that perhaps the day that Paddy Whelan almost did not return had impressed itself on his memory to the point of his now remembering the loss of two men rather than one.

On the other hand, his recollections reinforced and aided my own on some experiences that, after a lapse of forty-four years, were somewhat uncertain.

Finally I learned that Trotsky, like myself, had served in the United States Marine Corps in World War II. It would seem that Frank Simmons had made more of an impression on both of us than we then realized.

There is one noticeable difference between us, however. With the exception of troop transports during his Marine Corps service Trotsky has not, since September 17, 1937, set foot on anything that floats. Nor does he intend to.

When the anchor splashed down into the waters of San Francisco Bay on September 17, 1937, it marked the end of the last voyage of the schooner William H. Smith as a commercial sailing vessel. We didn't know it at the time, of course, but never again would those sails drive her across the blue water.

In 1938 the William H. Smith was sold to the Alaska Salmon Company. She was never used by that company and was subsequently sold to William Yen Yee. This owner intended to use her as a barge, but she remained idle. During World War II the Navy acquired her, renamed her Mustang, and used her as a training barge instructing coxswains in landing craft operations.

244

The end came in the late 1940s, when she was left to die on the mud flats of San Diego Harbor after plans for using her as a copra barge were abandoned.

All ships that sail the oceans of the world develop a unique character of their own—an impress in part of the masters who command them, in part of the crews who man them, completed by the full measure of the experiences that befall them at sea. A seafaring man invariably perceives this uniquely individual ship's personality.

Perhaps because it was my first ship, it has always seemed to me that the *Smith*, more than any other vessel I have known, had a special quality of her own. Thus when I learned, many years after the fact, of her ending, the sense of loss for me was strong and profound.

When I think of the *Smith* in all her moods, groaning maddeningly as she rolled in a calm, driven over on her beam ends almost helpless in a storm, or flying like a live thing across the sea with every stitch of canvas set and drawing, she seems as alive to me as anything created by man can be.

From the tall masts stepped on the keelson to the bowsprit secured firmly to the hull by the stays, the component parts of a sailing vessel work together. The continual, rhythmic sounds of the ship's timbers when the schooner is sailing on a steady course seem to me to give her a special voice and a life of her own.

It is the ending of all this that causes my sense of loss.

Built by Hall Brothers in 1899, launched from their yard in Port Blakely, Washington, when the age of sail was even then passing, the schooner *William H. Smith* served her various owners honestly and well.

In 1906 she accomplished an epic rescue of the crew of the British ship *Melanope,* forced to abandon their vessel off Cape Blanco on the Oregon coast.

Despite the misfortunes that beset our 1937 voyage, an inevitable part of any codfishing trip to the Bering Sea, I remember now that the ship did not let us down.

I prefer not to think of when the last time was that the *Smith* was hauled and caulked before that voyage. Certainly the Union Fish Company did not waste its undoubtedly limited resources on new gear for the *Smith*.

Yet, despite her less than top condition and despite the mutterings from time to time that the ship was jinxed, she got us safely there and back. I think now of her recalcitrant deck engine, which finally coughed into life just in time to pump the seawater into the fire in the lazaret where the gasoline drums were stowed and save her and us from a fiery death.

I remember now that heart-stopping jibe, which saved us from wrecking on Ugamak Island. The schooner responded heroically, and those old stays held fast while she completed that sudden, violent, and life-saving movement without dismasting herself.

She always came through when it counted. She was an honest ship.

AUTHOR'S NOTE

This book, in retrospect, seems to me to have possessed a small, independent destiny of its own. A Mexican virus, two conversations, and an abrupt, temporary termination of my work as a practicing lawyer all combined to cause me to pick up the pen to attempt to recapture what was for me one of the most formative experiences of my life.

In May 1980 I had lunch with my old friend Herb Ainsworth. For the first time in years our conversation turned to the schooner *William H. Smith* and my voyage as a member of her crew to the Bering Sea in 1937. Herb's interest and questions were obviously genuine, and they made some type of impact on my subconscious.

In late May my wife and I departed for a two-week vacation in Mexico. As always, we had a wonderful trip but, unknown to me at the time, I returned home with the virus of infectious hepatitis, waiting out its incubation period, in my bloodstream.

In mid-June we enjoyed a most pleasant evening at our home with Leonard and Janet McCarthy. Although I had known Len as a good friend for over thirty years, I simply had never realized that he was such a sailing-ship buff. That evening he brought with him Jim Gibbs' fascinating book *West Coast Windjammers*. Together, on page 113, we found a photograph of my old ship under sail. That naturally led to my telling Len sea stories for a good portion of the remainder of the evening. Much like Herb Ainsworth several weeks previously, Len listened with obvious and genuine interest. But he did more than listen. Toward the end of the evening he said, "You know, Russ, I think that voyage of yours would make a hell of a yarn!" That too must have sunk in.

Then in early July, having had time to mature, and almost exactly on its incubatory schedule, the virus struck. I was laid low with infectious hepatitis.

My doctor, the day the blood test confirmed his diagnosis, instructed me emphatically and unequivocally that I was to remain in bed, at home, and away from my law office. Despite the heavy work load of the typical, busy lawyer, I was too miserable and wiped out even to argue with him. Thus I remained for about the first two weeks of a rather prolonged convalescence. Then, as I began to feel more alive again but still barred from my office by medical edict, my conversations with Herb Ainsworth and Len McCarthy came into focus in my mind. With more leisure time available to me at home than I had enjoyed in years, I started writing this book. This was not really a remarkable combination of circumstances, but I wonder now if it had not been for this particular juxtaposition of events, this small kismet of *"Hard on the Wind"* if I ever would have written the book.

It seems to me that one of the more civilized and courteous conventions in the world of books is the custom of authors to acknowledge their indebtedness to those who have contributed, on one basis or another, to the end result. I do so now with pleasure.

My patient and loving wife, Beverly, was always and invariably the first to read the latest script after I wrote it in longhand on my yellow, legal-size tablets. Despite the number of times she had heard some of these sea stories, she read the material carefully and criticized unsparingly. The usual pattern of our discussions was a first indignant eruption from me, "Goddamnit, that's the way I want to write it!" Then, the next time back over her written notations, I would have to agree that her comments were right on the mark. In a very real sense this book is the product of a collaboration with Bev.

Carol Abate, professor of English at West Valley College, provided the professional editing that I believe, as a somewhat uninformed newcomer to the field, every writer must need.

248

Much as was the case with my wife's comments directed toward substantive content, Carol's skilled directions for deleting, unraveling awkward sentences, and clarifying meaning were of monumental importance to me in completing this book. And as was the case with my wife, minus the verbal pyrotechnics, although I occasionally disagreed at first I almost invariably followed Carol's direction in the end.

The diary I kept on the schooner acted in a remarkable way as a stimulus to my memory of long past experiences, but it was quite lacking in the specific detail that obviously was required for a book of this type. Jim Gibbs, with no more knowledge of me than an explanatory letter requesting information on the length and beam of the ship, became an invaluable source of detailed information on the schooner *William H. Smith*. He has generously permitted the use of the photograph of the *Smith* from his book *West Coast Windjammers*, which, perhaps more than any other single factor (as previously noted), was the proximate cause of this book.

Finally, I thank my patient and efficient secretary, Sheila Roth. Fitting in the typing of this manuscript with the complaints, answers, wills, petitions, briefs, and all the other documents so characteristic of a general practitioner's work, I wonder how she did it. But she did—and superbly.

I believe I share, with most individuals I know, the happy faculty of memory rounding off the jagged edges of unpleasant experiences, on the one hand. On the other hand, the single, exciting experience perhaps gains in the retelling much like the fisherman who has successfully boated a fighting marlin—large enough to begin with, anyway, but grown to unbelievable proportions in the fisherman's memory.

Thus, on occasion, I would wonder how accurate my memory was. I knew that the instant in which I stared death in the face embodied by the bottom of Paul Myers' dory, poised high above me as I lay helpless on the running board, was recounted precisely as it had occurred. That experience was indelibly etched into my very being. But then I wondered if I accurately remembered Frank Simmons' terse comments about fishing dories infrequently, but occasionally, being swept over the side of a schooner in a wild sea.

Sometime after the book was finished I was reading Alan Villiers' *Great Sea Stories.* Interestingly enough, the one story from his own writing that he included in the collection described the Portuguese codfishermen on the Grand Banks. Naturally, I found it fascinating reading. More than that, in this one particular I found satisfying confirmation of my own memory. In describing the relative merits of the newer motor-ships and the older schooners he had this, among other things, to say about the schooners: "But they could hoist dories inboard all along their low main decks. If necessary, they could sail them inboard, *take them over the side as the schooner rolled.*"

Since my memory of the fo'c'sle of the *Smith* wasn't really all that bad—indeed, my memories of turning into my bunk after a cold and stormy night watch were downright pleasant—I wondered if perhaps I hadn't overdone it a bit in describing the conditions in the fo'c'sle that first week aboard. Again I found confirmation of my memory.

At the foot of Hyde Street, in San Francisco Bay, the three-masted schooner C. A. *Thayer* is berthed. She ended her active life as a codfisher in the Bering Sea, and that part of her career is emphasized. The ship has been beautifully restored and is now part of the National Maritime Museum, Golden Gate National Recreation Area. Admission to her is free, and throughout the vessel there are numerous informative placards and memorabilia of her life as a codfisher.

In the fo'c'sle—no portholes and basically below the waterline, as was the *Smith's*—there is a placard containing the following statement: "Even sailors accustomed to the dank and crowded quarters of square-rigged merchant ships found the forecastle of a codfisherman almost uninhabitable."

In another part of the fo'c'sle of the C. A. *Thayer* there is a typed and enlarged extract from a diary one Jimmy Crooks kept of his voyage to the Bering Sea in 1926 on the schooner *Fanny*

250

Dutard. In describing the fo'c'sle of his ship, Jimmy Crooks had this to say: "The hold of a slaver could not have been much worse than the quarters I found on the schooner *Fanny Dutard* during the year 1926."

Perhaps I am just not as perceptive and sensitive as Jimmy Crooks. The *Smith*'s fo'c'sle simply did not seem quite *that* bad to me; just that first week, and that I *know* I remember truly well.

It seems doubtful to me that any of the fishermen of the *Smith* are alive today. In that unlikely event it is even more improbable to me that any of them would ever see this book, much less read it. But that possibility, however remote—that one of the fishermen might have read about his life in the Bering Sea—makes me wish that I had written this book many years ago, when at least those particular odds would have been reduced. Many men in this world labor in hazardous employment, but on a day in, day out basis I have never known, or heard of, anything comparable to the life of a dory fisherman in the Bering Sea. I marvel now at the uncomplaining courage they exhibited every day that they shoved off in those flat-bottomed dories.

Perhaps in that Valhalla where Scandinavian merchant seamen finally dwell they know that someone has attempted to tell part of their story. I hope so. I am proud to have sailed with them.